# FIRST FATHERS

## THE MEN WHO INSPIRED OUR PRESIDENTS

### HAROLD I. GULLAN

WILEY

John Wiley & Sons, Inc.

Published by John Wiley & Sons, Inc., Hoboken, New Jersey
Published simultaneously in Canada

For general information about our other products and services, please contact our Customer Care Department within the United States at (800) 762-2974, outside the United States at (317) 572-3993 or fax (317) 572-4002.

Wiley also publishes its books in a variety of electronic formats. Some content that appears in print may not be available in electronic books. For more information about Wiley products, visit our web site at www.wiley.com.

ISBN 0-471-46597-6

Printed in the United States of America
10 9 8 7 6 5 4 3 2 1

*To the two*
*who inspire me—*
*Betsy and Bill Gullan*

# Contents

# Acknowledgments

Writing may seem a solitary pursuit, but few writers—particularly of nonfiction—work or walk entirely alone. Supplementing the palpable presence of the real people I've tried to portray in *First Fathers* has been the sustained encouragement of a host of those who share my interest in the American experience. Some I've had the good fortune to meet. Many more have aided me from afar.

I'm particularly indebted to Barbara Oliver, formerly of the Library of Congress, and her associates; Cathryn Henry and Jeffrey Daniels of the Chicago Historical Society; Ed Presley of Belle Grove Plantation; Dana Angell of the Library of Virginia; Stephanie Jacobs of the Virginia Historical Society; Linda Kennedy of the Buffalo and Erie Historical Society; David Smolen of the New Hampshire Historical Society; Leanne Garland of the Lincoln Memorial University; Kim Bauer of the Illinois Historical Preservation Agency; Duryea Kemp of the Ohio Historical Society; Sharon Farrell (and her technological son, David Farrell) of the Grover Cleveland Birthplace; Jennifer Capps of the President Benjamin Harrison Home; and conscientious Mari Artzner-Wolf at the Ramsayer Research Library of the McKinley Museum and National Memorial.

Also Wallace Dailey of the Theodore Roosevelt Collection at the Houghton Library of Harvard University; E. Ray Henderson of the William Howard Taft National Historical Site; gracious Lucinda Cooke and Rick Potter of the Woodrow Wilson Birthplace and Museum; Lu Knox of the Calvin Coolidge Presidential Library and Museum; Christine Moun and Jim Detlefsen of the Herbert Hoover Presidential Library; Lynn Bassanese, Mark Renovitch, and Annmarie Gleeson of the Franklin Delano Roosevelt Library; Anita Holland and Liz Safly of the Harry S Truman Library; Kathy Struss of the Dwight D. Eisenhower Library; James Hill of the John Fitzgerald Kennedy Library; Margaret Harmon of the Lyndon Baines Johnson Library; Susan Naulty, John Taylor, Greg Cumming, Sandy Quinn, and Arianna Barrios-Lochrie of the Richard Nixon Library and Birthplace; Carol Barber of the Wyoming State Archives; Nancy Mirshah, Kenneth Hafeli, and William McNitt of the Gerald R. Ford Library; Sheila Mayo, David Stanhope, and Polly Nodine of the Jimmy Carter Library; Kirby Hanson, Erica Jolles, and Josh Tenenbaum of the Ronald Reagan Library; Bonnie Burlbaw, Matthew Lee, Brian Blake, and Rod Thornton of the George Bush Library.

Lewis and Clark had no more reliable associates comprising their Corps of Discovery than I've enjoyed at the Saint Joseph's University Library, my local base of operations. They include director Evelyn Minick, Mary Martinson, Tamara Jackson, Martha Van Auken, Dolores McCaughan, and the incomparable Susan Tsiouris. At the four universities where I've taught courses in recent years, I've benefited from the generous input of noted scholars of all ages—from Jim Hilty, Randall Miller, and Richard Webster to such future academic stars as the innovative Jeffrey La Monica and the indefatigable Joe Zuggi. In such hands, hopefully, the study of American history may yet be prevented from perishing.

We Gullans are fortuitously situated in a compact community of tall trees, old stone homes, and congenial neighbors. Next door lives Elsa Efran, a steady hand at the tiller, who somehow manages to put my laborious printing into presentable form, guiding it skillfully as she goes along. Her husband, Jay, a psychologist who is also a computer-mastering magician, keeps it all moving. I've appreciated the proffered hospitality of many other neighbors, friends, and family—Auritts, Massaris, Boltons, Hoescheles—but writing *is* just solitary enough to be difficult to stick to amidst such good company. To Carey Rowan and Mike Nunnally go my thanks for helping me to get around in pursuit of the documentation on which this book is based.

Its form and substance have been most influenced by my perceptive, patient, and painstaking editor at Wiley, Hana Lane, her able associate, Mike Thompson, and resourceful production editor John Simko. We were joined together by that resolute repository of good sense, my agent, Ed Knappman.

After my first book, Elsa Efran, only half in jest, suggested distributing T-shirts emblazoned "I survived working with Hal Gullan." In view of how many years they have survived *living* with Hal Gullan, perhaps special commendation should be accorded my eminently talented and supportive wife, Betsy, and our equally remarkable son, Bill. As for you who have chosen to buy and read *First Fathers,* becoming welcome companions on this voyage, I extend my profound thanks in the immortal words of William S. Gilbert, "In for a penny, in for a pound; it's love that makes the world go 'round."

# By Way of Introduction

Inspiration is what this book is about. Just as success has many fathers, inspiration can come in many forms—a premise personified by that most neglected cohort in American history, the forty-four fathers of the men who became our presidents.

Of all of them, only Joseph P. Kennedy Sr. viewed the presidency as an obsessive aim for one of his sons. Most first fathers motivated their offspring more toward high aspirations than high office. The very examples of their own lives, as with John Tyler Sr., Richard Cleveland, John Coolidge, or Gerald Ford Sr., could serve as inspiration. More frequently, however, ambition was framed by earnest admonitions that only excellence was acceptable. Consider, for example, the letters of Alphonso Taft, the Rev. Doctor Joseph Ruggles Wilson, or the younger John Adams to their favored sons. Many were first sons, the traditional repository of parental expectations.

A call to selfless service came from the elder Theodore Roosevelt to young "Teedie." In the next century, it would be echoed by Prescott Bush to his own children, and later by George Herbert Walker Bush to his. In some instances a specific career goal was at least implied. Pious John Adams Sr., the "Deacon," hoped that perhaps his namesake might become a learned Congregational minister. Pragmatic James Buchanan Sr. viewed the law as a sound foundation for success in any endeavor. Zachary Taylor longed to be a soldier like his father. Self-made successes, from Jesse Grant to James Earl Carter Sr., naturally harbored hopes that their most talented sons might expand their enterprises. But by and large specificity was sublimated to the universal goal, "Make something of yourself."

Of course, the ultimate career choice of every future president would turn out to be public life. However indirect the influence, they had no lack of paternal examples to inspire them. In addition to two presidents, the ranks of first fathers have included several governors, a United States senator, and many legislators, judges, and diplomats. If young Martin Van Buren, our first president to portray himself as a professional politician, wanted to hear heated partisan discourse, he needed only to walk downstairs to his father's tavern. Spirited political debate around frontier campfires formed vivid childhood memories for most of our nineteenth-century presidents. It was John Truman and Sam Johnson who introduced their receptive sons to the excitement of all-day picnics, rallies, and torchlight parades—politics as entertainment. Franklin Roosevelt gained his confidence to pursue life in the arena from his father's confidence in him. Ronald Reagan's "gift of gab" was an inheritance from his salesman father. Dwight Eisenhower's freedom to choose his own path stemmed from his father's thwarted ambitions for his own life. Jimmy Carter's political career derived from the belated recognition of his father's unsuspected beneficence. Indeed, inspiration comes in many forms.

Not every first father was granted the years to fully guide his favored son to manhood. Gentle giant Augustine Washington died when George was only eleven. Self-educated Peter Jefferson, the prototype for his son's "aristocracy of achievement," died when Thomas was fourteen. Ambitious Jesse Hoover died when Herbert was only six. The fathers of both Roosevelts died while their sons were at Harvard. At least four fathers of our presidents expired as the result of sheer physical exertion: Andrew Jackson Sr., a weaver turned farmer, in clearing land to which he did not even hold title; the robust Abram Garfield, after fighting a fire that imperiled his homestead; man-of-all-work Jacob Johnson, after heroically saving prominent Raleigh citizens from drowning; diminutive John Anderson Truman, an impatient road overseer, after moving an immense rock himself. Jackson and the estimable Ruddy Hayes died even before their namesakes were born, as did Bill Blythe, the father of the boy who would later be named William Jefferson Clinton. On the other hand, Joseph P. Kennedy Sr. outlived four of his nine children.

The rarely recounted stories of such disparate first fathers are often as compelling as those of their famous sons. Their lives encompass the full range of the American experience—from inherited affluence to abject destitution, from heartening success to heartrending failure. Why do we know so little about most of these men? Why have their lives been so overlooked by generations of historians?

Perhaps some of the blame resides with the presidents themselves, in the paucity of their recorded recollections. Overall, they have volunteered a bit more about their fathers than about their mothers, enabling biographers to at least cobble together some semblance of their lives. I am indebted to all these writers, particularly to Jeff C. Young, author of the only prior effort to assemble at least the specifics about each first father within a single set of covers. Indeed, in all of American history, in contrast to the abundance of accounts about first ladies, there have only been five books devoted to presidential parents. The most recent, my own *Faith of Our Mothers* (2001), stresses two dimensions of that faith—in the limitless potential of their sons, and the deep religious faith of so many of the mothers.

If these mothers had faith, the fathers had hope—for their sons, and for themselves. Beyond the variations of inspiration, perhaps the most pervasively unifying theme of first fathers has been their relentless pursuit of happiness. Of course, this is a quintessentially American theme, espoused originally by Thomas Jefferson. The majority of presidential fathers, rural or urban, rich or poor, successful or not, were really entrepreneurs. Restless, ambitious, and energetic, through choice or necessity, they sought to "make it" on their own. That so many were thwarted rarely diminished their dreams. What was success to Thomas Lincoln? A more bountiful farm, always just over the horizon. To George Harding, a prosperous medical practice; to Rev. Richard Cleveland, finally settling in a supportive parish; to William McKinley Sr., a more productive iron foundry; to John Truman, a successful investment in *something;* to David Eisenhower, the opportunity to finally become an engineer; to Francis Nixon, a lemon grove in the right soil; to Jack Reagan, simply the largest shoe store, outside of Chicago, in Illinois. Why did it never work out?

Whatever the failures or failings of their fathers, the men who became our presidents were rarely critical of them. Whenever voiced, their reflections tended to recall admired examples of rectitude. To the younger John Adams, for example, his father was "the honestest man I ever knew." Spoken or not, affection was evident. "Silent Cal" Coolidge kissed his equally taciturn father whenever they met.

Nothing in this book is really new, except, one hopes, at least a modicum of insight. I've uncovered no previously undiscovered cache of letters, no incriminating revelations of presidential indiscretion. Any titillation is accidental. Then why should you read *First Fathers*? Well, Harry Truman once said that the only new thing in the world is the history we don't know. It is fine and fitting that our recent popular history is replete with accounts of first ladies and that there are now at least two good books in print about first mothers. But where did the *original* inspiration come from to fire the ambition of the young men who ultimately became our presidents? If you share my curiosity, you are a welcome companion on this voyage of rediscovery—to explore together the most neglected component of our nation's heritage, history we should know.

And so this book is about forty-four very different men, most of whom have in common only that aim of personal ambition—and the desire to inspire their offspring. Fortunately, despite the limitations of the literature, we can learn at least something about each of them—a bit more about Ford's two fathers, a bit less about Clinton's. Accordingly, each chapter is really a separate essay, widely varying in length. As you can see, it is all written in a popular (one is tempted to say "pop") style. Fortunately, the lives of so many of these men are intriguing in them- selves, even had their sons never ascended to the presidency. Would that we knew more, but thankfully enough records and recollections survive to try to bring these first fathers back to life (only one is still with us), and I hope to justify our journey. Please start wherever you like. See you "In Conclusion."

# 1

# FATHERS OF FOUNDERS

Augustine Washington • John Adams Sr.
Peter Jefferson • James Madison Sr.
Spence Monroe

IN MASSACHUSETTS AS IN VIRGINIA, the upwardly mobile fathers of our "founding fathers," whether their holdings remained relatively modest or had expanded to abundance, inspired their sons with examples of entrepreneurship, the significance of service, and the value of education.

## Augustine Washington

Augustine Washington seems to have been sent by central casting. One can imagine this genial giant embracing a son incapable of telling a lie, or matching him in tossing silver coins across the Rappahannock. By all accounts he was a fitting father for the nation's founding father. The problem is the paucity of such accounts. Our picture of Augustine Washington has been framed by people who never knew him. He died when his most famous son was only eleven. As George Washington sadly reflected, "I was early deprived of a father."

That didn't prevent writers from putting words in George's mouth. According to Washington biographer Douglas Southall Freeman, the youth remembered his father as "tall, fair of complexion, well proportioned and fond of children." James Thomas Flexner, the other most prominent Washington biographer, adds that Augustine, called "Gus" by his friends, "was blond, of fine proportions and great physical strength and stood six feet in his stockings." Most of these family recollections, gathered by Augustine's step-grandson, are so similar that they must represent more than mythology.

Augustine
Washington

As historian Miriam Anne Bourne writes, it is inconceivable that such an energetic man as Augustine Washington "would not have had some influence on his best-known son." Yet particularly the last decade of Augustine's forty-nine years on this earth was so frenetic that he could scarcely have spent very much time with George. What he left was the influence of an image.

For generations the Washingtons had lived in the Essex region of England, rising to become landed country gentry, just below the aristocracy, before finding themselves on the losing side of the English civil war of the 1640s. High-spirited John Washington, working his way over as a lowly mate on a sailing ship, arrived in Virginia in 1657. He lost little time finding himself a prosperous bride, the most direct form of upward mobility, and exercising what biographer John Alden calls his "passion for acreage"—both qualities to be demonstrated by future Washingtons. Much of his rich Westmoreland County land was inherited by his more sedate son, Lawrence, an eminently respectable lawyer. He had ambitious plans for his offspring, but unfortunately he died too soon. His younger son, Augustine, was only three. By the time Augustine came of age in 1715, his robust good looks, generous nature, and possession of at least a remnant of his parents' land made him an attractive catch. At twenty-one he married sixteen- or seventeen-year-old Jane Butler.

Starting their life together on a 1,700-acre plantation at Popes Creek, the young couple were not truly wealthy by patrician Virginia standards, but they were much admired, a bright future seemingly stretching out before them. Eventually Augustine built a handsome home called "Wakefield." By then Jane had given birth to four children, three of whom survived. The two boys had familiar names—Lawrence and another Augustine. The senior Augustine was already a justice of the peace and a member of the county court. He would go on to be named a church warden, high sheriff of Westmoreland County, and eventually a trustee of Fredericksburg—an acknowledged leader in each of the three Virginia localities in which his family would reside.

What changed Augustine's life was the discovery of a rich deposit of iron ore at Popes Creek, turning him from a gentleman farmer to an overburdened entrepreneur. Augustine entered into a partnership with British investors to form the Principio Company. By the mid-eighteenth century the company would manufacture and export over 3,000 tons of pig iron. Managing the complex enterprise not only frequently separated Augustine from his family, it also took a considerable psychological toll. Normally renowned for his equanimity, Augustine, at least in running his business, became nervous, uncertain, and irritable. Records indicate that he was often engaged in litigation of one kind or another. While he was in England in 1729, meeting with his increasingly contentious partners, Jane, his wife of fourteen years, passed away.

Despite feelings of guilt and grief, Augustine was obliged to find a new mother for his children. Amiable widows were hardly in short supply in Virginia, but Augustine, now a mature thirty-seven, settled on an "old maid" of twenty-three named Mary Ball. Flexner describes Mary as "a healthy orphan of moderate height, rounded figure, and pleasant voice." Not everyone was to find her voice so pleasant in future years. She brought to their marriage in 1731 some property of her own and a very strong will, more than a match for her obliging husband.

Eleven months later, on the morning of February 22, 1732, Mary gave birth to a baby described as large enough to be a proper son of Augustine Washington. He was called George, not for a prior Washington but for George Eskridge, who had been Mary's devoted guardian. By the time he learned to walk, George had a sister named Betty; in a year and a half, he had a brother named Samuel. They were followed by John Augustine, Charles, and Mildred. That five of these six children survived to adulthood, an unlikely percentage at that time and place, testifies to the vigor of both parents. While growing up, George hardly wanted for playmates, black as well as white. At Popes Creek, the natural world was just outside his door, supplemented by a menagerie of dogs, chickens, calves, pigs, and horses. Throughout, Augustine was the parent on the move, Mary the parent in place.

That place would change when George was three. Augustine moved his family from Westmoreland County to a much larger plantation farther up the Potomac, at Little Hunting Creek in what is now Fairfax County, Virginia. A few years later, in 1738, the family moved for the final time, to be closer to Augustine's principal iron mine and furnace, at Accokeek Creek, in present-day Stafford County, on the Rappahannock River, near the new town of Fredericksburg. Called "Ferry Farm," it was truly George's childhood home. If, indeed, he cut down that cherry tree, it was likely here. A precocious, lively child, George loved to hunt in the nearby woods and to fish, swim, and sail in the river, narrow enough for a strong youth to hurl a heavy coin across. Some of this activity had to be in the company of his nature-loving father, although by now Augustine was immersed not only in the iron business and farming tobacco and other crops but in buying, selling, and leasing land to others.

For a time George was enrolled in a small school in Fredericksburg operated by an Anglican clergyman, but his education was largely in the hands of tutors. George learned to write in a fine, flourishing hand. His studies tended toward the practical, although they included moral and natural philosophy. He became a proficient draftsman, essential for a future surveyor, and was good at arithmetic. His classical education was intended to come later, at the Appleby School in England, where George's half-brothers were already enrolled.

It was probably they, particularly Lawrence Washington, whom George had in mind when he wrote with such care in his notebook all 110 maxims of the "Rules of Civility in Decent Behavior in Company and

Conversation." Devised by Jesuits for Spanish or French nobility, they were equally applicable to the proprietary gentry of Virginia. When Lawrence returned from England, for a few precious months George saw his two role models together. He greatly admired his father's commanding presence and his half-brother's effortless ease in any company. Together they represented the ideal gentleman. Lawrence's later return, in 1743, as a dashing young captain in a Virginia regiment that had taken part in a British expedition against Spain in the Caribbean completed the picture of gentility. Lawrence was engaged now to lovely Anne Fairfax, whose family stood at the very pinnacle of Tidewater society. Such acceptance marked the apogee of ascension for the Washington family, after only three generations in America. Surely George could do no less.

He was visiting nearby cousins when a messenger arrived with the urgent summons to return home. His father was dying. It may have been exacerbated by pneumonia, but the official cause of death was "gout of the stomach." At the age of forty-nine, Augustine Washington passed away on April 12, 1743. His will was predictably detailed and included provisions for everyone. To Lawrence, the elder son of his first marriage, went the house at Little Hunting Creek. He would rebuild and rename it Mount Vernon, in honor of English admiral Edward Vernon, under whom he had served. To George, to be kept in trust for him by his mother until he came of age, went Ferry Farm and its surroundings.

The impact on George was immense. Beyond the immediacy of the loss, he had looked forward not only to going to school in England but probably to William and Mary College as well. All his life he would feel keenly his lack of formal education and exposure to the wider world. He was only to travel once outside the original colonies, to Barbados with Lawrence. George Washington might be first in command or even character, but he never viewed himself as the intellectual equal of Adams, Jefferson, Hamilton, or Madison—and they concurred.

His widowed mother, who never remarried, intended that George should become titular head of her bustling household, under her relentless supervision, at the tender age of eleven. It is not surprising that he preferred the more congenial company of Lawrence at Mount Vernon and the neighboring Fairfaxes at their palatial Belvoir estate. Alas, Lawrence, too, would die young, of tuberculosis. Before he was twenty, George had lost both of his male role models. Biographer Paul Longmore writes, "Perhaps we can see in the loss of his father the origins of his extraordinary drive for public fame." In the creation of his own austere official image, George Washington may have been less genial than his father, but no less commanding.

For all its initial promise, the time-consuming iron business did not lead to wealth substantially greater than that accumulated by Augustine's ambitious father or his swashbuckling grandfather. But appraisals of the life of Augustine Washington should not be circumscribed by such ready conclusions as historian Bernard Fay's: "He had been a good husband, a good father, a good worker, and a good Virginian, but he died too young." It was not too young to inspire his famous son. Had they been able to spend more time together, inspiration would have been enhanced by influence.

## John Adams Sr.

Augustine Washington was at home on two continents. "Deacon" John Adams rarely strayed from Braintree, in the Massachusetts Bay Colony, but the scope of his ambition was no less. It was not so much for himself as for his firstborn son, who would also be named John. He must go to college, which at that time and place meant Harvard. He could then attain the noblest of callings and become an eminent Congregational minister. At the very least, he would be prepared to enter one of the other learned professions. It was all preordained. As the son recalled a lifetime later, "My father had destined his firstborn, long before his birth to a public education"—meaning "public" in the English sense.

It seems unfair, a sort of educational primogeniture. Families were large in the Massachusetts Bay Colony, although these Adamses were to have only three children. Who was to say which one might benefit best from advanced learning? Still, arbitrary or not, the firstborn son remained the repository of parental hopes. And there was a more compelling reason. Deacon John could afford to send only one of his sons to college. He would try to make it up in due course to the others, if there were to be others. There was only one problem. Young John didn't want to go.

At ten he had already experienced some five years of preliminary education. Why must he, and only he, go on to college? "What would you do, child?" his exasperated father asked. "Why, be a farmer like you," his son replied. "A farmer! I'll show you what it is to be a farmer," Deacon John responded, and the next morning he took his son out with him to the marshes to cut thatch, a particularly laborious task. They didn't return until dark. "Well," asked the Deacon, not unkindly, "are you satisfied with being a farmer?" His son persisted. "I like it very well, sir." The father grew sterner. "Aye, but I don't like it so well. So you shall go back to school."

John Adams Sr. was not called Deacon merely to differentiate him from his oldest son. It was an affirmation of his devotion to both church and community. If not quite so theocratic as they had been at their inception, such Massachusetts towns as Braintree, in the eighteenth century, still merged the temporal with the spiritual. As biographer Page Smith writes, "A good Puritan kept a kind of daily audit of his soul's state of grace and submitted the account to God in private prayer and public meeting." Such intense introspection within so close-knit a community could be either stifling or inspiring. Young John Adams grew up in what would seem a foreign country to young George Washington. Yet despite the rigors of life in New England, and its climate, life expectancy was actually greater than in Virginia.

By the time young John Adams was born, the strictures of Calvinism had so relaxed that taverns dotted the village, more social contacts between young people often led to illegitimate births, and—most shocking of all—a small Anglican church, more liberal in its theology, nestled near the meetinghouse. In reaction, a Great Awakening was spreading throughout New England, calling the faithful back to their roots. The Congregational meetinghouse, called the North Precinct Church, reflecting these sentiments, remained at the center of Braintree in both location and life. During both extensive services every Sunday, its elders sat in front. The deacon's central place faced the pulpit. For fourteen years the senior John Adams was selected for this honor, so often that man and mission seemed to merge.

The Adams family had been among the first to settle in this town, before it had even been incorporated. They came from another Braintree across the sea, in Somersetshire. Had they stayed for the English civil war, they would have been on opposite sides from the Royalist Washingtons. To the Church of England and King Charles I, still in possession of his head, these dissenting Puritans were a royal nuisance. Some 20,000 emigrated in the 1630s and later, most with their families, intent on building their own City of God in the New World.

John Adams, the second son of a Joseph Adams, was born in 1691. The boy was obviously bright, but only his older brother, another Joseph, would be granted the opportunity to go to college. He became a respected Congregational minister in New Hampshire. John could not have enjoyed many terms at the village school, although he learned to read and write. Through the seasons of planting and harvesting, he would be needed at his family's farm. If he was resentful, no record of it survives.

By the time of his birth, Braintree contained a population of about 2,000. Homes were scattered or clustered near the central church, surrounded by many small farms with soil so stony that only the most strenuous labor could yield much bounty. In so self-sufficient a community, almost every household required an additional occupation to get through the rigorous winters. Henry Adams, John's grandfather, had been both a farmer and a maltster, who processed barley into beer. His brewery continued for two generations. However devout, Braintree was never dry. One of Henry's sons, initiating a tradition, served as the town's first clerk. Deacon John's father, Joseph, expanded on his example, being elected town constable, selectman, and surveyor of highways.

The Deacon's energy would outdo them all. He was both a farmer, growing wheat, corn, oats, and barley on his modest acreage, and a cordswainer, one who makes shoes and other leather goods. From mid-March to early autumn he tended his fields. At the end of the growing season, he would fashion his shoes, working at a low bench in a tiny room off the kitchen of his compact home. Despite his unobtrusiveness, people were drawn to his company for advice. He was as short in stature as his namesake would be, but sturdy and sound. He served as Braintree's tax collector, as a lieutenant in the militia, and was nine times elected a selectman, second only to his tenure as church deacon. He loved the town and lived there all his life, but never viewed himself as gentry or even as Braintree's first citizen. That distinction belonged to Colonel of Militia Josiah Quincy, a glass manufacturer and for forty years speaker of the Massachusetts Assembly. As Braintree's representative on the Governor's Council, Quincy was the acknowledged leader of this modest realm. If it mattered, Adams was surely second.

Yet John remained unfulfilled. In his forties, an age many of his neighbors would be happy simply to reach, he decided he must get married. The object of his affection was equally surprising, and some eighteen years younger—sophisticated and socially superior Susanna Boylston of Brookline, near Boston. Called Sarah by her friends, Susanna came from a family renowned for its medical practitioners. Although on the cusp of spinsterhood at twenty-five, she didn't want for suitors. What could she possibly see in stolid, sober, short, rural-rooted John Adams? Perhaps it was just such qualities that won her over. And, in truth, he was intelligent as well as industrious. As his first son later observed, "My parents were both fond of reading." In any case, in 1734 they were wed, and she was introduced to all the amenities Braintree could offer.

Only a year later, in the fall of 1735, as biographer John Ferling writes, Deacon John awoke "nervous and excited. At the age of forty-four he was to become a father for the first time." While he sat uneasily tinkering at his bench, Susanna, assisted by a midwife, gave birth to a healthy son. He, too, would be named John. The date was October 19, 1735. Reportedly, John and Susanna Adams bickered throughout their lives together, each strong-willed and stubborn, but of the future of this son they were of one mind. He would one day go to Harvard. Deacon John's means of upward ascent had not been so different from that of the first fathers of Virginia. As Smith puts it, "In later years his son surmised that it had been this union which had lifted the Adams family of Braintree out of the obscurity of small-town life."

That family would soon grow, although by very modest dimensions compared with their neighbors—or with prior Adamses. John had two younger brothers, Peter Boylston and Elihu. They all lived in a typical village house, a compact frame "saltbox," at a picturesque spot near Penn's Hill, adjacent to Adams's fields, the town, and the salt marshes of Boston Bay. Their home was often crowded with overnight visitors, relatives and men who came to consult with Deacon John. As Ferling writes, "Both parents worked diligently," the father toiling inside and out, the mother tending their garden, managing the home, and teaching each child to read by the age of five.

At six John was sent to a "dame school" in the home of a neighbor, where the regimen was largely reading and recitation. Along with the town's other more promising scholars, John was advanced to Braintree's Latin School, presided over by Joseph Cleverly, late of Harvard. When Cleverly died in 1802 at the age of ninety, Adams recalled him as "the most indolent man I ever knew, although a tolerable scholar and a gentleman." Cleverly's teaching was so indifferent and uninspired that it turned even so bright a child as young John Adams away from the pursuit of knowledge as a source of stimulation.

Not that he needed much incentive. The boy loved the outdoors and delighted in simply roaming and spending his hours as "idly" as possible. He recalled his pleasure "in making and sailing boats . . . in making and flying kites . . . in driving hoops" and in games and sports—playing marbles and quoits, wrestling, swimming, skating, and above all, shooting game of all kinds. His fowling piece was rarely absent from his side. Such bounty might be welcome at his family's dinner table, but this was hardly Deacon John's priority when he sent his son to school. Another source of concern was young John's active social life, "running about to quiltings and frolics and dances among the boys and girls." A hint of potential trouble is indicated by John's recitation of his preferences: "Girls, girls, cards, flutes, violins . . . laziness, languor, inattention are my bane."

Competitive yet sensitive, young John was also, as Smith writes, "imaginative, lively, quick, and handsome." His parents repeatedly warned John that sloth and licentiousness were equally sinful and could imperil his bright future. It is likely that as a youth John, well aware of his own "amorous disposition" and "ardent nature," sought more than wild game in the forests. In his old age, however, Adams insisted that he had never given way to temptation, finally finding sexual fulfillment in the safe haven of a strong marriage. Whether this was true or not, his parents' admonitions were never far from his mind, nor was his grounding in their morality.

Most of all, John recalled, "My Enthusiasm for Sports and Inattention to Books alarmed my Father." Despite everything, it was clear how instinctively bright and quick-witted young John was, but the Deacon also discerned a stubbornness equal to his own. "Why do you resist?" he asked repeatedly. Finally, his fourteen-year-old son blurted out the truth. "Sir, I don't like my schoolmaster." That was enough. The next day, John Adams had a new one.

Joseph Marsh, although the son of Braintree's former minister, had little use for organized religion and was a nonconformist generally. But Marsh genuinely enjoyed the cadence of a Latin sentence, the elegance of mathematics, and the glories of English history—and he could impart that enthusiasm to others. Under his tutelage John Adams had his personal Great Awakening. The intensive year and a half he spent with Marsh changed his life. He laid aimless avocations aside. But, as Ferling points out, "Success came only because of the wisdom of his father, who ultimately insisted that he complete his education."

Still, at sixteen, would John be ready for the challenges of Harvard? Marsh exuded confidence and prepared to ride with his charge, side by side, to the entrance examinations at Cambridge. Unfortunately, at the last moment, the schoolmaster fell ill. John would have to face the formidable Harvard elders alone. It turned out, however, that they were also benign, allowing the apprehensive young scholar to use a dictionary in translating a difficult Latin passage into English. Assigning a theme for John to write over the summer, they accepted him on the spot, an admissions process that certainly compares favorably with today's. He was even granted a partial scholarship, although his father would be obliged to sell the only ten acres of ground that ever passed from his possession in order to help pay his tuition. John all but floated home, a hero to his friends and the pride of his parents.

Although, as biographer Jack Shepherd writes, Adams's admission was a tribute to Harvard's insistence on opening "its doors to men of promise," the college in the 1750s was not yet a bastion of pure merit. John's ranking of fourteenth in a graduating class of twenty-five was based on an evaluation of the social status of his family. His mother's Boylston lineage could not have hurt. Academically he was at the top of his class. In the opinion of historian Daniel Boorstin, his associations at Harvard helped enable Adams to all but leap into eminence, becoming a "self-made aristocrat." It is not quite so. He was launched by his father, and he knew it. Of his "honored and beloved mother" he would say relatively little. Of his father, as biographer David McCullough points out in *John Adams,* "He could hardly say enough. . . . It was his father's honesty . . . independent spirit and love of country, Adams said, that were his lifelong inspiration."

He would, however, have to disappoint the Deacon in his choice of a career. He would not be a minister. It took some time to decide. John had witnessed too much of the worldly side of religion from his father's visitors. Physicians, in his view, were as likely to take life as save it. He longed to emulate his militiaman father, but not as a career. Teaching could only be a short-term profession, born of necessity. The law was dry, "a rubbish of writs," and quarrelsome, but it could be lucrative and lead to many other opportunities. In 1756, just short of his twenty-first birthday, still wracked by doubts, he contracted to begin an apprenticeship with his friend James Putnam, only twenty-eight himself, but already the leading attorney in Worcester, some sixty miles west of Braintree. After all, John reasoned, perhaps as much for his father as for himself, "The Practice of the Law . . . does not Dissolve the Obligations of Morality or of Religion."

He lived with the Putnams, a most hospitable couple. To pay his way he taught in a Worcester school, finding it as little to his liking as he had surmised. His public mien turned more serious, in part to impress his students with a maturity he hardly felt. Poring over precedents and accompanying Putnam on his rounds, John was reassured to discover a decided affinity for the law. It was not easily mastered, but it would definitely be his future. The diary he had started to keep affirmed a confidence that his reflections were worth recording.

In the fall of 1758, his apprenticeship ended, John returned home. The Putnams wanted him to settle in the vicinity, but John declined. He had already begun to have severe headaches. Ailments, real and imagined, would dog him the rest of his life. He longed for the healthful sea breezes, "the pure zephyrs from the rocky mountains of my native town," and the sight of his parents. He had left a boy of sixteen; he returned a man of twenty-three. A room in his parents' home became his office. John Adams would never reach a height of more than five foot six or seven, but he could hardly stand taller than he did now to his parents.

For a time he lived as his father always had, amidst the familiar people and places of his own town. His old friends still called him "Johnny" or "Jack." But he also set out to find influential patrons in Boston, where most of Braintree's legal business was conducted. It took time, but under the sponsorship of such leaders of the bar as Jeremiah Gridley, the fledgling attorney was admitted to practice before the Superior Court, equivalent to passing the bar today. Already in 1760, Adams was considering cases concerning the legality of writs of assistance, the sort of question that would ultimately imperil relations between Great Britain and its American colonies.

He was also pursuing other matters, in line with his still "ardent nature." He courted the lovely and flirtatious Hannah Quincy, daughter of Colonel Josiah Quincy, who had come to take quite a shine to young Adams. Hannah, however, chose another of her many suitors. In the company of a friend, Richard Cranch, he journeyed to the nearby town of Weymouth. Cranch was smitten with Mary Smith, the oldest daughter of the Reverend William Smith, the well-educated and well-heeled pastor of Weymouth's Congregational church. The Smiths had two other sprightly daughters, Abigail and Eliza. Abigail was more intrigued than impressed by this outspoken young lawyer, and Adams viewed all the Smith girls as "not fond, not frank, not candid." First impressions are subject to revision.

Everything changed in the spring of 1761. No American colony was immune from periodic epidemics of influenza, smallpox, typhoid, or diphtheria, and medical science could do little to limit their toll. Who survived and who succumbed was largely a matter of luck. An attack of influenza throughout the Massachusetts coastline put half the citizens of Braintree to bed. Seventeen people expired, among them seventy-year-old Deacon John Adams. He died only a few days after falling ill, on May 25, 1761, his three sons by his bedside. His wife, Susanna, who had also been stricken but survived, was too weak to attend his funeral. She would live into her eighty-ninth year. The ministers at the meetinghouse so familiar to all the Adamses celebrated the Deacon's life, stressing that those taken in the fullness of years should be more appreciated than mourned.

It was scant solace for young John, who for some time sank into a deep depression. Deacon John left a relatively substantial estate. As in life, he had sought to distribute it equitably. A nearby farm he owned in Randolph went to Elihu, and the Adams homestead to Peter Boylston. John Adams, his executor, inherited the smallest share in that he alone had received "a liberal education," but it included a house adjacent to the main home in Braintree and some thirty acres of land.

What this did, however, was to enable John, once he had recovered emotionally, to take part in town meetings and attain his responsible place in the community. Now he was a man of property, however modest, and a taxpayer. He was elected a freeholder and even for a time named surveyor of highways. One can see the influence of his childhood in his subsequent attacks on the evil influence of the town's taverns, and his own ambition in his opposition to "pettifoggers," who today would be called shyster lawyers. In this final gift, Deacon John had enabled his favored son to launch his legal practice in the most direct way possible.

The aristocratic Charles Francis Adams characterized his great-grand-father, Deacon John Adams, as merely "a typical New England yeoman." John Adams knew better. He could hardly find adequate words to suffi-ciently praise his father, this stalwart citizen who for twenty years had managed "almost all the business of the town." He venerated Deacon John as "the honestest man I ever knew. . . . In wisdom, piety, benevo-lence and charity in proportion to his education and sphere of life I have never seen his equal." In geographical terms, that "sphere of life" was minute. In terms of influence on his first son, it was immense.

## Peter Jefferson

Thomas Jefferson owed everything to his father, although he might have spared a few more words to acknowledge the debt. In his autobiography, written some sixty-three years after the death of Peter Jefferson, Thomas noted, "My father's education had been quite neglected; but being of a strong mind, sound judgment, and eager after information, he read much and improved himself." That is all most biographers quote, but Thomas went on to observe that the elder Jefferson was chosen, along with a mathematics professor from William and Mary College, to determine the boundary line between Virginia and North Carolina. Imagine, Peter Jefferson was so "eager after information" that he taught himself, to a remarkable level of proficiency, mapmaking and surveying. He was truly the personification of his son's vision for the new nation, a self-made aristocracy not of birth but of achievement.

Well, perhaps not entirely self-made. Although, as noted Jefferson biographer Dumas Malone writes of Peter, "The enhancement of his fortunes, like the improvement of his mind, must be chiefly attributed to his own exertions," even the sturdy, independent father of Thomas Jefferson didn't make it entirely on his own. In his brief account of his lineage, Thomas seems more interested in natural than in familial history: "The tradition of my father's family was that their ancestors came to this country from Wales, and from near the mountain of Snowden, the highest in Great Britain." In fact, as biographer Merrill Peterson points out, there had been Jeffersons in Virginia since its earliest settlement. The youngest son of a moderately successful planter, Peter Jefferson was born to neither excessive wealth nor privilege, but he had inherited a good name, his forebears' energy, and property ripe for development. He would improve it as he "improved himself."

In his mid-twenties Peter seems a combination of Augustine Washington, Daniel Boone, and Paul Bunyan. He stood well over six feet tall, and his strength was legendary. He was reputed, for example, to have lifted at the same time two hogsheads of tobacco, each weighing a thousand pounds, upright from their sides. Such superhuman strength would be put to the test as Peter set out to explore and expand his wild domain. Biographer Thomas Fleming writes, "He had fought his way through the winter wilderness . . . often living on the raw flesh of game and even on his own pack-train mules, sleeping in hollow trees while wolves and wildcats howled around him." Yet when his mapping was completed, he would somehow find his way back to his humble home to read Addison, Swift, Pope, and Shakespeare, "eager after information," a man for all seasons.

Although described by historian Fawn Brodie as "grave and taciturn," Peter also had "a faculty for friendship." He took people as they came, making friends readily, to his great advantage, whether with the resident Indians, not yet alarmed by an excess of interlopers, or with his few neighboring plantation owners, intrepid pioneers like himself. The most prominent, in terms of both social status and his future friendship, was wealthy young William Randolph, whose 2,400 acres adjoined Peter's smaller property. The Randolphs would be to the Jeffersons what the Fairfaxes were to the Washingtons—a connection vaulting them from gentry to aristocracy. At thirty-two, Peter paused long enough to marry Randolph's beguiling nineteen-year-old cousin Jane.

Forging ahead, acquiring more land, by two years after his marriage Peter had rounded out a much larger tract on which to build a proper home for his wife. It would be called "Shadwell," after the Anglican parish in England where she had been baptized. Working hand in hand with his few slaves, Peter erected a remarkably spacious edifice, rising a story and a half, scenically sited at the edge of the hazy Blue Ridge Mountains by the Rivanna River. Shadwell's grounds included a terraced garden for Jane, who also loved the outdoors. However isolated from polite society, it was a relatively healthy environment, less prone to the mosquitoes and fevers that afflicted the lowlands. Eight of the ten children born to the Jeffersons survived infancy. Peter and Jane moved into Shadwell in 1741, with the two daughters they already had, and it was here, on April 13, 1743, that their first son was born and given the recurring family name of Thomas.

Thomas Jefferson's earliest memory was of being carried as a child of three by a mounted slave on a pillow from this home to another, illustrating both sides of his comfortably ambulatory childhood—secure yet insecure. If George Washington was born only a day's journey from the American frontier, Thomas Jefferson was set directly on it.

By the terms of an extraordinary agreement between Peter Jefferson and William Randolph, young Tom would be uncertain precisely where his home was located. A widower with two children, Randolph died at only thirty-three. His will, which Peter had approved, stipulated that upon his death both the Randolph plantation at Tuckahoe, some fifty miles east of Shadwell, and the Randolph children would be under the care of Peter Jefferson, "his dear and loving friend." For the next seven years, while Shadwell was overseen by trusted associates, the Jeffersons resided at Tuckahoe, raising two sets of children. At least Tom wouldn't want for playmates. From the age of five, he was taught by a tutor in a little schoolhouse on the grounds.

Peter taught Tom surveying, which many years later he would teach to Meriwether Lewis, and mathematics. Indeed, Peter taught his son everything he could. As biographer Henry Sterne Randall writes, Peter made certain his son knew how "to sit on his horse, fire his gun, boldly stem the Rivanna" when the river turned treacherous. Tom never enjoyed shooting, even wild turkeys, but he thoroughly absorbed his father's love of the natural world and emulated his keen knowledge of it. Peter gave him his own canoe, for which a local Indian chief provided a cherished hand-carved paddle.

The merged families sang and celebrated together. Tom even learned to play the fiddle. Peter encouraged his son to delve into his well-worn library of over forty books. He would not have a second boy until Tom was twelve. Peter and Tom even thought a bit alike, sharing a rather measured, serious approach to things, as well as a calm demeanor. Tom's facial features, delicate and small, favored his father's, although his pale face was more freckled and his hair was a bright red. He was growing up as tall as his father, and almost as strong, but gangling and lanky, far more slender. He relished Peter's favorite homely admonitions, such as "Never ask another to do for you what you can do for yourself" and "It is the strong in body who are both the strong and *free* in mind." Between them there developed a bond of immense affection, even if it was rarely voiced.

Then, in 1752, the Jeffersons, with things well established at Tucka-hoe, returned to Shadwell, and Tom was abandoned. Or so he felt. At nine he was sent to study and board at the Latin school of the Reverend William Douglas. Could he not have continued his studies through a learned tutor at Shadwell? Sensitive young Tom was terribly homesick and was bound to blame Peter for so sudden a separation. As biographer Page Smith writes, "Even though his later references to his father are respectful and admiring, there is about them an unmistakable reserve." As for Douglas, Jefferson preferred the subjects he studied to his schoolmas-ter's scholarship. "To read the Latin and Greek authors in their original is a sublime luxury," Jefferson reflected, concluding that he should "thank on [his] knees him who directed my early education." That direction, of course, had been set by his father.

Peter Jefferson emerged as unquestionably the first citizen of Albe-marle County. He was named to chancery court and was a justice of the peace, church warden, county surveyor, and, as a lieutenant, the chief offi-cer of the local militia. For a time he served as a member in the House of Burgesses, although his responsibilities at home precluded a political career. He had accumulated 7,500 fertile acres. His care in maintaining it, and his passion for detail, would be transmitted to his eldest son. Tom was also deeply influenced by Peter Jefferson's example of egalitarianism. On the frontier he had run into all manner of men and had learned to judge them only by their deeds. He was himself a man of few words, little given to artifice, a composite of frontier and plantation. Even what Tom had seen of slavery was relatively benign, his parents teaching their slaves useful skills, from carpentry to housekeeping, as part of an interdependent extended family. Yet Tom also experienced a puzzling separation when his black playmates did not accompany him to school, sensing the fundamental dilemma he would be unable to reconcile in the years ahead.

On August 17, 1757, Peter Jefferson abruptly terminated his son's reluctant tenure with the Reverend Douglas, but in a most tragic fashion. He died. Although he had been feeling rather poorly throughout the summer and had been frequently visited by his friend Dr. Thomas Walker, his death came to his family as a sudden shock. He was only forty-nine years old. It may well be that the accumulation of all those forays into the forests had overtaxed even his robust constitution and legendary strength.

Tom's reaction to his father's death, beyond sadness, was peculiarly self-centered. It seemed almost another betrayal. Even a lifetime later he recalled, "At fourteen years of age the whole care and direction of myself was thrown on myself entirely, without a relation or friend to advise or guide me." What of the five devoted guardians selected by his father? What of his mother, and the others of his household? Malone concludes that the loss of Peter Jefferson "created a chasm [in his son's life] which remained unfilled until his years in Williamsburg." Jefferson's education, of course, did not end. He was enrolled at a school administered by the Reverend James Maury, another Anglican minister, but one he admired far more than Douglas, and then to William and Mary College. The other three students at Maury's became Jefferson's closest friends. Such mentors in Williamsburg as William Small and George Wythe were his mature role models. None of this would have been possible had it not been for self-taught Peter Jefferson's love of learning. Unlike Augustine Washington, he specifically insisted in writing that his son's "thorough classical education" be continued and completed.

What did Peter endow to Thomas in immediate, tangible terms? "My mulatto fellow Shawney, my Books, mathematical instruments, & my Cherry tree Desk and Bookcase." Shawney was his father's favorite servant; the rest constituted the inheritance of an intellectual. At college, while his classmates caroused, Jefferson was known to study for as long as fifteen hours at a stretch—the mental equivalent of his father's physical energy. When he came of age, Thomas was given his choice of either Peter's "lands on the Rivanna River and its branches" or his other major property on the Fluvanna River, locales that even sound classical. Tom was technically the man of his house, at only fourteen, just as George Washington was intended to be at eleven. Washington escaped to Mount Vernon and Belvoir, Jefferson to college. He insisted that his father's books meant more to him than any estate. When Shadwell burned in 1770, it was the books he most mourned.

Thomas Jefferson sustained sudden losses again in his lifetime, and suffered them largely in silence. His adored wife died after only ten years of marriage. When he built Monticello on his mountaintop, it was only four miles from the site of Shadwell, the land still beautiful and wild. His father left him too often, and then too soon, but had endowed him with both a position and the means to maintain it, both an estate and an education. As Peterson concludes, had Peter Jefferson lived longer he could have done so much more, but already "the pathway to power had been blazed for his son."

## James Madison Sr.

In a prior book I titled an early chapter "The Missing Mothers of Virginia." The corresponding first fathers aren't so much missing as marginalized. Why would James Madison say, not of his father but of his first schoolmaster, "All I have in life I owe largely to that man"? Who saw fit to send Madison to his school? And who did Madison have the grace to thank later for advancing him a generous "bill of exchange" at Princeton? In fact, whose credit was he still using during sessions of the Constitutional Convention in Philadelphia? It was always his father who not only paid his bills but also paved his way.

If Madison's gratitude to James Madison Sr. is difficult to discern, it is probably because he didn't view his private life as anyone else's business. When finally induced to dictate an autobiography of sorts, he provided only the "merest skeleton," some two hundred words, to describe his first eighteen years. As for his parents, "In both the paternal and maternal line . . . they were planters and among the respectable, though not the most opulent class." As with his predecessors, Madison's paternal line had also been socially elevated by the maternal. Unlike the fathers of

James Madison Sr.

Washington and Jefferson, however, James Madison Sr. lived to proudly witness his son's rise to prominence in the new republic they had struggled together to create. His "Jemmy" was on his way to Washington to become secretary of state when, finally, the old man's "flame of life" went out in 1801.

The first "Maddison," John, a ship's carpenter who was even more proficient as a promoter, used the money he made from the "headright" system—talking others into coming to the New World—to "patent" immense Virginia acreage for himself. By the time he died in the late 1600s he was esteemed as a landed gentleman, losing only the extra "d" in his name.

John's grandson James was born in 1723. An only son, he would later have two sisters. As biographer Virginia Moore writes, this original James

Madison "was a man before he was a boy." His father, Ambrose, died when James was only nine. His mother relied on him to help run the premises. The plantation was a self-contained community, its modest main house surrounded by outbuildings—slave family cabins, barns and sheds for cattle, sheep, hogs, and horses. Pasture land had to be maintained, apple and peach trees planted. Wheat, corn, and especially tobacco had to be marketed. It fell to James to keep it all going.

Despite the relative isolation of his plantation, Madison's father had established warm relationships with surrounding planters. One of them, Francis Conway, he had made an executor of his will. The Conways had a daughter named Nelly, whom James had met when she was only nine. As James grew into manhood, one of his tasks was to transport great hogsheads of tobacco (the sort Peter Jefferson had "headed up") for storage and inspection to a warehouse owned by the Conways. The main attraction was Nelly Conway, now a lovely and lively teenager. Acquaintance ripened into affection. They were married in September 1749, when she was seventeen and he a mature twenty-six.

Their first child, named James for his father, was born on March 16, 1751. James, called "Jemmy," was the first of his parents' twelve children. In the sad demographics of the time, only seven were to survive to maturity. Unlike George Washington and Thomas Jefferson, sturdy sons of sturdy fathers, "little Jemmy" would reach only five foot three or five foot six, depending on which account is accurate. Moreover, he was always sickly. That he survived to eighty-five—almost, as he remarked, "to have outlived myself"—would have astonished his anxious parents. The Conways were reputed to be descended from Scottish nobility, but family pride born of lineage was no more a preoccupation of the Madisons than it had been of the Jeffersons. Pride of place was another matter. When Jemmy was brought from his birthplace, the home of his mother's family at Port Conway, beyond the Rappahannock, to the modest wooden house that had been erected by Ambrose Madison, his father was already planning a magnificent replacement.

The harmonious, graceful mansion his father named Montpelier was completed when Jemmy was eight. He recalled being allowed to carry in some of its lighter furniture. He would expand the house as an adult, and he particularly enjoyed its setting of fields, lawns, and forest, opening out to the vista of the Blue Ridge Mountains. Madison's was a more settled, emotionally secure childhood than that of Washington or Jefferson, his mother solicitous, his father busy but not so often away. Montpelier would always be the true home of both James Madisons.

James Madison Sr. was hardly an intellectual. When he died, his library of eighty-five books, unlike Peter Jefferson's literary classics, were largely religious and medical works. But Jemmy marveled at his father's mastery of agricultural management and admired his even temper and his respected position in the community.

The major event each Sunday, both social and liturgical, was attending services at Brick Church, erected in the 1750s. Since the Anglican Church was officially sanctioned in Virginia, as a vestryman James Madison Sr. played a role in the colony's government as well. Church and courthouse were only six miles apart. Madison was reluctant to take on more tasks, with so many family responsibilities weighing on him, but ultimately he was convinced to become a justice of the peace (that perennial position of first fathers), a presiding magistrate of Orange County, and a colonel of the militia. Like Augustine Washington and Peter Jefferson, he became, in effect, the first citizen of his community.

Jemmy enjoyed nothing more than following his father around their domain, exploring its wonders on foot or horseback. The boy enjoyed riding, although it came no more naturally to him than other outdoor activities. His lifelong hatred of slavery derived from this rural childhood. His earliest playmates were largely the children of his father's slaves. As with Jefferson, he saw little of slavery's overt brutality—his father was a most humane master—but Jemmy came to understand the inherent inequity of such a system. He, too, would struggle throughout his public career to establish a solution, only to pass any implementation on to later generations.

The elder Madison, now often called "Squire," was a more scientific farmer than many of his neighbors, expanding his acres of wheat and other crops in addition to tobacco and becoming less dependent on the vagaries of nature. Over the vagaries of man he had less control. In his thirties, during the French and Indian War, Madison headed what amounted to a home guard, but the entire area was terrified by the possible results of English general Edward Braddock's crushing defeat. It may be that Jemmy actually saw Virginia rangers commanded by the young George Washington protecting straggling survivors of Braddock's original force. In any case, as biographer Irving Brant points out, while Madison always viewed Negroes, on whom he had relied as a child, as kindhearted and faithful, he considered Indians bloodthirsty, treacherous savages.

Taught reading, writing, and computation at home, Jemmy had demonstrated immense promise. Concerned about their son's fragility, the Madisons were loath to send him too far away to continue his education.

From the ages of eleven through fifteen, Jemmy boarded at the nearby classical school of Donald Robertson. Unlike Thomas Jefferson's relationship with William Douglas, Madison loved both his school and his schoolmaster. Like Jefferson, Madison discovered that learning to read the classics in their original languages was both a joy and a revelation. Madison came to almost revere Robertson, ascribing to him the credit for "all I have in life." Although Jemmy deeply loved his parents, he was none too happy to return home in 1761. As it happened, the youthful rector of Brick Church, the Reverend Thomas Martin, had been engaged to tutor the Madison children and came to live at Montpelier. His particular concern was to prepare Jemmy for college, a destination the elder Madison had settled on with the certainty of John Adams for his namesake.

In this instance, however, the location of the college was less certain. Madison was not at all happy with what he had heard about the licentiousness then prevailing at William and Mary, still the college of choice for the sons of Virginia planters. Martin had graduated from the College of New Jersey at Princeton and thought highly of its celebrated new president, the Reverend John Witherspoon. That both school and president were Presbyterian mattered not at all to Madison. Moreover, the northern climate was considered more healthful than even backcountry Virginia, and the Madisons had come to trust Martin's judgment.

In 1769, James Madison Jr. became one of the first Southerners to matriculate at Princeton. The college and Witherspoon would have as profound an impact on Madison's future course as Robertson had on his intellectual foundations. As distinguished historians Oscar and Lilian Handlin point out, Witherspoon linked civil morality with clerical mission: "All people possessed the capacity for reason, just as all possessed souls to save." Squire Madison had done his son a service, biographer Merrill Peterson writes, in taking such "a venturesome step. . . . It paid off not simply in the standard currency of education but in the education of a man whose personal identifications were neither Virginian nor Anglican, but American." As Jemmy wrote his father, at commencement he and his friends wore only "American cloth." Madison would insist on the same some forty years later at his presidential inauguration.

James Sr. was slowly moving in the same political direction as his son. He had early expressed concern at the implications of the Stamp Act and later was alarmed by news of the bloodshed at Lexington and Concord. However sober and conservative Madison's instincts remained, as an established planter and representative of the king's justice, when the

American Revolution finally came to Orange County, Virginia, its headquarters was at Montpelier. Father and son worked together. Back from
college, itself a hotbed of emerging American nationalism, Jemmy and his
father organized a local committee of public safety, with the elder Madison at its head. Both took the oath of allegiance to Virginia—and ultimately to the United States of America. Firearms were assembled, and
the militia mobilized. By now both father and son held the position of
colonel. When, at fifty-five, Madison Sr. sought to resign his leadership of
Orange County's resistance, he could only be dissuaded by his son. Neither was to see action in the conflict, but both shared in its patriotic
resolve.

According to writer Jeff Young, they even looked a bit alike, despite
the difference in height. Both the "old Colonel" and the "young Colonel" shared a distinctively long upper lip. Their reserved manner was also
quite similar. Virginia Moore writes that the father's reticence had been
fostered by "heavy early farm responsibilities . . . the son's by an example
of a father he greatly esteemed and by his own experience in office
holding."

They probably didn't sound very much alike, however. According to
contemporary reports, Jemmy's voice was so "soft" that it could scarcely
be heard. He didn't make an actual address until he was thirty, four years
after launching his public career. Yet somehow he bested the eloquent
Patrick Henry in their dramatic debate over Virginia's adopting the Constitution of the United States. As biographer Robert Rutland attests,
Madison often turned to his aged father for counsel during the critical
days of constructing the American Constitution. "The business goes very
slowly," he wrote. "We are in a wilderness without a single footstep to
guide us."

Inevitably, our prevailing view of each founding father can seem one-
dimensional—the austere, commanding Washington; the stubborn, methodical Adams; the enigmatic, brilliant Jefferson. Madison, if considered at all,
seems particularly colorless, however impressive his intellect. There was
nothing impressive about his physical presence. As Washington Irving put
it, "Jemmy Madison—ah, poor Jemmy! He is but a withered little apple
John." Yet, as the father of our Constitution, the "lonely last sentinel" of
the founders, Madison is the equal of any American statesman. In old age
he modestly declined the title of "sage of his time," insisting that the
Constitution was "the work of many heads and hands." If, in such under-
statement, he could never quite credit his father's inspiration, Madison

reached a poignant eloquence when he wrote on February 28, 1801, to an anxious Thomas Jefferson in Washington, awaiting the arrival of his new secretary of state, of the death of seventy-seven-year-old James Madison Sr., "Yesterday morning rather suddenly, tho very gently, the flame of life went out." Torn between his family and his friend, Madison stayed with his father to the end.

## Spence Monroe

If James Madison was "the last of the founders," James Monroe came close behind, completing the cycle of four favored Virginians who, in concert with a remarkable Massachusetts family, transformed a collection of colonies into unique nationhood. Of his father, Spence Monroe, we know just enough to validate at least some similarities with the more successful first fathers who preceded him. He, too, was a patriot, a gentleman but not an aristocrat, whose fortunes were at least moderately enhanced by an advantageous marriage and whose fondest wish was for the education of his favored son. His forebears, the "Munroes" of Scotland, like the Washingtons, had emigrated to Virginia after siding with the losing Royalists in the English civil war. Oliver Cromwell certainly had an influence in developing the American colonies.

Over time, Munroes became Monroes—major landowners around Monroe's Creek in Westmoreland County. There were so many Monroes that young Spence, in their third American generation, inherited only about 500 acres. Like John Maddison, both a modest landowner and a carpenter, he was considered at least marginally a gentleman. Spence's carpentry was not nautical but domestic. He was technically a "joiner." It is likely that Spence's modest two-story frame house was largely crafted by his own efforts. Such a humble residence, on sandy soil near a virgin forest, represented little cachet in a neighborhood of 60,000-acre estates, presided over by their indolent, English-emulating proprietors. In this "Northern Neck" of Virginia, the gentry consumed their abundant fare on fine china in the elaborate luxury of elegant dining rooms. The Monroes ate in the same area in which they lived, using wooden bowls, their food cooked in pots and pans hanging over a slow-burning flame in their central fireplace.

Born on April 28, 1758, James was the oldest of five children of Spence and Elizabeth Monroe. When, a lifetime later, he was induced to write a spare autobiographical sketch, all he volunteered about his parents was predictably positive—his father was "a worthy and respectable citizen possessed of good land and other property." His mother, Elizabeth Jones, often called Eliza, was "amiable and respectable." It was her family's status that enhanced Spence Monroe's expectations for his first son. She was the daughter of an "undertaker in architecture," and her father was married to the daughter of a prominent lawyer. Her brother, Judge Joseph Jones of Fredericksburg, presided over the Virginia General Court, later served in Congress, and became a confidant of Washington, Jefferson, and Madison.

The sons of the planter elite learned their Latin, Greek, and other components of a classical education on their plantations from tutors often imported from abroad. They would then go on to college in England, at Oxford or Cambridge, or, after its chartering in 1693, to William and Mary in Williamsburg. The best Spence Monroe could manage was to send his son trudging through deep woods to the schoolhouse of stern Parson Archibald Campbell, several miles away.

The travel, if not the course of study, wasn't all that challenging for vigorous young Monroe. Even at the age of eleven, he seems as solemn a youth as James Madison, but there the comparison ends. Monroe was tall and strong, skilled at every outdoor pursuit. He loved riding, hunting, and any form of exercise. A crack shot, he carried a rifle over one arm and his books over the other. On his way home from school, he would often bag game for his family's dinner table. His congenial daily companion was future Chief Justice John Marshall, whose personality was as lighthearted as Monroe's was somber. At Campbell's school, as the leading Monroe biographer William Penn Cresson writes, Monroe gained "a solid foundation in the classics, a respect for the factual exactness of mathematics, and an understanding of such words as loyalty, honesty, honor, and devotion."

His father had already provided an example of courage. At the behest of Richard Henry Lee, Spence Monroe in 1766 was one of those bold Virginians who drafted and signed resolutions opposing the Stamp Act and encouraged a boycott of English goods to back up their demands. In this way, as famous nineteenth-century historian George Bancroft wrote, "Virginia rang the alarm bell for the continent." Whatever Monroe had to risk, he risked it all.

Although his son's schooling deprived Spence of help he could surely have used on his farm, it was not to be interrupted. Biographer Harry Ammon notes that Spence allowed his children great freedom at home, unusual for the time. Madison's home and school environments both stressed constancy and character. Somehow, Spence managed to at least get James started at William and Mary. On the eve of the American Revolution, apparently divested of the excesses Madison's father had decried, under an inspiring new president, William and Mary, along with the entire town of Williamsburg, seethed with excitement. Great issues were at hand.

Spence Monroe didn't live to witness it. He died in 1774. His modest estate was inherited by James, which only made him responsible for the rest of his family. His final bills at college were paid by his influential uncle, Joseph Jones. At his own death, Jones directed that his sizable estate be divided among the children of his late sisters, "allowing [his] nephew Colonel James Monroe the first choice." Not only Spence could appreciate the young man's qualities.

James Monroe left college after only two years to serve in the Continental Army. His notable bravery in a number of Revolutionary engagements won Washington's personal commendation. At scarcely twenty years of age he was a lieutenant colonel, soon launched on his legal and political careers. By the measure of prior first fathers, Spence Monroe was not notably successful. But had he been less intent on education, what would have been the future of James Monroe? As Cresson writes, the boy was already "solid at sixteen." What better tribute to the man who raised him?


IF ONE HAD ASKED any of the fathers of our first five presidents to name his occupation, the probable response would have been "farmer." To be sure, the four Virginians were more gentleman farmers (even Spence Monroe), plantation owners on horseback, employing—whatever their deep reservations about the peculiar institution—slave labor. Only Deacon John Adams likely got down to dig in the dirt very often.

Yet by the time of his death, Augustine Washington was already more of a business entrepreneur than a farmer, a precursor of many future first fathers. All of these first five were engaged, to some extent, in the official life of their communities, but government was viewed as a necessary part-time commitment for gentlemen—those with the means, judgment, knowledge, and most of all the leisure to pursue it. George Washington's role model from antiquity was Cincinnatus, who left his plow to save Rome, and then promptly returned. The citizen-soldier readily became the citizen-statesman. The backbone of Jefferson's America was to be its sturdy, independent, informed yeomanry—a more egalitarian premise, to be sure, but still leadership by the enlightened.

The first five of our first fathers would have affirmed all this. They were upwardly mobile, all right, most fortuitously through their marriages. But what they sought for their favored sons was not so much sustained power as personal fulfillment. The means of ascent was education. Deacon John Adams may have preferred that his son be a minister, others that their sons follow the law, but it was not the profession that mattered. The Deacon's son would make that plain. It was the direction.

# 2

# THE FIRST LINE

## John Adams

GRANTED A SON who would one day also rise to the presidency, John Adams—his family's future always in his mind—projected that for John Quincy and subsequent generations of Adamses, high office was less a priority than high achievement.

Both John Adams and John Quincy Adams were first sons to whom much was given and from whom much would be expected. Unlike Thomas Jefferson, who believed that every generation starts anew, to John Adams a family's progress, no less than a nation's, could and should be enhanced one generation after another. As the great-great-grandson of the first Adams to come to the Massachusetts Bay Colony, and the son of so generous a father, Adams felt keenly his responsibility to advance his family's name. It was not necessarily a political dynasty that he projected for the future.

On a diplomatic mission to Paris, Adams mused about all this, culminating in a conclusion much quoted because it seems so uncharacteristic: "I must study politics and war," he reflected, "so that my sons may have the liberty to study mathematics and philosophy. My sons ought to study mathematics and philosophy, geography, natural history, naval architecture, navigation, commerce, and agriculture in order to give their children a right to study paintings, poetry, music, architecture, tapestry, and porcelain." Perhaps he was simply affirming that the attainment of leisure is necessary for the appreciation of beauty. But whatever he had in mind, none of his children—including the one who succeeded him in the presidency—or his grandchildren spent their lives in the contemplation of tapestry and porcelain.

As a struggling young lawyer in his mid-twenties, John no longer had a devoted father to encourage him. The death of Deacon John in

John Adams

1761 had been a terrible blow, but the old man had left a final legacy. John Adams was now a landowner, however modest, able to take part in the public business of Braintree, making use of his legal knowledge. It also endowed him with a bit more substance when it came time to bring suit for the affections of a young lady.

Each day's events were likely to be recorded in a diary he had started during an earthquake. John was visiting at home, enjoying a brief respite from the rigors of teaching in Worcester just prior to taking up his legal studies, when, as he recalled, "the house seemed to rock and reel and crack as if it would fall in ruins around us." The quake, so unusual for New England, was one of a series of seismic shocks felt on both sides of the Atlantic. To Adams it had a kind of symbolic significance. As Lyman Butterfield, who edited the Adams papers, writes, it "jolted" him into starting his diary: "With this record of a young schoolmaster's daily thought and experiences, the family records may be said to begin." So did the productive years of Adams's life.

He would soon receive a second jolt, shortly after his father's death, when he was reintroduced to the Smith family of Weymouth. He remained less than impressed with their wealthy, worldly parents, but after two years, somehow the Smith daughters seemed to have become fonder, franker, and more candid—particularly Abigail. Now a sprightly seventeen, called "Nabby," she was unlike anyone he had ever met. Nabby was equally intrigued with this unusual visitor, so awkward in all the social graces yet so outspoken. She countered his every comment with a bright response of her own—and he found that he actually enjoyed it.

Nabby was hardly a classic beauty but was striking in her own way. Very slender, about five feet tall, she had a fair complexion, brown hair, dark eyes, and a natural vivacity. Her vitality belied her always-frail health. She had read widely, but largely on her own. Although a dutiful daughter, she would always regret that, as a girl, she had never been sent to a "real school." To her father and his friends she was a delightful revelation, to her mother an endearing perplexity.

Whatever attracted Abigail to John, it was surely not his looks. Although described as a handsome child, as a young man Adams's short frame was already thickening to the stocky conformation prevalent in his family. His balding pate was surrounded by a halo of rather unkempt hair. As historian Stephen Hess writes, "The Adams face, from top to bottom, had a tendency to baldness, a broad forehead, finely arched eyebrows, penetrating eyes, a slightly aquiline nose, and a bulldog jaw." Opposites may attract, but so can similarities. Unmatched physically, they balanced each other temperamentally. Mutual curiosity grew into affection. Affection was transformed into love, and the start of a unique partnership. Her counsel was what he always sought, her sunnier nature what he needed. Many of his contemporaries, while admitting Adams's talents, viewed him as less than lovable. As Hess enumerates, he was often described as rude, tactless, humorless, introspective, preachy, arrogant, austere, and unsocial. Abigail, however, might have added "passionate."

The heat of his ardor was hard to contain before they were married by her father on October 25, 1764, in the Weymouth meetinghouse. She was nineteen, he twenty-nine. Their first child, born in the summer of 1765, was a girl they named Abigail, a miniature Nabby. And then, on June 11, 1767, the Adamses had a son. Unlike the Virginians who preceded and succeeded him in the presidency, John Adams was blessed with a male heir. They named him John Quincy Adams, which immensely pleased Abigail's mother. The day the child was christened, old Colonel Josiah Quincy, much loved by both John Adams and his mother-in-law, passed away. John Quincy's parents would always call him Johnny. He grew up with the American Revolution.

Abigail and John were to have two more sons, Charles and Thomas Boylston, but a second daughter, Susanna, died in infancy. Traveling to expand his practice increasingly involved John in Boston's political activities, often in concert with his more volatile cousin, Sam Adams. During their first thirty years of marriage, John was away from Abigail more than half the time. Their enduring legacy of letters, so treasured by historians, is also testimony to a life of farewells. The more successful he became as a lawyer, the ever-wider circuits Adams was obliged to traverse. It was only ten miles from Braintree to Boston, but by horseback it could seem a hundred. "What a desultory Life," he reflected, "a rambling, raving, vagrant, vagabond Life," one town after another, one court after another— Sessions, Pleas, Admiralty, Superior. By his mid-thirties, John Adams was finally successful in his chosen profession, but at what cost?

In 1770 momentous events intruded. The Boston Massacre had the city in an uproar. Adams agreed to defend eight British soldiers and their captain. With a skilled defense, he won his case, the most severe penalty given to two soldiers whose thumbs were branded. Despite the unpopularity of their cause, Adams had gained so high a reputation for integrity that he was elected to the Massachusetts legislature and in 1774 was chosen as a representative to the Continental Congress in Philadelphia. The rest of his active life would be dominated by public service. His promising legal career was sacrificed, and his income decimated. Others were to give their lives for the cause of liberty. Adams gave up his security.

His young son Johnny had decided even before his deliberative father that separation from the mother country was unavoidable. Imbued with patriotic fervor, his borrowed musket at his shoulder, the boy went through the manual of arms with members of the local militia. When he was eight he witnessed from the heights of Penn's Hill the flash of cannons from the Battle of Bunker Hill. At nine he listened as the Declaration of Independence was read, and recorded his reactions in a letter to his father. As a post rider, he took the family mail to Boston twice each week. Feeling immense guilt at his enforced absence during his children's most formative years, John issued to hard-pressed Abigail a stream of advice. Their offspring must be instructed "not only to do virtuously but to excell [sic]." In more immediate terms, she was urged to "fly to the woods with our children" were the British to land nearby—a distinct possibility.

Every letter from his father was read avidly and often responded to by Johnny. "I love to receive letters very well," he wrote his father, "much better than I love to write them. My head is much too fickle. . . . I am determined this week to be more diligent. . . . I wish, sir, you would give me in writing some instructions with regard to the use of my time." Although critical of his proclivity for "trifles," and seeking his father's advice on "how to proportion my Studies and Play," Johnny was already reading everything he could lay his hands on, from patriotic tracts and serious works like *Rollin's Ancient History* to fanciful fiction. He even struggled to get through *Paradise Lost* because he knew it would please his father. Frugal John Adams's one great extravagance was buying books.

At the end of 1777, John Adams, the acknowledged "Atlas" of a not-yet-secured independence, finally returned home. Abigail expressed pride at being married to someone whose "learning, patriotism, and prudence" were now so widely recognized. Unfortunately, members of Congress were among those admirers. Adams had been selected to replace Silas Deane as commissioner to France. He was to join the other commissioners, Benjamin Franklin and Arthur Lee, in the critical task of gaining foreign support for the American cause. A dangerous voyage lay ahead, encompassing not only the customary perils of the sea but also potential death or capture at the hands of roving British raiders. By "earnest entreaty" ten-year-old John Quincy was able to convince his father, who had already found him so "bright and eager to learn," to take him along. The two soon departed on a storm-tossed journey on the frigate *Boston* that lasted six weeks. Back in Braintree, Abigail could only lament, "Someday we may yet be happy."

From the age of eleven, John Quincy Adams received as thorough a preparation for eventual leadership as that visited on any American statesman. His father, despite worrying about its cost, placed him in a boarding school at Passy, where Franklin's grandson and Deane's son also studied. Johnny, remarkably self-possessed, went willingly, as biographer John Ferling writes, "pleased that prizes were given to the best students." He was soon immersed in this "typical French academy where dancing, fencing, music and drawing were taught as well as French and Latin." On weekends, Johnny joined his father in Paris, where the two became inseparable companions. In the next few years, Johnny would learn not only French and more advanced Latin but also Greek, Dutch, and German. He became so comfortable in the company of prominent men that John Adams would complain whimsically to Thomas Jefferson that Johnny "appears to me to be almost as much your boy as mine."

Letters back to Braintree were slow in arriving, and sometimes didn't arrive at all. Secluded in a particularly harsh Massachusetts winter, in wartime, with money tighter, food scarcer, and a smallpox epidemic threatening them all, Abigail wrote, "How lonely are my days?" "How solitary my nights?" More often than not, it was her son who replied. Now fiercely protective of his father, Johnny had the temerity to reprove his mother, "Poppa [has so] many other things to think about," it was admirable that he found the time to write home at all. "It really hurts him to receive such letters." Even if chagrined, Abigail must have felt at least a tinge of pride that they had produced such an assertive, loyal child.

Having discovered that an alliance with the French had already been achieved, Adams asked to return home. The one "joy of [his] heart," he wrote Abigail, was how highly their son was regarded. In July 1779, some eighteen months after they had left, the two Adamses returned home. However, within a month John Adams was gone again, off to a convention in Cambridge to help draft the new Massachusetts constitution. Adams then received his second diplomatic assignment. Events abroad were shifting. He was to return to France in a different capacity, as "minister plenipotentiary," in the hope that this proximity might be helpful in the eventuality of negotiating treaties of peace and commerce with Great Britain. This time John wanted to take back with him not only Johnny but their second son, Charles. The only problem was that Johnny didn't want to go.

He had seen enough of Europe, at least for now. He preferred to attend an American school and then go on to Harvard, as his father had. This time, however, both his parents prevailed on him to change his mind. However self-confident for a boy his age, John Quincy—the son of two such loving but intrusive parents—was also submissive. Assured that he would return in time to attend Harvard, he consented to go. The three Adamses embarked for France. After a trip even more arduous than the first one, their ship managed to find port in Spain. At the end of 1779, the exhausted trio made their way overland to Paris by horse, mule, and any carriage they could find.

Once more, things didn't proceed as hoped. Unable to make progress with either the French or the English, Adams took himself and his sons to the more hospitable environment of Holland. At the tender age of fourteen Johnny received an extraordinary appointment of his own. In 1781 Francis Dana, a friend of his father's, had been named American minister (the term *ambassador* was not yet in use) to the Imperial Court of Russia. He invited Johnny to accompany him to St. Petersburg as his secretary and translator. Russian was one language the boy had not yet learned, but he had mastered French, then the universal language of diplomacy. After a productive eighteen months he rejoined his father, serving as his private secretary in Holland, and was immensely helpful in the same capacity as peace talks finally commenced in Paris to end the American War of Independence.

Finally, in 1784, independence having been secured, Abigail Adams sailed to France, accompanied by her nineteen-year-old daughter, Nabby. Adams's reunion with his "heroine" wife, who had endured so many trials, was immensely moving. Johnny was also there to greet them, but soon he returned to Massachusetts to finally attend Harvard, redeeming his parents' pledge. In 1785 John Adams was appointed to the one diplomatic post he most fondly desired, despite its daunting challenges. He was to become the first minister of a free United States to Great Britain. Abigail found the artifice and snobbery of official English and French society to be less inviting than the opportunity to meet new American friends, such as Thomas Jefferson. John did his customarily conscientious job in London, but it was really too soon after the years of conflict to accomplish very much.

Although delighted at being reunited, John and Abigail were happier still to return home in 1788. He was fifty-three, she forty-four. The property had not prospered in their absence. John and Abigail gave its restoration to productivity all their immediate energies. Their children also pitched in. Johnny returned from his nearby studies from time to time to join his father in such activities as spreading manure. In the longer term, John contemplated asking Johnny, when he had finished his studies, to join him in the practice of law: Adams and Adams. There was still time to together assure the family's financial security. Public office was hardly in Adams's mind.

It was, however, in the minds of others. The new nation had need of John Adams's talents and experience. In 1789 electors met to name the first president and the first vice president of the United States. From Europe Adams had supported the Constitution, and he could hardly denounce its provisions now. His own name was forwarded through the machinations of Alexander Hamilton. It was a foregone conclusion that George Washington would be elected president. Coming in a distant second in a field of twelve, Adams was named vice president. Although describing the office to Abigail as "the most insignificant . . . that ever the invention of man contrived," Adams could not responsibly decline it. Living in the temporary capital of Philadelphia was costly, and the wages of office meager. Abigail often returned to the more salubrious air of Quincy, as their home area of Braintree had been respectfully renamed in 1792.

With his exceptional academic preparation, Johnny had been readily admitted to Harvard. He graduated in only two years, second in his class, and went on to study law by clerking with a distinguished attorney in Newburyport, north of Boston. It was what his parents wanted, of that he was certain, but what did *he* want? Introspective John Quincy had already developed at least a public demeanor as somber as his father's. Physically he was unlike previous Adamses, with a much thinner face and frame, although in time he would resemble his father more. John Quincy Adams passed the bar in 1790 and set up his legal practice in Boston. He was all of twenty-three.

His father had been more than generous, contributing not only his legal library and advice but also advancing his son a hundred pounds a year, which he could scarcely afford. Johnny was not yet quite his own man. In Newburyport he had met and fallen in love with a comely young woman named Mary Frazier, but he broke off the relationship when his parents viewed it as premature. Unhappy in the profession they had guided him to, he began to suffer from ailments, real or imagined—another family inheritance. He had trouble sleeping, lost weight, neglected his appearance, looked wan and pale, and even started to take tranquilizing drugs. His devoted parents, so hopeful for their "exemplary son," had sustained him but were also the source of his suffering.

George Washington saved him. On his tour of New England, the president had met and been impressed with young Adams. He appointed the surprised young man, then only twenty-six, to be "minister president" to The Hague. His parents were pleased, although it meant yet another separation. To the son he had only recently, in an unusually severe reproach, accused of "Lasiness, Slovenliness, and Obstinacy," John Adams wrote of the appointment, "I hope you will reflect upon it with due attention, collect yourself, let no little weakness escape you, and devote yourself to the service of your Country, and may the blessings of heaven attend you. So prays your affectionate father, John Adams."

When in 1796 Washington declined a third term in the office to which he could have been elected in perpetuity, thirteen men received electoral votes to succeed him. Uncertain whether his father or Thomas Jefferson, the favorites, would come in first, John Quincy wrote in his diary, "I can only pray for the happiness and prosperity of my country." Such a spirit was characteristic of the Adamses. Years later John Quincy wrote that his father "had never uttered a word upon which a wish on his part could be presumed that a public office should be conferred on me." John Adams won the presidency by only three electoral votes. By the procedures then prevalent his personal friend but political opponent Thomas Jefferson became his vice president.

Despite Washington's warnings against factionalism, the young nation's political leaders had already separated into two distinct political parties, the Federalists and the Democratic-Republicans. By inclination and affiliation a Federalist, Adams was no blind follower of any party's inflexible tenets, another tendency that would be emulated by his son. From abroad, it was John Quincy who was most instrumental in helping his father to achieve the transcending triumph of his presidency— although it would be a triumph that doomed his reelection.

Upon leaving office, Washington planned to transfer John Quincy, whom he now viewed as "the most valued public character we have abroad," from the Netherlands to Portugal. Washington urged on his successor "that you will not withdraw merited promotion [for John Quincy] because he is your son." Despite inevitable accusations of nepotism, Adams changed John Quincy's destination to the more prominent position of minister to Prussia, although at the same salary. When his son showed hesitation, Adams reminded him, "The sons of Presidents have the same claim to liberty, equality, and the benefit of the laws with all other citizens." From this more central listening post, John Quincy's contacts in London and Paris provided his father with the intelligence to avert war with an increasingly unstable France.

It was, however, a conflict the Federalists longed for—and expected Adams to champion. In 1799 he was at the height of his popularity. By 1800, with war averted and a new, skillful envoy placed in France, Adams was equally hated. Hamilton called him "an old woman." He had placed the welfare of his country ahead of the emotion of the moment. When he ran again in 1800, he was a president without a party. Under the circumstances, his defeat by Jefferson, complicated by Aaron Burr, turned out to be surprisingly close. In the first forty years of the American republic, John Adams and John Quincy Adams were the only American presidents to be denied two terms.

The Adamses did not linger in Washington to witness Jefferson's inauguration. John had bought and refurbished a much larger house in Quincy, which he hopefully named "Peacefield." Modest by the standards of European gentry, it was more than spacious compared to his original Braintree domicile. Here he half hoped for repose, but he still chafed over slights too recent to heal. He remained convinced that his contributions would be overshadowed by those of his more visible contemporaries. Now, Lord willing, he and Abigail would be together for the rest of their lives. Best of all, their boy, too, was coming home. In one of his last acts as president, John had recalled John Quincy.

He would not be returning alone. In London, before going on to Prussia, he had met and married cosmopolitan Louisa Catherine Johnson. Their first child was already five months old. Born to an American father and an English mother and raised in France, Louisa had never set foot on American soil. Her father, a tobacco merchant, had fallen on hard times but had been named American consul general. A buoyant John Quincy, tired of foreign climes, reassured his parents, "You will find her [to] prove such a daughter as you would want for your son." Abigail was at first stunned, then apprehensive, but hopefully noted "the Syren is at least half-blood." Would she not be too fine a lady, however—too delicate, and too aristocratic, not to mention too poor—to provide for Johnny the kind of supportive partnership Abigail had given John? Louisa, too, was apprehensive. Only one factor saved her awkward introduction to Quincy. Having heard John Adams described as acerbic, she discovered instead a kindred spirit, warm and interested, who took an instant fancy to her. Her affection for the "old gentleman" would never wane.

John Quincy hoped his "honorable exile" might lead to "future usefulness." To his father, Johnny already possessed "greater capabilities than any other native American." In 1802 John Quincy was elected as a Federalist to the state senate, and the following year he was sent to fill a vacancy in the United States Senate. There he would prove no less independent than his father, insisting on considering every issue on its merits. Many years later John Quincy would write to one of his sons, "No person can ever be a thorough partisan for a long period without sacrifice of his moral identity. The skill consists of knowing exactly where to draw the line." He drew the line on his fellow Federalists by supporting

President Jefferson in the Louisiana Purchase and by also voting in favor of his 1807 Embargo Act. The Federalists in the Massachusetts legislature retaliated by naming Adams's successor six months before his term had expired. They preferred party regularity. The one constant was his father's counsel, no less reasoned when John Quincy was forty than when he had been fourteen. John wrote, "My advice to you is steadily to pursue the course you are in . . . because I think it is the path of justice."

When President Madison appointed John Quincy to become minister to Russia, only his father could see the point of it, another stepping-stone in an evolving, remarkable career. Yet John Adams seemed far less intent than his wife that their son might ultimately reach the nation's highest office. Abigail's brisk advice was almost that of a political handler, counseling John Quincy on everything from his clothes, his manners, his appearance, and his deportment in general to the delivery of his speeches. John, while still specific, turned more benign and philosophical in his counsel. Well, after all, he had intended that the next generation of his family would study philosophy. Now *he* was almost in that generation.

All the Adamses were cheered, however, when in 1814 John Quincy was sent to Ghent in Belgium as senior American representative to negotiate an agreement to end the War of 1812. This notable assignment was followed by his appointment as American minister to Great Britain. It was all so strikingly similar to his father's progression in the 1780s. To John Quincy in London, his father wrote, "My son! No man except your father was ever placed in a more delicate or dangerous situation than you are. . . . Your providence I know will be greater than mine ever was." To his father, John Quincy replied, "I have been accustomed all my life to plain dealing and candor, and am not sufficiently versed in the art of political swindling to be prepared for negotiating with a European Minister of State." Nonetheless, when he was recalled by President James Monroe to be secretary of state, he accepted. After eight years abroad, John Quincy Adams and his family returned to the United States to stay.

Inevitably, even old John Adams had mellowed. After a decade of retirement in Quincy, his resentments receded, leaving him less vindictive and bitter, more detached from "the gambols of ambition." Encouraged by their mutual friend Benjamin Rush, he had resumed his correspondence and his friendship with Thomas Jefferson. Although Abigail was often ill, John took "great delight in riding out with her every fair day." But not every day was fair. Their daughter, Nabby, had died, as had their

son Charles. Now only two of their children remained, John Quincy and
Thomas Boylston. More heartrending still, two grandchildren had already
died. Of one of them John lamented, "Why was I preserved 3/4 of a
century and that rose cropped in the bud?"

Abigail Smith Adams died on October 28, 1818, at the age of seventy-
four. The immediate cause of death was typhoid fever, but it could have
been one of many afflictions. Always frail, she simply wasted away. John
Quincy said of his mother, "There is not a virtue that can abide in the
female heart, but it was an ornament of hers." As Abigail was laid to rest
beside her daughter, the minister celebrated "one who shone with no
common splendor." Jefferson wrote to Adams with unusual emotion of
"mingling my tears with yours."

John Quincy Adams had no illusions. "I am a man of reserved, cold,
austere, and forbidding manners." But, as had his mother, he also felt it
his "destiny" to be president. His father no longer shared that view, if he
ever had, but he remained positive, whatever the future might bring. In
his eighties, feeling grief that would never subside, palsied but still alert
mentally, John affirmed, "I still live and enjoy life." His son, who returned
every summer to be with him, was helpful in every way, the two cur-
mudgeons together. He adroitly managed his father's financial affairs.

By 1820 only four signers of the Declaration of Independence were
still alive. John Adams had predicted the occasion would be ever celebrated with pomp, parades, fireworks, and prayers of thanksgiving. The
following year he made his final public appearance. The cadet corps from
West Point was in Boston. They marched to Quincy and paraded past
his residence. Very moved, Adams told them to emulate the example of
Washington. Now, finally, not forgotten after all, Adams felt that the silent
halls of Peacefield were an appropriate place for him to live out his days.

In 1824 John Quincy's "destiny" came to pass but in so unfortunate
a manner that it crippled his presidency. Coming in second to Andrew
Jackson in both the popular and electoral vote, Adams was declared the
winner by proceedings in the House of Representatives manipulated by
Henry Clay. It smacked of "corrupt bargaining" to many. Adams had no
hand in it, but he emerged as the beneficiary. A nationalist like his father,
John Quincy's bold program of internal improvements was doomed from
the start. John Adams was hardly elated by his son's tainted triumph. He
wrote John Quincy, "Never did I feel so much solemnity as upon this
occasion." Jackson, who began his next presidential campaign almost

immediately, handily defeated Adams in 1828. John Quincy went on to a unique tenure in the House of Representatives, the substance of which would most certainly have elated his father.

John Adams did not witness the conclusion of his son's sole term in the presidency. His fondest hope was to live until July 4, 1826, the fiftieth anniversary of the Declaration of Independence. He just made it. Unable to attend celebrations of the sort he had predicted, when Adams was visited by a delegation and asked to produce a toast, his response was simply, "Independence forever!" Now, of the signers, only he and eighty-three-year-old Jefferson still drew breath. On the evening of July 4, around six o'clock, John Adams's life finally ebbed away, his last words, "Thomas Jefferson lives." He was mistaken. The sage of Monticello had also died that day, some five hours earlier. To John Quincy and many others, such a coincidence was taken as "visible and palpable marks of Divine favor."

John Adams was laid to rest at Quincy, next to those he loved. His pastor read from the First Book of Chronicles, "He died in a good old age, full of days, riches, and honor, and Solomon his son reigned in his stead." John Quincy was not present. He had planned to come up shortly. When notified of his father's death he wrote in his diary, "I had flattered myself that he would survive this summer and even other years." On July 9 he and his son set out in the humidity of a Washington summer to make the long, sorrowful journey. "My father," John Quincy reflected, "had nearly closed the ninety-first year of his life—a life illustrious in the annals of his country and of the world. He had served to great and useful purpose his nation, his age, and his God."

Then John Quincy's thoughts turned inward. The two had been so similar, in demeanor and now in destiny. "For myself, all that I ask is that I may live the remnant of my days in a manner worthy of him." Although it seemed "presumptuous," he also hoped, "May my last end be like him." This did not come to pass. Although he also lived beyond his eightieth year, John Quincy Adams did not die in bed but in harness, in the Capitol Building of the United States. Adams was now renowned as "Old Man Eloquent" of the House, and his final campaign was to halt the extension of slavery. The common goal of both Adamses, the first father and son to be elected to the presidency, was less the rewards of office than its noblest ends.

# 3

# DRAMATIC DEPARTURE

## Andrew Jackson Sr. • Abraham Van Buren

OUR FIRST PRESIDENT to derive from destitution, Andrew Jackson marked as dramatic a departure in American history as did Martin Van Buren, the first with antecedents outside the British Isles and the first to view himself as a professional politician.

## Andrew Jackson Sr.

Not even the most egalitarian of the founders, Thomas Jefferson, could have foreseen an American president in the mold of Andrew Jackson. He emerged not only from the humblest recesses of the new world but of the old as well. This departure from the substantial status of our first six presidents was preceded by a more literal departure from the north of Ireland. It brought over Jackson's parents and his two older brothers. Andrew Jackson would be the first first-generation American to ascend to the presidency.

How he would have liked his father. The senior Andrew Jackson, too, was a restless, ambitious risk-taker as well as a man of prodigious energy. It was that ambition that brought him all the way to the Carolinas, and that energy that, in the end, did him in.

Twenty families, Andrew Jackson's among them, were to have emigrated together from the town of Carrickfergus, in County Antrim, near Belfast. Their new home across the Atlantic had been described to them by Andrew's brother, Hugh, as "the garden of the Waxhaws." It was in a fertile valley by the Catawba Creek, near the present-day border between North and South Carolina. Hugh had already seen it. Fighting with General Braddock against both the French and the Indians had taken him from Canada to the Carolinas. Andrew had another brother, Sam, who was a sailor, further fueling his wanderlust.

41

His father, within the possibilities of a small northern Irish town, had been rather successful. He was both a "linen draper," or skilled weaver, and a merchant, earning a more secure living than the sustenance of most of his neighbors. The Jacksons had come from Scotland in the prior century and had settled in Carrickfergus largely as weavers and tenant farmers. Andrew wanted more. He had no desire to clerk for his father, had declined an apprenticeship in weaving, and viewed farming on others' land as an unproductive investment of his time. He longed for land of his own, an opportunity for his family not only to survive but to prosper.

It was now a family of four. Andrew had married Elizabeth Hutchinson, whom everyone called "Betty." She is described by biographer Burke Davis as "a small, spirited woman." She was also resourceful, weaving throughout the night and tending to their two small sons during the day. Betty was quite as willing to leave as was her husband, fortified by the knowledge that four of her sisters were already settled in the Waxhaw area and would welcome them warmly.

As the day of departure neared, the hardy band of transatlantic pioneers had steadily declined. Instead of twenty families, only two would actually go through with it. Unfortunately, Hugh Jackson, that audacious warrior, hadn't factored in the approval of his stubborn wife. She was not about to be uprooted from beautiful, settled Ireland, whatever its limitations, to venture into a savage wilderness. Her defection, and her embarrassed husband's, gave others their excuse to exit as well. When the two remaining families finally set out in 1765, however, the Andrew Jacksons were still very much on board—Betty with two-year-old Hugh clinging tightly to her and five-month-old Robert at her breast. It was not a placid voyage. Upon arriving in the port of Philadelphia, they still faced a long, taxing journey. The other family had already begun to lose heart. Within two years they would be back in Ireland. "But," biographer Marquis James writes, "Andrew Jackson was for the Waxhaws and would not be dissuaded." When they finally arrived at their destination, they were cheered to discover that it was as populated with kin and connections as they had hoped.

Heartened by such familiar accents, Andrew set out to establish his modest farm. Those with the means had purchased the best land, with clear titles within the already settled area. Jackson's property would be further out, at the edge of the surrounding forest. Making an informal agreement to occupy a portion of what was described as public domain,

Andrew witnessed surveyors running a line around his two hundred acres. As Gerald Johnson, the renowned journalist turned biographer, writes, Jackson "attacked the forest resolutely and not without success, for the record testifies that he cleared his land, raised at least one crop and built his log house by the beginnings of the year 1767." The Jacksons entered into the life of their far-flung community. Each Sunday they traveled twelve miles to worship at the Presbyterian church frequented by the families of Betty's sisters. After only a year of unremitting toil, it appeared as if the Jacksons might be on their way to self-sufficiency and the fulfilling new life they had projected. However, in Johnson's words, they turned out to be "worse than poor, they were luckless." Despite the encouragement of their transplanted countrymen and their own efforts, the wilderness won out. Among the charred stumps of the hundreds of trees he had already felled, Jackson severely injured himself straining to lift a giant log. Within two days he was dead. It was early in March 1767, not long before the time for spring planting.

The very ownership of Andrew Jackson's farm came into question. Jackson probably never had clear title to any of the land he worked, but was only an unknowing tenant. His heritage of honest dealing had not prepared him for duplicity. His wife and sons could no longer reside in the home he had labored so tirelessly to wrest from the forest and provide for their future.

Neighbors gathered around his body in the manner of the old country, passing around a gourd of whiskey to ward off the chill of late winter and to fortify their own spirits. The wake was followed the next morning by a somber procession to the Waxhaw churchyard. As Jackson biographer Robert Remini describes it, "The funeral party scuffed over the snowy woods . . . to a frozen creek." Reportedly, once the coffin slid off its moorings onto the icy forest floor and had to be retrieved. The residue of drink had its effect on the pallbearers. Finally, their destination reached, the minister uttered his eulogy, and "the man from northern Ireland who had been only two years in the Carolina backwoods was buried." No headstone marked the grave's location.

A few days later, on March 15, 1767, at the nearby home of kindly relatives who took her in, Elizabeth Hutchinson Jackson gave birth to the last of her three sons, the only one who would survive the Revolutionary War. At least Betty could honor her late husband by giving the boy his name. Andrew Jackson would have liked his father. Since they were never to meet, he could only admire him.

## Abraham Van Buren

Unlike Andrew Jackson, Martin Van Buren was fortunate enough to know his father very well. There is no doubt that he loved Abraham Van Buren. He just didn't want to grow up to be like him. Abraham certainly was, as his son said, "an unassuming amiable man who was never known to have an enemy." But, as Martin went on to rather tactfully phrase it, Abraham was also "utterly devoid of any spirit of accumulation." His life refutes ethnic generalities. Abraham Van Buren was an improvident Dutchman.

And the Van Burens *were* thoroughly Dutch. Martin Van Buren marks a further departure from prior presidents in two ways: he was the first avowedly professional politician to occupy the office, and the first whose family did not originate from any part of the British Isles. By the time Van Buren became president, his hometown of Kinderhook, or "Old Kinderhook," as it would be called in his campaigns (from which our expression "OK" may derive), had been a Dutch enclave in upstate New York for almost two hundred years. It was only twenty miles from Albany but seemed a world away. To Washington Irving, the famously imaginative author, who was born a year after Martin Van Buren, placid backwaters like Kinderhook bore a somnolent resemblance to his creation Rip Van Winkle. Biographer Donald Cole refers to the area's "drowsy tranquility," its customs seemingly fixed in time. The roads were rudimentary. Visitors on the post road between Albany and New York were frequent, but they didn't stay long. Steamship travel to New York was twenty years in the future. Kinderhook retained its gabled homes, as if on an Amsterdam canal. Interiors were still decorated with tiles imported from Holland. Dutch was spoken at the dinner table, and virtually every family attended the local Dutch Reformed church, erected in 1727. For six generations no one had married an outsider. On the surface, Kinderhook seemed no closer to the realities of most American communities than, say, the mythical Brigadoon.

That would be a deceptive conclusion. By the eighteenth century, Kinderhook was, in fact, a thoroughly American town, including its politics. The meetings of both Federalists and Jeffersonians were frequently held in the local tavern, just as in Philadelphia or Boston. Only the accents were different. The popular tavern in Kinderhook was owned by Abraham Van Buren. If, as a child, Martin wanted to hear heated political debates, all he had to do was come downstairs from his family's living quarters.

The Van Burens had not always been tavern owners. The first of their family, Cornelius Maessen, had left the village of Buren in Holland to sail to America in 1631. He leased a plot of land from Kiliaen Van Rensselaer, a name that would resonate in American finance, near the town of Fort Orange, later Albany, on the Hudson River. From the start, the Van Burens were farmers, but they progressed from leaseholders to freeholders. The son of Cornelius, as Cole details, was named Marten Cornelisen Van Buren—that is, Marten, the son of Cornelius, from Buren. Abraham was born in 1737, in his parents' home in what would turn out to be a promising location on the south side of the post road. He would inherit a productive farm, although of modest size. There is some question whether he also inherited the tavern, or was obliged to turn his farmhouse into a tavern and inn because he was so indifferent a farmer.

Abraham, in the current vernacular, loved to hang out. Had he not been the tavern's proprietor, he probably would have patronized it just as frequently. He was genuinely good-hearted, a soft touch for any sad story or a loan he rarely pressed to have repaid. Keenly interested in politics, he earned some extra money by renting out his premises as a polling place and meeting hall and by serving as town clerk for ten years. He was sufficiently well regarded to also be captain of militia for a short time. In fact, because of his generosity and congeniality, Abraham Van Buren was probably one of the most popular men in Kinderhook.

Yet, although it bothered him little, he lacked status. The Van Burens, in so insular a setting, were related to virtually every other family in town, including the most prominent, but to the local gentry they were poor relations. Van Buren biographer John Niven points out the irony. Despite such kinship, or perhaps because of it, class lines in Kinderhook were closely drawn. Abraham was involved in governing the town, but his humble circumstances precluded having much clout. As Cole notes, Abraham tilled the soil, when he tilled it at all, only a few miles from where his ancestors had first settled, but in tangible terms he had less to show for it than had the original Cornelius. Ominously, Abraham also wound up with less each year than he'd had the year before, as his indolence increased. He could hardly manage things on his own, but in 1776, at the age of thirty-nine, he decided to take a bride.

Perhaps in part it was his good heart that motivated his choice. Marrying late was not unusual for the men in Kinderhook, most of whom were more immersed in "the spirit of accumulation" than was Abraham. It was the source of his affection that surprised everyone. Maria Hoes

Van Alen was a widow with three children of her own who had nothing tangible to bring into the match. However, she was reputed to be very capable, as she would soon prove, and was not unattractive. A decade younger than Abraham, she had known better times as the daughter of a respected family that had been among the original settlers of the town. Whatever Abraham's motivation, Maria brought more than children into his household. She brought at least a measure of stability.

Before Abraham went off to fight in the Revolutionary War, the couple had two girls, given the traditional Dutch names of Dirckie and Jannetje. After his return, they had a son, whom they named Martin. He was born on December 5, 1782. In the years that followed, two more sons and another daughter joined the family. It is not surprising that Martin's earliest memories were of congestion. Here he was, with eight brothers and sisters crowded together in only half of the upper floor of his father's steep-roofed tavern. His parents' bedroom and parlor were on the ground floor. Food was prepared in a small cookhouse and taproom that adjoined the main building. As Niven writes, there was just enough space for a "modicum of respectability."

What is most surprising is that Abraham owned six slaves, part of his inheritance. Two helped Maria cook. Slavery, Cole points out, had been outlawed in New York after the Revolutionary War, but it was not completely eradicated there until 1827. In 1790 slaves still comprised some 14 percent of the population of Kinderhook. Apparently their free labor didn't do very much to enhance Abraham's liquidity. He was housing, feeding, and clothing seventeen people, plus the overnight travelers who used his premises as an inn. Large families were traditional in towns like Kinderhook but were not usually confined to such limited quarters. In Cole's opinion, however, all this congestion was not without its benefits for Martin, as he grew into a bright, outgoing child. It taught him to accommodate to others. The constant stream of visitors, many very different from his homogeneous neighbors, vividly illustrated the variety of people inhabiting the great world outside their little Holland.

All the children were given their tasks to perform, on the farm or in the household, organized by Maria, and all were treated equally. It was soon clear, however, and not alone to his parents, that Martin possessed special talents. He even looked a bit different from the others. Niven writes, "A handsome child, small, rather delicate in appearance; his hair worn long as was the custom, fell in fine reddish blond waves to his

shoulders; bright blue deep-set eyes, a fair complexion, a merry disposition and an infectious smile made him popular among his friends." Later
he would grow more compact, but never very tall. As his hair receded,
his forehead would be most prominent.

Van Buren's poise and mental agility also impressed his elders, among
them the most prominent people in town. He was deferential to them
without being obsequious. Even in homespun, he was always immaculately dressed by his mother. By the time he was twelve he could dis-
cuss adult subjects with clarity and a kind of natural ease. He not only
stood out from his siblings but from the more privileged children in
Kinderhook.

His parents tried not to play favorites, but it is to Abraham's credit
that Martin was enabled to stay in school until the age of fifteen, a substantial loss of labor for his hard-pressed father. The school was Kinderhook Academy, not then the distinguished institution that survives under
that name, but essentially a one-room schoolhouse. It was presided over,
however, by a dedicated schoolmaster, David Warden, who was perceptive
enough to grasp Martin's potential and worked with him almost as a
personal tutor. Beyond Latin and arithmetic, the grammar, rhetoric, and
logic that Van Buren absorbed provided the foundation for him to learn
to speak and write more forcefully. Still, like George Washington before
him, Van Buren always regretted the limitations in his formal education,
feeling that it put him at some disadvantage with men like Webster and
Clay.

There was no way his parents could afford to send him to college.
They did, however, obtain for him the opportunity to learn the law in
the office of Kinderhook's leading attorney, Francis Sylvester (or Sil-
vester). In return for sweeping out his offices and working part-time at
the store of Sylvester's brother, Martin was given bed and board, and the
opportunity to clerk for the attorney. He made the most of it.

By the age of seventeen, he had also found time for politics. All those
discussions he had heard while helping his father out at the tavern were
as much a prelude to his career as the legal knowledge he garnered from
Sylvester. Martin's patron, like most of the prominent citizens in New
York and New England, was a Federalist, but, as had John Quincy Adams,
Van Buren could see that the patrician-backed, regionalized party was
headed for extinction. Recognizing Jefferson's Democratic-Republicans as
the emerging national majority party, he managed to attend their district

convention in Troy in 1800 and helped his townsman and distant relative (as who wasn't in Kinderhook?) John P. Van Ness gain their nomination for Congress.

Van Ness was so impressed with the youth's political acumen that two years later he paid for Martin to go to New York to continue his legal training by clerking for his brother, William. Martin had inherited so much of his father's charm that Sylvester forgave him this defection and wished him well in the metropolis. Van Buren went on to readily master the complex New York legal code, passed the bar, went into private practice, and was elected to his first political office by the age of thirty—already a power broker well on his way to a national political reputation.

His "amiable and loving father" died in 1817 at the age of eighty. By then his son's career was well advanced. Martin's mother died the following year at seventy-one. The next year, in 1819, his wife Hannah died at only thirty-six, leaving him to care for four sons, aged eleven to two—terrible blows, one after another. Dubbed "the Little Magician" for his political dexterity, Van Buren survived, and seventeen years later was elected president of the United States. In his rise to prominence he became celebrated for valuing victory over ideology, the personification of the new politics—public life as a pragmatic profession. But the finely honed skills he had developed served him well when, as had John Adams, he avoided imprudent wars that might have enhanced his popularity. Perhaps through it all he retained something of his small-town values, American as well as Dutch.

Martin understood that success entailed careful planning and working harder than just about anyone else, qualities hardly personified by his father. But he must have appreciated that political success also rests on generosity, pliability, and sociability, qualities Abraham Van Buren had in abundance. As biographer Robert Remini writes, Martin's earliest education, his great knowledge and understanding of human nature, "was acquired during these years he helped in his father's tavern, listening to the patrons." The politician in Martin Van Buren could only envy a man he described as "never known to have an enemy." He loved his father for such qualities and deeply mourned his passing.

# 4

# PATRIOTS AND PIONEERS

Benjamin Harrison V • John Tyler Sr.
Samuel Polk • Richard Taylor
Nathaniel Fillmore • Benjamin Pierce
James Buchanan Sr.

THROUGH WAR AND WESTWARD EXPANSION the contributions of such patrician families as the Harrisons, Tylers, and Taylors were matched by equally patriotic pioneers—from luckless Nathaniel Fillmore to self-made successes like Samuel Polk, Benjamin Pierce, and James Buchanan Sr.

## Benjamin Harrison V

In the colorful presidential election of 1840, William Henry Harrison, a Virginia aristocrat now reduced to being an Ohio aristocrat, was presented by his fellow Whigs to the American electorate as the hero of Tippecanoe, a devotee of hard cider, and a humble inhabitant of the requisite log cabin. His opponent, incumbent Martin Van Buren, who had actually experienced poverty, was depicted by his opponents as the "used-up" tool of Eastern money and a prissy embodiment of luxurious living.

Harrison's father would have loved it. No one appreciated a good joke more than Benjamin Harrison V. Unfortunately, he had died almost a half-century before. Both the father and great-grandfather of American presidents, Harrison was the prototypical patrician-patriot. To his son, William, during the eighteen years they were at least sometimes together, the father imparted family pride and fidelity to one's studies. He was not the ideal exponent of the latter, having left William and Mary College before graduating. Benjamin was neither a scholar nor a deep thinker, but a man of immense good humor, charm, and impressive girth. Writer

Benjamin Harrison V

Jeff Young describes the "portly patriot" as "six feet, four inches tall and weighing 249 pounds." His portrait, perhaps idealized, displays a most handsome countenance. William, on the other hand, short and thin, almost gaunt, looked nothing like his father. Nor did he share his love of rich foods, lavish entertaining, and all the accoutrements of good living. In appearance and attire, Benjamin was almost a dandy, but, as described by biographer Freeman Cleaves, he had within him a stubborn, independent quality he would have occasion to demonstrate. His tinted wigs and silk suits masked a forceful character, if not quite an American Pimpernel.

The Harrisons had settled in Virginia in the mid-seventeenth century. Already prominent in England, they prospered anew, assembling vast plantations, anchored by a magnificent mansion called "Berkeley," overlooking the James River. There, on April 5, 1726, Benjamin Harrison V was born. There, on February 9, 1773, William Henry Harrison would be born. He was the seventh of seven children, the last of three boys. It is more likely that his father celebrated the event with a fine claret than

with hard cider. Like the families of the founders, the Harrisons enhanced their holdings with fortuitous marriages. Harrison's father, Benjamin Harrison IV, married Anne Carter, of a family of legendary wealth.
Benjamin V in 1748 married eighteen-year-old Elizabeth Bassett, daughter of Colonel William Bassett of the adjoining plantation. Celebrated for
her beauty, piety, and benevolence, she was a niece of Martha Washington, and seemed in her serenity the ideal counterpoint to the opulent
lifestyle of the fifth (but not the last) of the Benjamin Harrisons.

What turned so firmly established and contented a landowner into a
champion of separation from the mother country? At first, Harrison
seems to have simply accepted service in the Virginia House of Burgesses
as his obligation, much in the manner of other men of property. He must
have enjoyed the conviviality between sessions with those of similar station. It may well be that, as in Massachusetts, the implications of the
Stamp Act began to shift hitherto conciliatory opinions in a more truc-
ulent direction. The transition took time. As Young notes, although serving on a committee of protest, Harrison opposed Patrick Henry's anti–
Stamp Act resolutions. However, by 1773, as a member of Virginia's
committee of correspondence, Harrison had come all the way around to
active support of rebellion. Whatever had caused his conversion, he never
wavered.

By then the House of Burgesses had been dissolved by the royal governor. Benjamin headed for Philadelphia as one of Virginia's seven delegates to the First Continental Congress. He took his high spirits with
him. When John Hancock hesitated to accept his election as president of
the congress in 1774, Harrison picked him up bodily and placed him in
the chair. Harrison won praise from his colleagues, particularly for light-
ening the often-somber tone of the proceedings, although his humor
could be grim. After signing the Declaration of Independence, which cli-
maxed the Second Continental Congress, Harrison is purported to have
turned to slender Elbridge Gerry of Massachusetts and remarked that
"when the hanging scene comes," Gerry would take a lot longer to die.

For the rest of his life Harrison was in public service. He returned to
Virginia in 1777, presided over the House of Delegates as speaker, served
three terms as wartime governor, and then returned to the House of
Delegates. As biographer Harry Sievers writes, Harrison not only helped
establish the state, war, and navy departments and was a significant
"signer"; he later helped to secure the adoption of the Constitution. Too
old to fight in the Revolutionary War, Harrison was fortunate enough to

lose neither his life nor his lifestyle. His home was sacked, but at least it was not burned to the ground. Benjamin's extended absences denied young William the opportunity he craved to really get to know so ebullient a character. In the later years of their marriage, Benjamin's wife also had too often to do without his company. She died in 1792. The year before, on April 24, 1791, Benjamin Harrison V had passed away, at sixty-five. The probable cause was gout, not inappropriate for one of his rich tastes.

As a younger son, William Henry Harrison had contemplated a career based on the likelihood of inheriting little land. After attending Hampden-Sydney College, he studied medicine in Philadelphia under Dr. Benjamin Rush, apparently as the elder Harrison had wished. When his father died, William followed his own bent. The struggle had instilled patriotism in the son as well as the father. Through the influence of "Light Horse" Harry Lee, the orphaned Harrison, only eighteen, received his commission as ensign in the First Regiment, United States Artillery. It was signed by President George Washington, whom he had already met. "How I wished," the youth reflected, "my father were alive to be with me."

He must have felt such a wish often in his life. His notable military career led to a most unlikely political career. William Henry Harrison wrote the acceptance address for his inauguration as president in 1841 not in his nonexistent log cabin but at his family's mansion. Oddly, because, like his father, he was a man not given to excessive rhetoric, it turned out to be the longest such oration in American history. Even condensed by Daniel Webster, it ran to two hours. However, as stubborn as his father, Harrison insisted on riding his white charger through a driving rainstorm to deliver the speech in full. He caught pneumonia and was dead within a month. Benjamin Harrison V would have appreciated this dramatic flourish by his son, but also the foolhardy irony of it all.

# John Tyler Sr.

The Harrisons and the Tylers seem so similar. Both are counted among Virginia's most prominent families and had settled on soil very near each other. Both first fathers were patrician patriots, and each became governor of the Old Dominion. Their favored—although not their first—sons ran together in the presidential election of 1840—"Tippecanoe and

Tyler, too." It was, however, a memorably misleading slogan. Tyler was there to balance the ticket. The ticket-makers had not anticipated that their candidate for president might die in office. If any of the views of that genial general, William Henry Harrison, were clear it was his affirmation of nationalism. Nothing was more certain about John Tyler, the younger, than his fervent espousal of states' rights. Here were the seeds of the Civil War, within a single slate, twenty years ahead of time.

As for the deceased fathers of the two candidates, seemingly so similar, they had differed in every way save their sympathies and status—in appearance, demeanor, and their relationship to their children. William Henry Harrison hardly knew the father he so admired. The John Tylers, senior and junior, were inseparable. Because his wife died so young, the elder Tyler was both father and mother to his offspring. Many of the stories told of the one might well have been of the other—such as playing the fiddle they both favored under a willow tree to entertain the local children. However, neither Tyler was much given to frivolity. Unlike the Harrisons, the Tylers looked very much alike. Biographer Robert Seager writes of young John, "He was very slight in build; his long, thin patrician face was dominated by the high cheekbones and the prominent nose he would later joke about—the 'Tyler nose.' . . . His lips were thin and tight, his dark brown hair was silken. Physically, he was never robust."

If there was a difference, it was in personality. The senior Tyler's was more forceful and less conciliatory. As biographer Oliver Chitwood writes, "He was a man of strong convictions and prejudices, both of which he expressed with utter fearlessness." His son, perhaps of necessity, demonstrated more tact, but it would help him little in his accidental presidency, the first in American history.

The Tyler saga must seem, by now, in this account of the earliest first fathers, a familiar story—the old English gentry emigrating to Virginia and emerging as its new gentry, after their monarch had lost his cause, his crown, and his head. There are as many Henrys and Johns among the Tylers as Benjamins among the Harrisons. In the middle of the seventeenth century, a Henry Tyler settled in the Virginia peninsula, between the James and York rivers, the location of more American families of eminence than any other region. He obtained a grant of over 250 acres near the town that became Williamsburg. Family tradition holds that the Tylers are descended from both an ancestor who came to England with William the Conqueror and from Wat Tyler, a humble blacksmith who led a revolt against King Richard II—merging royalty with revolution.

John Tyler Sr.

By the time of the birth of the John Tyler who would father a president, on February 28, 1747, Tylers were firmly established as among the first of the celebrated First Families of Virginia.

On a balmy spring day in 1764, two young law students from William and Mary College strode down Duke of Gloucester Street in Williamsburg to the capitol building to listen to the proceedings of the House of Burgesses. They picked a historic session, hearing Patrick Henry make his impassioned declaration that if the Stamp Act were not repealed, King George III might well go the way of Charles I or, for that matter, Julius Caesar. Just as similar sentiments had had their impact on Benjamin Harrison V, and far to the north on young attorney John Adams, they resonated with eighteen-year-old John Tyler and his close friend and roommate, twenty-two-year-old Thomas Jefferson. Although actual rebellion would not take shape for a decade, Tyler's outspoken comments alarmed his staunchly Royalist father, Henry. He issued a dire warning to his son: "Ah! John, they will hang you for a rebel. They will hang you yet." A similar warning had been issued to Benjamin Harrison V by his father.

It inhibited neither man, although both would have close calls in the conflict to come. After completing his studies, Tyler didn't rush off to man the barricades but dutifully established his legal practice in adjoining Charles City County. He also got married, during the momentous year of 1776, to Maria Armistead, daughter of a prominent planter. They moved to Greenway, the Tyler mansion, near Charles City Courthouse. It would always be John Tyler's home. Like Elizabeth Bassett Harrison, Maria is reputed to have been both beautiful and beneficent. Over twenty years she gave birth to eight children. John Tyler the younger was the sixth. He was born on March 29, 1790, long after the fighting had subsided, enabling him to have a more settled childhood than William Henry Harrison.

Although his father's fearlessness was never in doubt, John Tyler Sr. was more engaged in legislative than military action throughout the Revolutionary War. He did spend time in the militia but in 1777 was elected to the House of Delegates and later served as its speaker. During his tenure, however, its members were obliged to flee when informed that notorious British Colonel Banastre Tarleton was on his way to hang them all. The delegates escaped just in time. Tyler's Greenway was not ransacked, as was Harrison's Berkeley, and the war ended not only with Tyler physically intact but with his reputation as a skillful legislator enhanced. It was Tyler who introduced in 1785 Madison's resolution for a constitutional convention in Annapolis, leading to the second, more productive convention in Philadelphia, all before the young John Tyler had been born.

Most noted for his judicial capacities, John Tyler Sr. would be called Judge Tyler throughout his later years. His career on the bench, from the Virginia Court of Admiralty in 1785 to the General Court of Virginia in 1788 and the United States District Court in 1812, lasted until his death, interrupted only by his three one-year terms as governor and his role in the Virginia convention considering the adoption of the Constitution of the United States. Like his youthful hero, Patrick Henry, Tyler found himself adamantly opposed to it. The struggle for liberty, in their view, was betrayed by a document yielding far too much power to federal authority. No inheritance passed on to young John Tyler was of greater significance than his father's staunch support of states' rights.

As Chitwood writes, John Tyler Jr.'s personality "embodied more of the gentle virtues of his mother," who had died when he was only seven, "than the stern qualities of his father." But his father would be with him for another sixteen years. Having to accommodate to five sisters and two brothers must have encouraged young John's proclivity to compromise, even with nineteen hundred acres to roam around in. However stern, his father's softer side increased the congestion at Greenway. According to Chitwood, Judge Tyler so loved children that, in addition to his own, he reared twenty-one more for whom he was guardian. Perhaps he played the fiddle as much for therapy as entertainment.

Of course there were also many slave children with whom the Tylers would play. Like his father, John Tyler initially accepted the institution of slavery as a given and would own slaves all his life. By all accounts, Judge Tyler was among the most humanitarian and enlightened of masters, as would be his son. But that gentler son would wrestle all his adult life with the inherent evils of the peculiar institution. The sight of a slave auction made him physically ill. He would strenuously oppose the continuation of the slave trade and seek means of gradual abolition, including the emigration of slaves to Liberia. In the end, he admitted the illusory nature of such schemes and, like his Virginia predecessors, simply passed the problem on, wishing, as Seager puts it, "that slavery would just go away somehow." But, even as the ever-courteous champion of states' rights, he would end up being reviled in the North and misunderstood in the South.

In at least one instance of his contented childhood, the generally well-behaved Tyler demonstrated something of the steel of his father. He led a schoolboy revolt against the teacher at the small local schoolhouse to which he had been sent. William McMurdo, a Scot with a visage more stern than John Tyler's, believed the rod was one of the three Rs. Tired of his bullying, Tyler and the other children overpowered McMurdo, tied him up, and fled the building. When the apoplectic schoolmaster finally got out and appealed to Judge Tyler for justice, the bemused Tyler could only reply *"Sic semper tyrannis"*—thus always to tyrants—in the spirit of his own mentor, Patrick Henry.

In terms of significant study, Judge Tyler was really John's most memorable teacher. He imparted not only the lessons of his life, memories of Revolutionary days, and a love of music and poetry, but also something of the law itself. At the age of twelve, John entered the preparatory school for William and Mary, and a year or two later entered the college itself. An excellent student, he graduated in 1807, shortly after his seventeenth birthday. Letters from his highly engaged father reveal that he closely monitored his son's progress, criticizing such lapses as poor penmanship.

However, even Judge Tyler must have been pleased when John was selected to speak at the commencement exercises. His address on female education (one hopes he was in favor of it) was widely praised by the college faculty. He then went home to read law, not surprisingly with his father.

Chitwood concludes, "Few men in American public life have been more fortunate both as to heredity and environment than was John Tyler." Unfortunately, the certainties of the 1790s were not always equal to the challenges of the 1840s. Tyler's lifelong convictions, learned at his father's side, led him inevitably to oppose the nationalist emphasis of his own Whig party. The accidental nature of his ascension to the presidency didn't help. When Henry Clay suggested that, as had been said of both Adamses, John Tyler was a president without a party, before departing the White House in 1845 Tyler and his wife Julia responded by giving one of the most lavish entertainments in the history of the executive mansion. "Now," he is reported to have said, "they can't say I didn't have a party."

John Tyler Sr. would have immensely appreciated such a defiant gesture. He died at his home on January 6, 1813, at the age of sixty-five, having performed his judicial duties almost to the last. The nation was once again at war with Great Britain, a conflict Judge Tyler had hoped to see to its conclusion. During his three years as governor in Richmond, the new state capital, Tyler had particularly enjoyed having his son with him, helping out as an aide while completing his legal training. For young Tyler, only eighteen, it was also a matchless opportunity to meet the renowned personages his father esteemed, including Thomas Jefferson. In the War of 1812 young Tyler, as had his father in the prior conflict, joined a company of militia, although it was never engaged in actual combat, and earned a title of captain that he was proud to retain. Still, he mistrusted military leadership. Like Judge Tyler, he was always fearful of its potential for excessive executive power. Young Tyler predicted, "The day is rapidly approaching when an ounce of lead will be worth more than a pound of sense." The United States must not duplicate the folly of less enlightened nations.

Despite his firm espousal of states' rights, former president John Tyler would be called back to Washington in 1861 by a James Buchanan desperate to avoid civil war. Because he transcended identification with any faction, Tyler presided over a last-ditch conference to bring both sides together. Of course, it was doomed to failure. His father, however, would not have disparaged such an effort. Above all, he was a patriot.

# Samuel Polk

Once he made up his mind, you couldn't budge Samuel Polk. Fortunately, he and his wife, Jane, agreed on just about everything except religion. When it came to politics, as it often did on the frontier, they were both devoted Jeffersonians, as were most of their neighbors, although opposing views could also be vigorously voiced around their campfires. It was here, an outdoor equivalent of the Van Burens' tavern, that their oldest son, James, absorbed his earliest impressions of political discourse and also heard thrilling tales of his grandfather's exploits in the Revolutionary War. In time James Knox Polk would lead the nation in fulfilling his own vision of American destiny. His education had been financed by a father who knew a good investment when he saw one.

He came to it naturally. If many first fathers were restless, ambitious entrepreneurs pursuing their personal visions of the American dream, so were many of *their* fathers. As Polk biographer Martha Morrel writes of Samuel Polk's father, Ezekiel, "The same venturesome spirit that had brought his great-grandfather to America more than a century earlier flowed through his veins with undiluted vigor." Those venturesome Polks had come from Scotland to Maryland and then to North Carolina, where Samuel was born in 1772. Three years later, in 1775, an intrepid relative was one of those who assembled to proclaim the Mechlenburg Resolves declaring British authority null and void, a year before the Declaration of Independence emerged from Philadelphia.

Ezekiel's great chance came when, like many others, he received a land grant as a result of his service in the War for American Independence. As a surveyor as well as a farmer, he energetically bought up additional grants from other veterans, expanded his holdings in North Carolina, and ultimately moved on to a greater opportunity in Tennessee. Samuel Polk grew up in an environment of ambitious acquisitiveness. Not very far away, near the flourishing town of Charlotte, ironically named for the wife of George III, another distinguished veteran of the Revolutionary War returned to the farm he had already established. James Knox had risen to the rank of colonel. Among those most anxious to greet him was his daughter, Jane, who had been born in 1776, just before her father went off to fight. That the Knox family was known for piety as well as industriousness is not surprising. Jane Knox was the great-great-grandniece of John Knox, the father of Scotch Presbyterianism. It was a legacy she didn't take lightly.

Jane may have been known to her friends as "Jenny," but there was as little of frivolity in her makeup as in that of Sam Polk. As each grew to adulthood, the boundaries of their region moved inexorably westward. A projected road thirty feet wide was being constructed all the way to Nashville. Soon it would be safe for families to settle beyond the Appalachians, and the population in the western territory of North Carolina would make it eligible for separate statehood. Even in this relative wilderness, opportunities for young people to meet socially were not lacking. Samuel Polk, the energetic son of an energetic father, could read, write, and calculate, qualities that must have also appealed to Jane. He inherited more than land from his father. Ezekiel Polk was a freethinking deist, in the tradition of Franklin and Jefferson, but Jane found Samuel so admirable in other ways that she overlooked it.

They were married on Christmas evening in 1794, in a properly Presbyterian ceremony at the Mechlenburg church. On November 4, 1795, the first of their ten children was born, a son. Sam agreed that he should be named James Knox Polk in honor of Jane's father, not the Scotch founder of the faith. Problems arose when the boy was about to be baptized. The minister insisted that in order for this to be done, Samuel would have to first profess his own faith. With his customary tact, Samuel suggested that perhaps the learned pastor misunderstood his own theology. When the cleric proved adamant, Sam stormed out of the church, his wife and son in tow. Jane was appalled and the entire community a bit stunned, but Sam, as always, stood firm. At least Jane Polk hadn't married a weakling. James would grow up under the influence of his mother's faith, but he would never be baptized a Presbyterian.

He learned the rudiments of temporal education—reading, writing, and arithmetic—from his parents and would absorb their keen interest in events outside their community. As the family grew, he also inherited their sense of order and duty, sharing responsibility for the care and direction of his nine younger brothers and sisters. Samuel Polk was becoming recognized not only as a successful farmer but also as a community leader. Still, he longed for wider horizons. When John was nearly eleven, the Polks joined Ezekiel, who had already established much larger holdings in Tennessee, between Franklin and Nashville, which he described as a "bountiful land of promise." Although born only a few months before Tennessee's admission as a state, the memories of his childhood in Mechlenburg always stayed with James.

Samuel received substantial land from his father, emulated his skills as a surveyor, and ventured into the buying and selling of others' farmland. All this was supplemented by a host of community activities, from serving as a county magistrate to promoting candidates for office. It was a promising but very exacting life. Samuel needed the help of everyone, especially his oldest son. Although James undertook farm chores willingly, he simply lacked the physical strength and stamina for them. Morrel describes the child as "well-formed" but "frail," small but handsome. He loved horses, hunting and fishing, and the outdoors in general, but his recurring illnesses alarmed both his parents. If anything, James seemed to be weakening as he grew older. Their new locale was more spacious but far less settled than Mechlenburg, devoid of any amenities. The nearest doctor resided some 250 miles away, in Kentucky. However immersed in work, Sam determined that he must lay everything aside and undertake the journey with his son. When they finally arrived, the diagnosis was gallstones. James endured a risky, painful operation to remove them, without benefit of anesthesia, earning the enduring respect of his father.

After the operation, James's health markedly improved, but his father realized that the boy would never be up to the rigorous demands of farming or surveying. Seemingly capable of turning a profit at almost anything, Sam had expanded his enterprises to commercial ventures, helping to establish a local bank, a newspaper, and, most important, a general store. He decided to send his son to a nearby merchant to learn the business, but it soon became apparent that James was no more suited to retailing than to farming. He was hardly averse to hard work—that was never the problem—but it was his mind that he longed to exercise. With his mother's support, James convinced his stubborn father, who now had the means, to invest in the best education possible in their environs. "Do well in your studies," Samuel Polk promised, "and I'll send you to college. But mind—I'll not waste my money if you waste your time."

He need not have worried. Wasting time was no part of James Polk's inheritance. Starting with a tutor in the nearby town of Columbia, James advanced to a well-regarded academy in Murfreesboro, fifty miles away. Both were staunchly Presbyterian, but that didn't bother Samuel. James proved to be a conscientious if not brilliant student, a restless perfectionist who simply outworked everyone else. Such tenacity foreshadowed his future political career. It also opened wider vistas, enabling him to make friends outside his family circle. Some of them were young women who came to the school after hours for their own lessons. Polk would marry the brightest of them, Sarah Childress. Together they went for long walks, an exercise that benefited Polk's always fragile health. As good as his word, Sam sent James to the University of North Carolina. Entering as a sophomore, he graduated with honors in 1818.

James disappointed his mother only in his choice of vocation. He would not be a Presbyterian minister, as she had hoped, but an attorney. In this his father was anything but disappointed. James moved to Nashville, studied law for two years, passed the bar, and with a Carolina classmate set up a legal partnership. It was all financed by his father—the education, their office, even their books. Sam never made a sounder investment. As for Jane Knox Polk, when she looked up at her son's freshly painted shingle, all she could say was, "It's a fine looking sign. Never do anything to dishonor it."

There is a difference between success and esteem. James Polk would go on to remarkable, relentless success in his legal and political career. By the age of twenty-seven he was elected to the state legislature, and two years later, called "Young Hickory," to the same congressional seat as had been held by his parents' old acquaintance Andrew Jackson. Eventually he became governor of Tennessee, and in 1844 the first "dark horse" candidate to win the presidency. He was an expansionist Democrat, called by the press "a short man with a long program," and achieved virtually all of his objectives in only one term. Victory in the war with Mexico capped his career. Polk insisted on making his own decisions throughout, trusting virtually no one. Never robust physically, he literally worked himself to death. On his deathbed James Knox Polk was finally baptized—but as a Methodist, to honor a pledge he had given a friend. Whatever else might be said of him, the son of Samuel Polk also kept his word. His father had died on November 5, 1827, at the age of fifty-five. James would live to only fifty-three. Both Polks were rocks of reliability. Once Samuel Polk made up his mind, he couldn't be budged. When convinced that his son's intent to succeed was the equal of his own, Sam made it all possible.

# Richard Taylor

Zachary Taylor never wanted to be anything but a soldier, like his father. In his spare autobiography, all of fifteen pages, Taylor starts out, "I was born in Orange County, State of Vig. Nov. 24th 1784. My father Richard Taylor was appointed an officer in the first Regiment of continental troops raised by the State of Virginia to oppose the Brittish [*sic*] at the commencement of the Revolution and remained in the service in the Continental Line until the close of the war & quit the Service as a Lt. Col. In the Spring of '85 he emigrated to this state, and settled in the neighborhood of Louisville where I was raised. In the spring of 1808 I was appointed a first Lieutenant in the 7th Regiment United States Infantry." That is all there is of Richard Taylor.

The Taylors turn our ongoing story backwards. They were patrician patriots who became pioneer patriots. As a result, Zachary received much less education than had his parents. All the other elements are there—an intrepid family venturing west for more land, an ambitious war veteran of thirty-five marrying a gently bred young woman of eighteen, the large family that resulted, their frontier struggles, and even the log cabin, although this time it, too, was in reverse order. The Taylors went in a few years from plantation to log cabin and then back to a bigger plantation. Richard Taylor would always be known as "Colonel," but his official military career ended with the conclusion of the American Revolution. That was enough for Zachary. More than anything, Taylor longed for the opportunity to emulate his father's exploits as a soldier. Since Zachary invested ten times as much of his life to a military career as had his father, he would become not merely a colonel but a general. Since he also inherited much of his father's unpretentiousness, he would be known to his admiring troops as "Old Rough and Ready."

By the end of the Revolution, the Taylor family had been in America for almost 150 years. The first American Taylor had come from England around 1640 and settled in Virginia on the Mattaponi River. The entire colony had no more than ten thousand inhabitants, its Tidewater region only partially settled. Although established as a prominent family, the Taylors early demonstrated an inclination for exploration. In 1716 James Taylor was one of those celebrated Knights of the Golden Horseshoe who accompanied Governor Alexander Spotswood on his expedition over the Blue Ridge Mountains into the Shenandoah Valley. Taylor emerged with the acquisition of substantial holdings in the Piedmont on the Rapidan River. In 1721 his daughter, Frances, married Ambrose Madison, merging the families of two future presidents. Through blood or marriage, Taylors would be related as well to Lees, Marshalls, and Monroes. Richard Taylor was born into this well-established Virginia family on April 3, 1744, one of the four children of a prior Zachary Taylor and Elizabeth Lee. Richard's explorations would take him farther than any of his forebears. His son Zachary's exploits would take him all the way to the White House.

Like many similarly situated young Virginians, Richard attended William and Mary College. He seemed headed for the comfortable serenity of plantation life, but at twenty-five demonstrated an adventurous streak. With his brother and a friend, he journeyed down the Ohio and Mississippi rivers, a yearlong exploration not quite of Lewis and Clark dimensions but very ambitious for the time. Whatever its dangers, the trip convinced Taylor that there was a vast area of potential habitation beyond the Piedmont.

If he sought more immediate adventure, it came with the War for American Independence. As his son later recorded, Richard was an early recruit of the First Virginia regiment. In five years and five months of fighting in both the eastern and western theaters of war, he rose from first lieutenant to lieutenant colonel. In 1779 he somehow found the time to wed Sarah Dabney Strother, seventeen years his junior. Born to a prominent plantation family near Fredericksburg, charming "Sally" Strother had enjoyed all the advantages, including tutors from Europe. Her cultivated demeanor seemed a perfect complement to Richard's dashing persona. Reportedly Richard Taylor was quite tall, blue-eyed, and strikingly handsome. Once he returned from the war, the children came quickly—in February 1781, their first son, named Hancock for both the brother who had accompanied Richard on his adventurous journey and an uncle who had been killed by Indians; in 1782, their second son, William Dabney Strother, named for Sally's brother who had been killed in the war.

Richard was not his parents' first son. The Hare Forest property he had inherited was substantial and had escaped the ravages of war, but in Taylor's view it was simply not of sufficient size to supply the needs of a growing family. He was already representing Orange County in the Virginia Assembly, and he and his wife were happily settled, but his old wanderlust returned. It was enhanced by a postwar government short of cash but flush with land. Virginia made Richard Taylor an offer he couldn't refuse. Unable to pay returning veterans a bonus for their services, hard-pressed states like Virginia offered them vast tracts of land in their western preserves. The grant made to Richard Taylor in sparsely settled Kentucky was over eight thousand acres.

That was enough to convince him to sell Hare Forest and hasten west to claim the first thousand, outside the outpost village of Louisville, as quickly as possible. The relocation of his family was delayed by Sally, who was pregnant again. The baby, another boy, was delivered more or less en route, giving two states claim to a future president. Sally's confinement was completed at Montebello, a plantation owned by a Taylor cousin, some twelve miles from Hare Forest. The newest Zachary Taylor was born on November 24, 1784. With bag, baggage, and baby, the Taylors ventured overland to Pennsylvania, to Fort Pitt, where Richard had served in the war, to Ohio, and then down the wilderness trail by wagon and flatboat to their new home in Kentucky. Richard had already erected a log cabin (no one would later claim, as with William Henry Harrison, that Zachary still resided in one). Within a few years it would be replaced by a substantial two-story brick edifice that Taylor called "Springfield," where he lived for the remaining forty-four years of his life.

Until the turn of the nineteenth century, the "dark and bloody ground" of Kentucky came under frequent Indian attack. Richard fought in many such skirmishes and was wounded at least once. Young Zachary grew up not only hearing tales of the Revolution but also seeing evidence of his father's heroism. Certainly he was never privy to the Indians' point of view. Kentucky had long served as a prime hunting and fishing ground for many tribes. It became for the Indians an unequal struggle for survival.

The reality of slavery was also part of Zachary's childhood. His father had started with three slaves; by 1810 he had thirty-seven. Richard's prosperity grew as if by destiny, but there was an uneven quality to life at Springfield and throughout the region. As biographer Brainerd Dyer writes, Taylor had "developed a plantation that in time offered the comforts, if not the luxuries, of the older plantations of the east." He might have added "the amenities." The Taylors eventually had nine children. Although there were no really close neighbors, with two older brothers, three younger brothers, and three sisters, Zachary rarely wanted for playmates.

There was, however, no real school on any continuing basis. For a time an itinerant schoolmaster from New England conducted classes, and later Zachary had at least some sessions with a classical scholar named Kean O'Hara, a far cry from either his father's education at William and Mary or his mother's European tutors. Sally became his only consistent teacher, just as his father served as his lifelong role model. To attain a commission in the army, even someone as well connected as Zachary Taylor had to know how to write his name. He would always have difficulty with spelling, grammar, and penmanship. It is interesting that in later years Taylor stressed the importance of education for the children of those stationed at every army post he commanded, and that his only son, Richard, studied in Edinburgh and Paris before graduating from Yale. Eventually Zachary appreciated the value of everything that he had been able to learn, despite his childhood on the frontier.

The area around Louisville was intended as at least a rough replica of what its settlers had left behind. In 1785, when the Taylors arrived, Kentucky, which was still a part of Virginia, already had a population of some 25,000, but the area around Louisville had hardly grown at all. Its growth spurt began after the Indians were dispersed and Kentucky finally became a state. Zachary's father helped it to happen. Richard was a member of the convention that framed Kentucky's constitution, and seven years later he helped to revise it. He served a term in the state legislature and was a justice of the peace and a county magistrate. Four times, between 1812 and 1824, he was a presidential elector, granted the opportunity to cast his vote for his own distant relations. President Washington also named Taylor to the post of collector for the Port of Louisville.

That location was a key to his success. Taylor's plantation was on Beargrass Creek, where goods could be docked and moved overland to Louisville. Along with the bounty of his tobacco and other crops, this river commerce helped create his wealth. The entire region began to prosper, and soon there were many fine homes, built by men of substance. Their wives wore the latest fashions. There was horse racing, and parties as lavish as those in the Piedmont and Tidewater. Mundane matters like sanitation and education could come later.

Although Zachary professed to love the land, when he was given some he chose not to retain it. It is surprising that it took him so long to become a soldier. Perhaps his marriage in 1801 delayed his decision. Zachary did serve in the militia in 1806. Finally, at the age of twenty-three, in 1808, he gained his commission as a first lieutenant in the infantry when President Jefferson tripled the size of the army. His father's influence could not have hurt. Service was to be for five years; officers were not intended to become professional soldiers. In fact, feeling disappointed at his lack of advancement, Zachary left the service after the War of 1812, ostensibly to go back to farming. "I do not regreat [sic] the change of calling," he insisted, but when President Madison, his kinsman, reorganized the army in 1816, Zachary was happy to return, as a major.

He stayed a soldier, devoted to the welfare of his men, through his years of triumph in the Mexican War. President Polk, suspicious of everyone, predicted that his prominent generals, Winfield Scott and Zachary Taylor, both utterly "ignorant of public affairs," would be nominated for president.

Both were, and in 1848 Taylor won. Although a slave-owning Southerner, he fervently believed in the preservation of the Union. His tenure was longer than William Henry Harrison's single month, but typhoid fever claimed Zachary Taylor only fifteen months into his promising presidency. Shortly before, he had claimed, "I have no aspirations for civic office of any kind," but like other military leaders, before and since, he was carried forward by a wave of euphoria. Taylor, the soldier's general, might well have become a unifying people's president. His admiring parents had only lived long enough to see him a lieutenant colonel, the same rank his father had risen to. Richard Taylor died on January 19, 1829, at the age of eighty-four. His wife died the following year. Zachary found the old homestead "a dreary and comfortless place to visit" when he returned to mourn them.

Zachary Taylor looked nothing like his father. He was short, and anything but dashing in appearance or attire. As noted Taylor biographer K. Jack Bauer writes, in later years "Old Rough and Ready" resembled either a prosperous farmer, with his weathered and lined countenance, or, more accurately, "a man who had spent most of his adult years in command of troops in the field or those manning frontier posts. The eyes are sharp, the mouth firm, the features lean." Hardly the physical embodiment of his father, Taylor wanted nothing more than to *be* like his father. In Zachary's mind, Richard Taylor remained perpetually that heroic colonel who opposed "the Brittish at the commencement of the Revolution & remained in the Service."

## Nathaniel Fillmore

Millard Fillmore may not have been our greatest president, but he has few rivals for most unlikely. His saga combines Dickensian privation with aspects of Cinderella—minus the evil stepmother. Fillmore was blessed with two loving parents, and it was his bungling, endlessly striving father, Nathaniel, who somehow found a way to give the boy his start. Little more than thirty years later the two would stand proudly together at a

Nathaniel Fillmore

White House reception given by the son to honor his father, a scene that might induce even a certified cynic to utter, "Only in America."

Things should have been a bit easier. Lieutenant Nathaniel Fillmore, of old English stock, helped to settle Bennington, Vermont, and then went on to defend it in the Revolutionary War. His son, also named Nathaniel, who had been born in 1771, inherited his father's love of the region if not of its impossibly stony soil. He wanted to farm where the soil was as spectacular as the scenery. Young Nathaniel married well. Phoebe Millard, the daughter of a prominent doctor in Pittsfield, Massachusetts, loved learning. At the age of sixteen, she also fell in love with strapping Nat Fillmore, who was all of twenty-five. Perhaps as well as his blond good looks, it was his sense of adventure that appealed to her, for Nathaniel was intent on setting out to find prosperity in the wild west—that is to say, in the wilderness of Cayuga County, New York.

Just as the Virginia government had lured veterans like Richard Taylor with a bounty of land in Kentucky, New York set aside one and a half million acres of public domain land as a "military tract," intended for its war veterans. Few of them took advantage of the offer. They understood that central New York, however scenic, is not quite the equivalent of fertile Kentucky. Most of the land fell into the hands of speculators, who, unburdened by scruples, fanned out throughout the countryside, spreading tales of the new Eden only a few hundred miles to the west. Among the most gullible of their victims were Nathaniel Fillmore and his brother, Calvin. They bought a farm sight unseen, in Locke Township, within a deep forest. To this pristine location they took their supportive young brides. On it they built the requisite log cabin in which both families would live. After laboriously clearing much of the timber, as Robert Raybach writes, "Instead of fertile loam, the Fillmore brothers found unyielding clay. Instead of prosperity, they found poverty."

In the midst of mounting gloom, however, Phoebe and Nathaniel had one tangible reason for hope. On January 7, 1800, their first child was born, a son. They named him Millard, his mother's maiden name. Joy, however, was soon overtaken by dire events. As Raybach continues, to the Fillmores' "woes of poor crops, poor weather, and a crowded cabin was added a defective land title. . . . Faulty surveys, claim-jumping, ignorance, and downright chicanery had so confused the region's land titles that the state sent a team of commissioners to review and settle all land titles in the area." There was no way the Fillmores could prove anything. When Millard was two, they simply picked up and moved, settling some miles away in Sempronius, where they took a lease on 130 acres. Nathaniel Fillmore would never again be even technically an owner, only a tenant farmer of the land he worked.

For Millard, who was to be one of eight children, it meant a life of grinding poverty and toil. He was raw-boned and sturdy as an oak, like his father. As Millard recalled, "Being large of my age and unusually strong, I learned to plow, to hoe, to chop, to log and clear land, to mow, to reap, and finally to do all kinds of work which is usually done in clearing and cultivating a new farm." Nathaniel's tenant farm at least had the soil to sustain such crops as wheat and corn, unlike the clay of his wilderness swindle. School for Millard was a sometime thing, largely a matter of improvisation, in this sparsely settled area. At the age of six or seven, Millard learned his alphabet and how to spell and read. When he was ten, one of those ubiquitous itinerant (there seem to have been no other kind) schoolmasters from New England arrived to instruct the local children in writing and arithmetic, reportedly without benefit of even a dictionary. When Millard was twelve, community leaders tried to organize a real school and hire teachers, but hard-pressed Nathaniel could spare his oldest son only for two or three months in the winter.

Millard had by now discovered how much he enjoyed reading. He also loved every outdoor pursuit. Nathaniel might have welcomed the provender for his growing family's table, but he insisted, according to Frank Severance, editor of the Fillmore papers, that "no man ever prospered from hunting and fishing" and even took Millard's gun away. Nathaniel was not so much severe as seeking some sort of solution. He was sick of farming. In tenancy, no amount of energy or enterprise could yield him the life he had envisioned for Phoebe, himself, and their family. He hoped their daughters might marry well. He must save their five sons.

How? He couldn't remotely finance their way to a profession, but each could at least learn a productive trade. He started by apprenticing the oldest, Millard, to a cloth maker. The boy went reluctantly; as he feared, the regimen was hard and confining, more like a workhouse than a place to learn a trade. As the youngest apprentice, Millard spent most of his time doing such menial chores as chopping wood and cleaning up. He was learning nothing. Demonstrating a streak of independence, he told his exploiter just what he thought and, when threatened with chastisement, picked up an axe to defend himself. He was home in four months. As distraught as his father, Millard even considered taking money to be the substitute for a neighbor who was to fight in the War of 1812. His father suggested that he at least try another apprenticeship, at a larger and hopefully more reputable fabric-processing mill.

The work was still demanding, but more purposeful. Most satisfying of all, Millard managed to send home some money to help his father. He also helped himself, but not to luxuries. He bought a dictionary, and even as he worked he found time to absorb the meaning of word after word. In his spare time, he joined a circulating library and read everything he could find, developing a quiet confidence that supplemented his physical strength. By seventeen he was coming into his own as a self-taught scholar. During the slack season at the mill the enterprising youth took classes at a new academy established in the town of New Hope, not far away. For the first time, he also discovered the pleasures of female company—in particular, that of Abigail Powers, the bright daughter of a local minister. She may have been socially far superior (as who was not?), but the two were more than compatible. They fell deeply in love, giving

Millard even more incentive to make something of himself. He saved enough from his meager earnings to pay off his employer, and got a job teaching school. At least it was a start.

His father's perpetual dissatisfaction with his own situation resulted in a fortuitous decision. Nathaniel sold his tenancy at Sempronius and moved his family to Montville, a dozen miles away. Perhaps Nathaniel's motivation was at least in part to enhance Millard's future. The proprietor of Nathaniel's new farm was also the wealthiest person in the entire region, straightlaced, aged Judge Walter Wood, a Quaker renowned for shrewdness and frugality. His law firm, specializing in land title litigation, was also the most successful in the area. With some temerity, Nathaniel asked Judge Wood if he might give young Millard a two-month trial as a law clerk in his office. To Nathaniel's delight, Wood readily agreed.

When Millard visited his home and was told the news by his mother, he was so touched that he burst into tears. Whatever lay ahead, his future was finally in his own hands. The two months turned into two years. To compensate for Millard's inability to pay his way, Judge Wood suggested, "I can give thee some employment." Although eventually it turned out that the canny judge was more interested in sustaining his own prosperity than in advancing Fillmore's, soon the young clerk was given small cases to pursue, gaining experience of immense value.

Nathaniel eventually moved to the town of Aurora, near Buffalo, finally finished with farming for good. This move, too, turned out to be ideally timed for his son, intentionally or not. After leaving Wood, Millard moved to Aurora and lived with his parents while he both taught school and obtained a more valuable clerkship with one of the major law firms in Buffalo. During his leanest years, he never abandoned hope, like Dickens's Micawber, that "something would turn up." He had resolved from the day he met dour Judge Wood "to be a lawyer and nothing else." He was ambitious, stubborn, resourceful, and self-confident, but, as Raybach notes, there remained as well a sort of residual modesty. It would prove to be both a strength and a shortcoming to Fillmore in his future political career. His father had enabled him to be in the right place at just the right time. Buffalo was becoming a thriving metropolis, opening opportunities that would have been unimaginable to Millard only a few months before.

Here he met and learned to deal with all sorts of people from a multiplicity of backgrounds. As he had once taught himself the very meaning of words, now his self-education focused on improving his social skills, while at the same time filling in gaps in his legal knowledge. To his associates, he was an agreeable if rather methodical companion; to the partners of his firm, a rising star. At their instigation, Millard was admitted to the practice of law before New York's Court of Common Pleas in 1823, equivalent to passing the bar. He was not quite twenty-three. Still not completely confident that he could flourish as the equal of his mentors, Fillmore opened his initial practice back in the eastern part of Aurora. When he returned to Buffalo several years later, his reputation had been enhanced and he had finally married the patient Abigail Powers.

Law led to politics. It seems odd that Fillmore's political career started and concluded with such extremist elements as the Anti-Masonic Party and the nativist "Know-Nothings," but during Fillmore's lifetime the American political structure was rather traumatically emerging into its present two-party configuration. It was as a National Republican that he was elected to the New York State Assembly at the age of only twenty-seven, and as a Whig that his political career would move forward to its heights. His mother did not live to enjoy it. She died in 1831, at only fifty-one, proud enough that the son who bore her family's name was already a success in Albany.

Nathaniel Fillmore saw it all. Eventually remarried, he witnessed Millard's lucrative law practice in Buffalo, his election to Congress, to the vice presidency, and upon the death of Taylor, to the presidency itself. Although not quite so mismatched as Harrison and Tyler, Zachary Taylor and Millard Fillmore are also examples of the perils of ticket-balancing. The magnanimous Fillmore was weak where Taylor would have been strong, a firmer advocate of preserving the Union. Fillmore hated slavery but invariably counseled moderation, agreeing to the Compromise of 1850 that Taylor had opposed. The sudden death of Taylor in July 1850 had stunned Fillmore. "I have no language to express the emotions of my heart," he said. But thrust into leadership in such a fevered climate of discord, he managed only to delay the carnage for a decade, hoping that perhaps his evenhanded espousal of prosperity for all sections of the nation might yet heal the breach. His presidency, like the man himself, was certainly well intentioned.

Millard Fillmore's entire career is a tribute to making the most of every opportunity. Few, however, would have come his way without his father's timely interventions. There they stood, side by side, in the White House, as Millard's term was winding down, receiving the notables of Washington, as well as just plain citizens—equitable to the end. Father and son were both still strikingly handsome, congenial six-footers, Nathaniel's great shock of white hair giving his appearance added distinctiveness. Asked how one raises a president, he replied with a suitably colorful country allusion, "Cradle him in a sap trough." In they came to shake his hand, to honor *him,* as if he, too, a lifelong failure, deserved such a tribute.

Nathaniel Fillmore died on March 28, 1863, at the age of ninety-two, in the midst of the war his son had tried to avert. He was the longest-lived of all first fathers, exceeding John Adams by a year. To the end of his days, plain old Nat Fillmore probably still couldn't quite believe what had happened to his son, a true tribute to the tenacity of both.

## Benjamin Pierce

The face in the official portrait looks familiar—a shock of gray hair, a prominent nose, a strong jaw, a penetrating gaze. No, it is not Andrew Jackson, but his great admirer, General Benjamin Pierce, governor of "the Granite State" of New Hampshire. Pierce's regard for Jackson's person and politics was passed along to his son, Franklin, who in time would earn the campaign appellation of "Young Hickory of the Granite Hills." Frank Pierce also inherited his father's handsome countenance and robust health and benefited from both the education and the political contacts he provided. Frank's inheritance from his mother was more mixed a blessing. She was undeniably charming and lighthearted. Her son would recall her as "a most affectionate and tender mother, strong in many points and weak in some." What was that weakness? Both Anna Kendrick Pierce and her son Franklin were alcoholics. Whether it was more an allergy or an addiction, he would struggle against it all his life, as she apparently did not. The wonder is that so astute an observer as Benjamin Pierce appears never to have been aware of it.

He wasn't really a general; it was a distinction he conferred on himself when he headed his local militia. After all, he served in it for twenty-one years. Such a gesture is entirely consistent with Pierce's self-made career, which took him all the way from rural poverty to the governor's mansion. As biographer Roy Franklin Nichols writes, Pierce "was a typical back country leader who, though rough in manners and lacking in education and culture, had a vivid personality with much native force and strength which made him a domineering yet generous 'squire.'" He may not have been an authentic general, but he was an undoubted

Benjamin Pierce

patriot, his heroism having been demonstrated repeatedly throughout the Revolutionary War, where he *did* rise to the rank of captain.

Of English heritage, the Pierces had settled in the town of Chelmsford, Massachusetts. Here Benjamin was born on Christmas day, 1757, the seventh of ten children. When he was six his father died, leaving him no inheritance. Young Ben grew up poor but proud on the farm of his uncle, Robert Pierce. Fortunately, he managed to obtain at least some schooling. As Pierce put it in his succinct autobiography, he learned to read, write, and do sums "by attending school from the age of ten to sixteen years, three weeks in each year."

His future arrived quite suddenly when he was only seventeen, in 1775, with the march of the Redcoats from Boston to Concord. In

Pierce's words, "I was ploughing in the field when the news first came that the British had fired upon the Americans at Lexington and killed eight men. I stepped between the cattle, dropped the chains from the plough, and without any further ceremony, shouldered my uncle's fowling piece, swung the bullet pouch and powder-horn and hastened to the place where the first blood had been spilled." Quite literally a Minuteman, Pierce would not soon return to his plow, as Washington's hero Cincinnatus had. He was gone for most of the next nine years, enlisting and reenlisting, fighting everywhere from Breed's Hill to Saratoga and spending a desolate winter at Valley Forge. Despite every privation, he wrote, "I enjoyed it much. . . . Arms was my profession."

He was much changed when he returned to Chelmsford, a grown man and a seasoned veteran, in 1784. He had learned enough to do some surveying for a local landowner, Colonel Samson Stoddard, up north in New Hampshire. It struck him as a more promising place to settle, and in the town of Hillsborough (or Hillsboro, as Pierce spelled it), he bought a small farm, reputedly at a dollar an acre, almost on the spur of the moment. The next year, he took up residence, improving the log hut that already existed on the property, and the following year, in 1787, he got married. Elizabeth Andrews Pierce lived for only an additional eighteen months. She died in childbirth, a too-frequent occurrence in those days. Her grieving husband named his new daughter, too, Elizabeth.

There was little time for Benjamin to mourn. He was already more a politician than a farmer. In 1789 he was elected to represent his county in the state legislature, and he would be reelected sixteen times in succession. As a supporter of the principles of Jefferson and Jackson in a predominantly Federalist region, he would not always triumph, but "with much native force," his future looked bright. Meanwhile, his daughter needed a mother. When Benjamin met pretty, plump, colorful, vivacious twenty-one-year-old Anna Kendrick, a new arrival in the area, it didn't take him long to propose. Nor did it take her long to accept this dashing suitor. Whether they toasted their nuptials with spirits is not a matter of record.

What kind of mother would she be? That also wouldn't take long to determine. Anna not only became stepmother to Elizabeth but bore her husband eight children. Franklin was the sixth, born on November 23, 1804, in an authentic log cabin. Whatever else might be said of Anna Kendrick Pierce, who seemed to take a positive delight in shocking the prim paragons of the community with her colorfully provocative attire, outspokenness, and eccentricities, she was a dutiful mother. Franklin referred to her "kindness and deep affection." The area was gradually growing, and with it the Pierces' interests. The year before Franklin's birth, Benjamin was elected to the Governor's Council, and he later would be a delegate to New Hampshire's constitutional convention as well as sheriff for the county of Hillsborough.

With so many children, and more on the way, although it was by no means a large family for the times, Benjamin decided that they had out-grown their rustic log cottage by Contoocook Pond. He built a larger home, almost a mansion, closer to the village center. It was also adjacent to the turnpike that brought visitors and news to their still-remote region by stagecoach, and it served as his political headquarters. Pierce was becoming so renowned for his hospitality that he converted part of his home into a tavern. It wasn't, like Abraham Van Buren's establishment, a tavern with a home attached, but a spacious home with a tavern attached. Still, could Pierce have been less conscious of his wife's drink-ing problem than were his neighbors? Gossip about Anna Pierce was by now the major diversion of Hillsborough. Perhaps Ben Pierce simply ascribed it to her generally buoyant spirits.

In any case, young Frank, as his parents called him, was genuinely fond of both of his parents. He thrilled to his father's Revolutionary War stories, but unlike Zachary Taylor, it was the political war stories that left the most lasting impression. Benjamin Pierce would run for governor four times and win twice. All the races were closely contested, some almost vicious in personal vindictiveness. With his soldierly bearing he was a stern but loving father. Nichols writes of Frank, "Between his father's strictness and his mother's easygoing ways there was sure to be a chance for the quick witted to escape many of the consequences of boy-ish disobedience." In what was still essentially a wilderness, Frank had ample opportunity for outdoor diversions—swimming, skating, hunting, and fishing, each in its season. His mother's independent thinking blunted any excessive influence of the town's still-pervasive Puritanism in their home. In contrast, his father's more structured influence was felt even when he was away. When Frank was eight, his idyll was interrupted by the War of 1812. His older brothers and his sister's husband enlisted, and his father was frequently called to councils at the state capital in Concord. Although impressed with accounts of their exploits, the family felt immense relief when each returned home safely.

Having had the advantage of so little formal education himself, Benjamin Pierce viewed it as a subject of some importance. First Frank attended the local school in Hillsborough Center, but it being deemed not quite sufficient, he was dispatched to prestigious Hancock Academy in a nearby town. It meant boarding, and his first sustained separation from his family. One particular incident is often cited by biographers as most significant in Franklin's progression to maturity. At the age of twelve, he was so homesick that on a Sunday morning he left Hancock without permission and walked all the way home to Hillsborough. After returning from church, his father calmly asked Frank to stay for dinner. Much relieved, the boy thought that once again he would have his way. His father had uttered no reproach. After dinner he started to drive his son back to school, but midway he dropped him off in the road and returned home alone. A drenching rain added to Frank's discomfort as he approached the academy. He never left school again without approval. The expectations of a man so strong as Benjamin Pierce did not need to be voiced to be understood.

Frank proved to be so adept a student that his father chose only him and his brother Benjamin as worthy to go on to college. Ben went to Dartmouth, but political turmoil there resulted in its president departing to head Bowdoin College in Maine. Benjamin liked what he'd heard of its more democratic environment and determined to send Frank there. First the boy spent a productive year of preparation at Francistown Academy, particularly strong in classical languages. In the fall of 1820, symbolically wedged between his two mismatched parents, Frank set out in their chaise, in a high state of excitement, bound for Bowdoin.

He blossomed there, in both academics and social life. Mingling with students from more sophisticated backgrounds, he may have felt some uncertainty, but he masked or mastered it successfully and met them on equal terms. Sanctioned or not, there was drinking at Bowdoin, but apparently Frank was able to resist excessive temptation. As fellow student Nathaniel Hawthorne later observed, "At this early period of life he was distinguished by the same fascination of manner that has since proved so magical in winning him unbounded popularity." Frank graduated in 1824, third in his class, and delivered an oration at commencement. At college, despite his outgoing nature, he also became more introspective and religious, impressed by sermons he had heard. Franklin was to receive another legacy from Bowdoin. A decade after his graduation he married the lovely but very delicate Jane Means Appleton, daughter of a former president of the college.

Franklin returned home intent on studying the law and then following his father's path to public service. Like Samuel Polk, Benjamin Pierce helped finance every step of his son's future career, initially turning over his office to him. Admitted to the bar in 1827, Franklin set out to establish his law office in Concord. Soon he would have another reason to reside in the state's capital city. He was elected in 1829 to represent Hillsborough in the Great and General Court, as New Hampshire's state legislature was rather grandiloquently called. His father was completing his second and last term as governor. In effect, they would serve together. It was a heady time.

Success was coming almost too easily, but as Nichols points out, Franklin's struggles were more internal. His inability to hold his liquor in a political environment that stressed sociability was only one manifestation of an insecurity he never entirely overcame. If Millard Fillmore's childhood of abject destitution contributed to too modest a demeanor, perhaps Pierce's comparatively comfortable childhood had a similar result. The contrast between his bluff father and his permissive mother may have proved just as damaging to developing an ability to provide decisive leadership.

Benjamin Pierce finally retired from active public life in 1830. His son, increasingly the beneficiary of his efforts, kept moving steadily ahead. Franklin was elected to the United States Congress in 1833. He would go on to the Senate. A local newspaper put it plainly: "Frank Pierce is the most popular man of his age that I know of in N.H. . . . Every circumstance connected with him seems to contribute to his popularity. In the first place he has the advantage of his father's well-earned reputation to bring him forward. . . . In the next place he has a handsome person, bland and agreeable manners." Here are gifts from both parents—his father's looks and influence, his mother's "manners." No one could deny that when she wanted to, Anna Pierce exuded charm. The two died within four months of each other, Anna on December 7, 1838, at the age of seventy; Benjamin on April 1, 1839, at the age of eighty-one.

Franklin left the Senate in 1842 and returned to the practice of law to better support his growing family, but he remained active and visible in Democratic Party affairs. Such visibility was enhanced by his service in the Mexican War. Appointed a colonel after he volunteered, he was later promoted to brigadier general under the command of Winfield Scott, whom he would later face for the presidency. And so at least one Pierce became a genuine general.

A compromise choice, Pierce was nominated as the Democratic candidate for the presidency in 1852 on the forty-ninth ballot. Political conventions were more exciting in those days. He won an exceedingly close victory over Scott (Polk's prediction came true—both his "ignorant" generals did seek the office). Pierce's presidency was almost as frustrating as Fillmore's had been. Instead of the Compromise of 1850, Pierce's well-intentioned Waterloo was his approval of the even more divisive Kansas-Nebraska Act. He was not renominated in 1856. Pierce was an amiably attractive and conscientious man who lacked either the force or the good fortune to be an effective president. The times called for more assertive leadership.

Pierce's inner anxieties were exacerbated on the very eve of his presidency by the death of his son Bennie. Biographer Nichols writes, "Pierce's greatest misfortune was that, disorganized and numbed by personal tragedy, he seemed to understand little of the forces outside himself which were combining with his inward insecurity to make him one of democracy's most unfortunate victims."

If he never entirely subdued the demon of drink, it is understandable. Perhaps his stalwart father *was* aware of this family weakness but had long since simply decided to look the other way. His wife wasn't about to change. There was so much of promise to focus on in terms of his son. Benjamin Pierce, typical of other first fathers—self-made, ambitious, a patriotic pioneer—endowed his favored son in every way he could. But he could only give Franklin physical strength. Emotional strength comes from within.

## James Buchanan Sr.

To this day no one really knows why Anne Coleman decided to take her life. It is not even certain that she was a suicide. What we do know is that this belle of Lancaster, Pennsylvania, died mysteriously on a visit to Philadelphia in 1819, that she was engaged to a rising young lawyer named James Buchanan, and that almost everyone, including her parents, for some reason blamed him for her death. The crestfallen Buchanan wrote in a letter to Anne's parents, "She, as well as I, have been much abused. God forgive the authors of it. . . . I feel that happiness has fled from me forever." The letter was refused and returned to Buchanan unopened. He never married, becoming our sole bachelor president.

The only place Buchanan could find solace was at the warm hearth of his home in Mercersburg, then as now a handsome Pennsylvania town. From his mother he absorbed the grace of her Presbyterian faith in predestination. Whatever happened in life was not without its purpose. From his pragmatic father, the elder James Buchanan, he slowly regained the confidence to continue a career that had previously seemed so promising. Unlike the Pierces, Buchanan's parents were not so much mismatched as complementary. Any poetry in his life was a legacy from his mother. All the ambition was from his father.

In this ongoing chronicle of restless, relentless aspiration there is no first father who surpasses James Buchanan Sr.—at least until one gets to the Kennedys. His family had lived in Scotland and then County Donegal in Ireland (another by-now-familiar theme) for at least seven generations when James Buchanan, in the wake of the American Revolution, glimpsed greater opportunities across the ocean. His uncle, Joshua Russell, had already settled near Gettysburg, Pennsylvania, and was the proprietor of a thriving tavern. James liked the look of this new land of opportunity almost as soon as he set foot in Philadelphia and was greeted by Russell. He liked it even more when he reached central Pennsylvania and encountered comely sixteen-year-old Elizabeth Speer. She kept house for her widower father and her four older brothers on a farm adjacent to Russell's tavern.

It didn't take long for James to discover economic opportunity. He found work some forty miles to the west at a trading post and warehouse called "The Stony Batter," operated by one John Tom. Situated at the busy junction of Cove Gap, the establishment sold provisions for wagons and packhorses headed off to many different destinations. Eventually, after some convoluted negotiations, Buchanan was able to purchase the entire operation from Tom. Returning to Gettysburg, James rekindled his acquaintance with Elizabeth Speer. They were married in 1788, when she was twenty-one and he twenty-seven, and moved into his inevitable log cabin (although at least James had many other buildings on his property).

The following year, the couple had their first child, a daughter they named Mary. On April 23, 1791, they had their first son and named him James, after his father. Little Mary died later that year, a tragedy that sorely tested even Elizabeth Buchanan's faith. As leading Buchanan biographer Philip Shriver Klein writes, "It would be an unnatural mother that after this experience did not lavish more than the usual care upon her surviving child. James Buchanan, from the very first year of his life, occupied a position of special importance in the household." The Buchanans would have eleven children in all, two of whom died in infancy and three more of whom died much too young, but there were no surviving boys for another fourteen years. Throughout his childhood young James was at the center of a circle of adoring females. He was also the focus of his ever-striving father's hopes for the future.

Supervising both a thriving mercantile business and a productive farm, James Buchanan Sr. was forging ahead. He soon realized that bustling Stony Batter was hardly a healthy or even a safe place to bring up his children, resounding, as Klein puts it, "with the turmoil of stamping horses, drunken drovers, and cursing wagoners." But he had never intended that this trading post would be more than a way station on his road to respectability. By 1794 Buchanan had prospered sufficiently to buy "Dunwoodie Farm," a spacious three-hundred-acre estate. Two years later he built and moved his family into a handsome home in the settled town of Mercersburg, which would also serve as the headquarters of his expanding business interests. His brother-in-law was put in charge of the store that had started it all. The move to town proved beneficial for both of young James's parents. It afforded his pious, well-read, gentle mother the acquaintance of educated, stimulating neighbors. His father was enabled to earn the regard he craved of well-established families, becoming for a time, among other distinctions, their justice of the peace.

A firm Federalist in politics, as were not only Eastern aristocrats but many who had risen by their own efforts, the senior Buchanan was hard-driving and scrupulously honest—but hardly noted for compassion or idealism. His likeness might have been used by Webster to illustrate both "go-getter" and "no-nonsense." He had little use for small talk or time for leisure, even if shared with his son. When the two worked together, the father was particularly demanding, expecting more than he would of another's child. From his example James inherited not only ambition but also an excessive passion for precision in all things, especially in accounting for every penny.

Such an influence is evident in the phrasing of former President Buchanan's recollections in the "Autobiographical Sketch" that opened his self-justifying memoirs of 1866. "My father," he wrote, "was a man of practical judgment and of great industry and perseverance. He had received a good English education, and had that knowledge of mankind which prevented him from being ever deceived in business. He was a man of great native force and character. He was not only respected, but beloved by everyone who approached him. . . . He was a kind father, a sincere friend, and an honest and religious man." That is laying it on a bit thick. James Buchanan Sr. was hardly beloved by everyone, but he certainly had earned their respect. His goal for his oldest son, unlike the equivocation of other first fathers, was specific. Young James would study law. It was the ideal preparation to head any enterprise, including the flourishing business that the older Buchanan had labored so strenuously to assemble.

The move to Mercersburg had been a bit traumatic for young James, then only five. It meant not only more sustained contact with his demanding father, whose expectations would never diminish, but also accepting the structure of a real school and sharing the spotlight with other children. Nevertheless, at the Old Stone Academy, which would evolve into the renowned Mercersburg Academy, he made the transition rather smoothly, learning to relate to others while attaining the foundation of a classical education. His academic progress came to the attention of the family's learned Presbyterian pastor, Dr. John King, who had recently been named a trustee of Dickinson College in nearby Carlisle.

Dickinson was undergoing some growing pains but had attained an estimable reputation as a liberal arts college, a logical place of preparation for learning the law. When James turned sixteen, his father enrolled him at Dickinson. At first, all went exceedingly well. James was permitted to start as a junior. Soon, however, he became critical of a great many things about the school. His academic progress was not the problem. Thrust among forty-one other students, James was even more obliged than he had been at the Old Stone Academy to court popularity. "Without much natural tendency to become dissipated," he recalled, "and chiefly from the example of others . . . I engaged in every sort of extravagance and mischief." He drank excessively (although, unlike Franklin Pierce, he had no problem with alcohol addiction), smoked cigars, and took part in pranks, but—most offensively—he showed off his intellectual prowess at the expense of some of his professors. Yet, with outstanding grades and the esteem of his peers, Buchanan returned home after his first year at Dickinson confident of his place on the campus and looking forward to his senior year. Instead, his father received a letter stating that James had been expelled for "disorderly conduct." He uttered no word at the time, handing the letter to his son and leaving the room, but one can imagine his consternation.

Only the intervention of the family's kindly pastor, Dr. King, who by then had been named president of the college's board of trustees, persuaded Dickinson to take James back. He was denied the coveted first

honor at graduation in 1809, however—an award he probably merited—
at least in part because of the residual resentment of much of the faculty.
His chagrined father suggested that he take this disappointment like a
man—"The more you know of mankind, the more you will distrust
them"—but even in his memoirs Buchanan expressed regret that he had
not attended a different college.

Little deterred, however, he plunged straight ahead, studying law in
Lancaster. He was admitted to the bar in 1812. Although he had opposed
the war with Britain that started the same year, he considered it his duty
to help defend his country. He was already making a reputation for
speaking out on public issues when he volunteered in 1814. In the
decade after his brief military service, Buchanan built a lucrative legal
practice. He was elected district attorney for Lebanon County and as a
member of the Pennsylvania State Assembly, a young man well on his
way. His father, however, would have preferred that he stay in private
practice, more rewarding financially, more stable, and so much more rel-
evant to running a business enterprise.

It was not to work out that way. In 1820, only a year after the death
of Anne Coleman, James was elected to the United States House of
Representatives. Klein suggests that some of Buchanan's friends had initiated the campaign to bring him out of his debilitating melancholia.
James would be reelected five times, eventually changing his party regis-
tration from Federalist to Democrat.

His father was spared this defection. In 1821 he died in a carriage accident, at the age of sixty. There is ample evidence that he was immensely
proud of his son's political success, although it was not quite the course
he had envisioned. James Buchanan Sr. would have been prouder still had
he lived to witness his son's diplomatic triumphs as American minister to
Russia and to the Court of St. James. In between, Buchanan served as a
United States senator and as secretary of state. He had already been proposed three times as a likely candidate for the presidency before he finally
won the nomination in 1856. A conservative Democrat, with John C.
Breckenridge of Kentucky as his running mate, Buchanan was elected on
a last-ditch "Save the Union" platform. Buchanan's ambitious program
for national development was compromised by his emphasis on the limitations of the law. Despite his sincere efforts at conciliation, he was no
more successful in stemming the tide to secession than were his equally
well-intentioned predecessors, Fillmore and Pierce. Perhaps by then no
one could have done so. As Edwin Stanton told Buchanan, "Mr. President, you are sleeping on a volcano."

Presidential historian Paul Boller describes James Buchanan Jr. as "a gentleman of the old school. Distinguished-looking, faultlessly attired, and courtly mannered, he looked, it was said, like a British nobleman of an earlier generation. An eye defect forced him to tilt his head slightly forward and sideways when engaged in conversation, which gave the impression of exceptional courteousness and sensitivity to others." His passion for precision throughout his legal, diplomatic, and political careers was the direct result of his father's early indoctrination. Both James Buchanans kept the most precise records, the younger becoming quite wealthy at least in part due to his thrift.

President Polk conceded that Buchanan was undoubtedly able, but he "sometimes acts like an old maid." It hadn't prevented his success as a supremely skilled litigator in Pennsylvania courtrooms. James Sr. would surely have agreed with a local judge's appraisal of his son: "He was cut out by nature as a great lawyer, and I think was spoiled by fortune when she made him a statesman." By 1860 even the frustrated Buchanan himself might have concurred. He is reputed to have told a somber Lincoln, "If you are as happy in entering the White House as I shall feel on returning to Wheatland [his Lancaster home] you are a happy man indeed." But Lancaster also harbored the enduring memory of his grief.

What had caused Anne Coleman's sudden death in 1819? It is known that she and James had quarreled. Perhaps it was an agitated reaction to her wealthy parents' insistence that he was a fortune hunter, perhaps a result of his attentions to other women, or simply due to her emotional fragility. Or did her fiancé, this dapper, courtly young lawyer, already seem even to her too much like an "old maid"? Later, James would have at least one male friend of whom he seemed inordinately fond. There has been recurrent speculation that Buchanan may have been a homosexual. Of course, so devastating an experience as Anne's death could have triggered his lifelong determination never to marry. It would take a Patricia Cornwell to retroactively uncover the truth.

In later life Buchanan became guardian for many of his orphaned nephews and nieces. His favorite, the charming Harriet Lane, became his official hostess in the White House. To a lady who in 1860 lamented that he had no wife, Buchanan replied, "That, madam, is my misfortune, not my fault." That he had overcome such misfortune owed much to the tough love of his father. As James Buchanan Sr. said to his son after his disappointment at Dickinson, "I hope that you will have fortitude enough to surmount these things."

# 5

# Soil of Greatness

## Thomas Lincoln

THEY MAY HAVE HAD little in common, but restless Thomas Lincoln
endowed his ambitious son Abraham with the greatest boon of his bleak
childhood, an affectionate mother and stepmother, who in turn nurtured
and encouraged the boy to learn.

Abraham Lincoln did not hate his father. The opposite of love is not
hatred; it is indifference. Looking at Lincoln's life, it seems fair to conclude
that by the age of twenty-one, when he was finally able to break loose
and be on his own, he had grown indifferent to his father. Their lives
were already in entirely separate orbits.

But as a son he was not indifferent to Thomas Lincoln's welfare. As
Abraham wrote to his stepbrother, John Johnston, in 1851, "You already
know that I desire that neither Father nor Mother shall be in want of
any comfort in health or sickness while they live." Thomas Lincoln died
not long after this letter arrived, and—as virtually every Lincoln biographer notes—Abraham did not attend his funeral. Abraham's stepmother,
Sarah Bush Lincoln, was undoubtedly the person Lincoln most loved.
Yet he had expressed equal concern about the well-being of both his
parents. In the light of how differently he viewed them, it was a laudable
sentiment.

In large part, this is a book about inspiration. Where inspiration is
lacking, it is a book about influence. But no amount of conjecture can
create circumstances in which Thomas Lincoln either inspired or posi-
tively influenced his son. There is not a single reference in all of Abraham Lincoln's recorded recollections where he said anything favorable
about his father. For that matter, he rarely mentioned him at all, except
for such anecdotal Lincolnisms as "My father taught me to work, but
never taught me to love it." Nor did Abraham directly malign his father,

Thomas Lincoln

beyond references to Thomas Lincoln's lack of education—not really his fault. The closest Abraham came to outright criticism was by inference, observing that Thomas's brother, Mordecai, "ran away with all the talents in the family." In fairness, however, as a first son, Mordecai also had all the luck.

Thomas Lincoln, nonetheless, must be credited with two significant if indirect contributions to his son's future success. Although he couldn't see the point of it, Thomas did not flatly forbid Abraham's taking valuable time to read or to receive a year or so of schooling. That is entirely due to the influence of the two women Thomas married in his lifetime, each in her own way exceptional and both intently supportive of Abraham's ambitions. "Larn all you can," his "angel mother," Nancy Hanks Lincoln, had intoned before she died when Abraham was only nine. A year later, his stepmother, Sarah Bush Lincoln, came into his life, the other light to brighten Abraham's otherwise bleak childhood. Suppose Thomas Lincoln had instead married in succession two women who shared his limitations, and brought *them* back to his humble habitations?

Those habitations were to change many times. In this way, at least, Thomas Lincoln was not unlike other first fathers. He, too, was a dreamer, even though his dreams were relatively modest. There was always a more bountiful farm just over the horizon—taking him from Virginia to Kentucky to Indiana to Illinois. He, too, was restless. Things *had* to be better somewhere else—a clearer land title, closer access to water, more fertile soil.

There are more biographies of Abraham Lincoln than of any other American president, perhaps more than of all the others combined. In them, Thomas Lincoln, although consigned largely to secondary status, has been described as everything from improvident to industrious, harsh to humorous, indolent to energetic, obtuse to sagacious. In truth, he was all of these things. After all, he died in his seventy-third year. In such a span of life, to paraphrase Shakespeare, one plays many parts. Thomas was hardly the same man at twenty-eight, when he married Nancy Hanks in Kentucky and set out to expand his holdings, as he was at the age of seventy, when Abraham had to pay to keep his father from losing his land in Illinois. Isn't it possible that Thomas Lincoln, like so many others, eventually was simply worn down by the wilderness? There is nothing limited about the trials he was obliged to face.

When asked to supply material for campaign biographies, Abraham Lincoln invariably replied that there was little to write about. "It is a great piece of folly to attempt to make anything out of my early life. It can all be condensed into a single sentence and that sentence you will find in Gray's Elegy, 'The short and simple annals of the poor.' That's my life and that's about all you or anyone else can make of it." Earlier Lincoln had volunteered, "I was born on February 12, 1809, in Hardin County, Kentucky. My parents were both born in Virginia, of undistinguished families—second families perhaps I should say. My mother, who died in my tenth year, was of a family of the name of Hanks."

As the most renowned of the more recent Lincoln biographers, David Herbert Donald, suggests that, in Lincoln's mind, "He was a self-made man, who had little need to care about his family tree." Yet Lincoln did care about it, although he was only able to trace it back to his grandfather, an earlier Abraham. Had he delved further he might have been surprised to find evidence of authentic achievement. The first Lincoln to emigrate from England was a weaver's apprentice who arrived in Massachusetts in 1637, settled in Hingham, and ultimately became a prosperous trader and businessman. Some early Lincolns were Quakers. Later Lincolns improved their circumstances, maintaining flourishing farms in Pennsylvania, where one particularly wealthy Lincoln was an ironmaster, and in Virginia. Most were engaged in public service. A Lincoln in Virginia married the niece of the royal governor. A noted earlier biographer, Benjamin Thomas, writes, "Without exception Lincoln's forebears proved to be self-reliant, upright men of even comfortable means, who earned the respect of their neighbors. Some Lincolns in collateral lines even earned distinction. . . . In the father, Thomas, there seemed to be a falling off in the general level of Abraham's ancestry."

Donald concurs, although he is more generous to Lincoln's father: "In sum, Abraham Lincoln, instead of being the unique blossom of an otherwise barren family tree, belonged to the seventh American generation of a family with competent means, a reputation for integrity, and a modest record of public service. . . . A closer study of the historical records would have given Abraham Lincoln a different and probably a kinder view of his father Thomas." It also would have confirmed that in earlier years Thomas had farmed more successfully, owned horses, was in addition a skilled cabinetmaker and carpenter, and enjoyed the esteem of his neighbors to the extent that he served on juries and in his local militia. He was a church member, sober, and not given to crude language, qualities that helped him win both his wives. Understandably, he must have had more energy when he was younger, but had he ever possessed the capacity for emotional sensitivity? Abraham believed the testimony of his own eyes. His father was more than the ignorant idler described by such biographers as Richard Current, "Both mentally and physically . . . slow, dull, careless, inert." But it would take more charity than even Abraham Lincoln could muster to view Thomas Lincoln as either an ideal farmer or an ideal citizen, let alone an ideal father.

At times in their years together, Thomas had grudgingly granted that his son was bright, but in his frustration with Abraham's inattentiveness to farm work, he had also hit him—and hit him hard. How could Thomas possibly appreciate what motivated someone so different from himself? In later years, Abraham ascribed it to the limitations of his father's own childhood. As Abraham wrote in 1848, "Owing to my father being left an orphan at the age of six years, in poverty, and in a new country, he became a wholly uneducated man." Later Abraham added, "By the early death of a father, and the very narrow circumstances of his mother, even in childhood [Thomas] was a wandering laboring boy and grew up literally without education. He never did more in the way of writing than bunglingly sign his own name." Abraham could hardly hate his father for such shortcomings, but the gulf between them grew too wide for resolution. In that 1851 letter to John Johnston, referring to his dying father, Lincoln concluded, "Say to him that if we could meet now, it is doubtful whether it would not be more painful than pleasant; but that if it be his lot to go now, he will soon have a joyous meeting with many loved ones gone before; and where the rest of us, through the help of God hope ere-long to join them."

As a parent, compensating for the emotional and physical poverty of his own childhood—and perhaps his father's as well—Abraham Lincoln, in the words of more recent biographer Michael Burlingame, "indulged his sons so much that he scandalized society." Lincoln insisted that his children should be "free, happy, and unrestrained by parental tyranny. Love is the chain whereby to bind a child to his parents." Abraham and Mary Todd Lincoln had four children, all boys. Not until the fourth, born two years after Thomas Lincoln's death, was a son of his son named for him. The Lincolns, however, invariably called this son "Tad," not Tom or Thomas.

Abraham's skin, like his father's, was rough, the result of years in the outdoors. Both had a shock of black hair, although Thomas's was straight and Abraham's unruly. In most respects they looked very little alike—Abraham so tall and slender, already six foot two and 160 pounds by the time he was sixteen (eventually he grew to six foot four), lanky, raw-boned, the familiar long face, beardless in youth but already full of melancholia, with such deep-set eyes. Thomas was short and stocky, round-faced, with a weak chin, a long mouth, and a very prominent nose. Both men loved to tell stories, both were given to bouts of depression, and both were immensely strong physically, but that could be said of many others along the American frontier. What matters is that Thomas Lincoln was the father Abraham knew when he was growing up—and as soon as he came of age, distanced himself from, as Burlingame puts it, "physically, socially, culturally, and politically."

Thomas was born in Virginia in 1778, the youngest of three sons of another Abraham Lincoln. Their family moved to Kentucky in 1782 after a distant relative, Daniel Boone, had returned with visions of "a second paradise" of bountiful acreage over the mountains. The elder Abraham Lincoln, like his fathers before him, had long worked the rich soil of Rockingham County without benefit of slaves. His new holdings near

Louisville grew to over 5,500 acres. Of course, there were perils on the frontier. Indians in the vicinity questioned the legitimacy of any land claims, using the only means at their disposal. In 1786, while Abraham and his sons, Mordecai, Josiah, and Thomas, were planting corn near the adjoining woods, they were ambushed. Abraham was killed instantly. Mordecai, the oldest son, who was only fifteen, kept his head. Sending Josiah to seek help at the settlement a half-mile away, he raced to their cabin and picked up his rifle. An Indian coming out of the forest approached eight-year-old Thomas, who was sitting next to the body of his father. Before he could pick the child up, Mordecai shot the intruder. Young Abraham Lincoln would hear this story repeated so frequently by his father, the surviving Thomas, that it became "the legend more strongly than any others imprinted on my mind and memory."

The violent incident also had economic consequences. When he came of age Mordecai "ran away" with his father's entire estate, and his brothers were left to fend for themselves. Starting as a manual laborer, Thomas, the "wandering boy," learned carpentry and cabinetmaking, reportedly from one Joseph Hanks, who had a niece named Nancy. Eventually he earned enough to settle in one spot and bought his first farm, some 238 acres in Hardin County, Kentucky. These were his most industrious and least isolated years, when he served in the militia and on juries and was high in the regard of a real community. Donald quotes a typical neighbor who remembered unpretentious, plain Thomas Lincoln as conscientious, peaceable, respectable, "quiet and good-natured." Interestingly, he was most often described as "honest," the political encomium to be given to his son, "Honest Abe."

By his mid-twenties, Thomas felt secure enough to seek a bride. He was enamored of Sarah Bush, daughter of the local jailer, and ventured into Elizabethtown to seek her hand. However, she preferred another. Thomas turned his gaze to diligent Nancy Hanks, whom he had also met before. No one really knows what she looked like, including Lincoln's earliest biographers. The consensus was that she was slender, quiet, dark, and pretty.

In any case, she readily accepted Thomas Lincoln's proposal. Apparently she was impressed by his robust appearance and respectful manner. She may also have longed for a home of her own, no matter how humble. She was then living with one of her sisters, married to a man named Sparrow. Trained as a seamstress, Nancy possessed skills a potential husband might value. Although most of the people in the community were illiterate, Nancy could read, but apparently she had never learned to write.

Nancy Hanks, twenty-three, and Thomas Lincoln, twenty-eight, were married on June 12, 1806, and moved to his hut in Elizabethtown. Their first child, a daughter they named Sarah, was born in 1807. By 1809 Thomas had bought another farm, called "Sinking Spring," a bit larger at 300 acres, on the south fork of Nolan Creek in nearby Hodgenville. On a small rise near the spring, using his carpentry skills, Tom built a sturdy little one-room cabin, only sixteen by eighteen feet, but a bit more comfortable for his wife and daughter. On February 12, 1809, the couple had their second child, a son they gave his grandfather's name of Abraham. The boy would have no memories of Sinking Spring. By the time he was two, his father moved the family again, to Knob Creek, some ten miles away. The exodus had begun. Water seems always to figure in the names of Thomas Lincoln's farms, although its availability failed to bring him fortune. The surroundings at Knob Creek were beautiful, but only a portion of his hilly acreage proved to be tillable. Still, it was more fertile than Sinking Spring, the main crop being corn.

During the five years his family lived there, Tom's spirit, if not his energy, already seemed to be in decline, although hardly without cause. A second son, named for him, had died in infancy. Tom may have been more skilled at carpentry than farming, yet the quality of his largest woodworking commission was disputed by the man who paid for it. Lincoln had an irascible tendency, despite his seeming equanimity, and highly valued his independence. Perhaps something in him rebelled against being too settled. Neighbors—and there were to be fewer in the future—noted his inclination to do only what was absolutely necessary, almost content to live hand-to-mouth. Lincoln biographer Albert Beveridge writes about Thomas during this transitional time, "He was improvident, yet in a slow and plodding way industrious." And then the customary additions: "He was good-natured, inoffensive, law abiding, notably honest . . . [but] he had no use for books."

His young wife, however, loved books, at least the few she could obtain, and she enjoyed reading them to little Abraham. Of course, the Bible came first. She is reputed to have said that if her son could have only either a farm or the ability to read the Bible, she would be happier if he chose the latter. As an adult, Lincoln would be far less formally religious than either of his mothers, but his most memorable public utterances were enhanced by a deep reliance on both the Old and New

Testaments. He would "larn" all he could, at least the alphabet, at a local school he and his older sister were enabled to attend briefly. His only memory of the War of 1812 was of his mother's gentle care of injured soldiers. His earliest memory of his father was ominous. Young Abraham, who already hated to be called "Abe," recalled dropping pumpkin seeds behind his father and using a hoe with the bottomland, only to see all their work washed away by a thunderstorm. Yet records reveal Thomas Lincoln to have still been a prosperous farmer, ranking fifteenth in acreage out of ninety-eight property owners in the county.

They had been at Knob Hill for five years. It was time to move again. Thomas, in his late thirties, for perhaps the final time reasserted all of his physical strength and residual energy. In 1816, when Abraham was seven, his father decided to leave Kentucky and settle across the Ohio River in Indiana. It was more than merely wanderlust—there were a host of practical reasons motivating such a move. Thomas Lincoln opposed slavery on both moral and practical grounds. He and his wife were "separate" Baptists, accepting traditional beliefs more than the church's formal structure and affirming a strict moral code opposed to intoxicants, profanity, gambling, dancing, gossip, and the ultimate immorality of slavery. Moreover, small family farmers like the Lincolns could not long compete economically with the slave labor of large-scale Kentucky plantations. Adding to that somber prognosis is that Lincoln had experienced difficulty obtaining clear land titles to all three of his Kentucky farms—a familiar theme on the emerging frontier. The courts were clogged with competing claims, but only the rich could afford influential lawyers to represent them. In the Indiana Territory, from which slavery had been excluded by the Northwest Ordinance, fully surveyed land with guaranteed titles could be purchased directly from the United States government.

Tom had at least to take a look. It was quite a trip. The flatboat he had built for himself capsized in the Ohio River, and most of his provisions were washed away. Starting over, he finally found the sort of site he sought, "a more inviting lodgment" some sixteen miles from the river, and trudged back to Kentucky to fetch his family. By the end of 1816 they were settled near Little Pigeon Creek in Indiana, and for a time— even in this wilderness—Thomas Lincoln became again a resolute pathfinder and farmer. Clearing the land was his first priority, then hacking out a rough trail to his property.

As the family's abode, at first he was only able to erect a rude "half-faced," three-sided shelter of timber and brush, without a finished floor, about fourteen feet square, with the fourth side open. It was not until the following year that Thomas had time to build the customary log cabin, its logs chinked together by mud. In the winter chill, with at least some heat by the fire and a full enclosure, it must have seemed comparatively comfortable. By spring he had planted corn, wheat, and oats, and had acquired some sheep, hogs, and cattle.

Abraham was now old enough to help. He went hunting with his father—the abundant local game was their family's primary source of sustenance—but never really enjoyed it Nor did he relish fishing. He pursued other outdoor activities, however, and did whatever he could to help his parents, up to a point—wielding an axe, planting crops, and tending livestock. From the age of eight, Donald writes, Abraham, "large for his age," had his own axe and knew how to use it. But even so early in his life, he was already determined never to be a farmer—or simply a splitter of logs—when he grew to manhood. Any book in the vicinity was soon in his possession. He was a lively, outwardly friendly child, gangling as he outgrew his crude homespun clothing, but he also developed a less obvious sense of remoteness that he would retain all his life. He enjoyed wrestling, telling jokes, and swapping stories with his companions, but somehow he was different from them, and he knew it.

The first of these friends was Dennis Hanks, the eighteen-year-old nephew of the Sparrows, who had come to join the Lincolns. The two families built a second cabin. Things were improving, and Thomas traveled sixty miles to Vincennes to make payments for adjoining tracts of land. Yet, despite everyone's efforts, the venturesome move to Indiana not only finally resulted in failure, it also proved fatal. In the summer of 1818, a mysterious disease swept through southwestern Indiana. It was called "milk sickness" or simply "milk sick" because it was apparently caused by drinking the milk of local cows. Very likely it was a form of brucellosis. The lethal cause turned out to be poisonous roots that free-roaming cattle had consumed. There was no known cure, and for that matter the nearest doctor was some thirty-five miles away. First the Sparrows died. Then, in the seventh day of her illness, Nancy Hanks Lincoln died as well, at the age of thirty-four or thirty-five, a "pioneer sacrifice," in Carl Sandburg's words. Thomas Lincoln constructed a casket, and his grief-stricken children watched him bury their mother next to the Sparrows. A few months later, a visiting Methodist or Baptist preacher said a few words over their graves.

Donald believes that the death of Abraham Lincoln's mother gave him "a sense of isolation" he never fully overcame. Lincoln was so moved by a return to his childhood home in 1844 that he could only express himself in poetry. It fell to eleven-year-old Sarah to try to cook, mend, and clean for the men now in her charge, but inevitably their domicile sank into squalor. In less than a year, Thomas felt impelled to go back to Kentucky, to Elizabethtown, to seek another wife—and a mother for his children. She turned out to be the woman who had rejected him originally. In the intervening years, Sarah Bush had married a man named Daniel Johnston, borne three children, and been widowed. Tom Lincoln probably still felt some residual affection for Sarah, but his intent was more practical than romantic. She, too, had needs. Tom still had the means to pay off some debts that Sarah had been left with; they were promptly married, and they set off together for Pigeon Creek, with her three young children in tow, in an overloaded, borrowed wagon.

Despite her circumstances, Sarah had accumulated possessions that to the Lincolns would seem the luxuries of a potentate—a solid table and chairs, a walnut bureau, a spinning wheel, feather beds, dishware, and matched sets of cutlery. Most astonishing, although Sarah, unlike Nancy Hanks Lincoln, could not read, she brought books: a handsome family Bible, *Pilgrim's Progress, Robinson Crusoe, Sinbad the Sailor, Aesop's Fables,* Weems's *Life of Washington,* Grimshaw's *History of the United States,* and such practical guides as *Lessons of Elocution.* When they finally arrived and Thomas announced, "Here's your new mammy," Abraham simply fell in love with her. Reportedly, he was so starved for affection that he called her "Mama" from the start, and hid herself in her ample skirts, hoping it would not be taken as disrespect for her predecessor. Her industriousness made itself evident at once, as somehow Sarah accommodated eight people in a rough-hewn cabin that had already been cramped with four.

Abraham, in particular, benefited from her beneficence. In only a few months in a "blab school," he learned to read and write so well that as the community expanded, he composed all the letters for his illiterate neighbors. "The things I want to know are in books," he told Sarah, and reversing his relationship with Nancy, he read them to her. He also learned to cipher, and until his stepmother could find paper or slate, did so on boards she obtained. But Thomas—now more hard-pressed than ever with so many additional mouths to feed—needed help, and his demonstrably strong son was becoming more reluctant to provide it. The better life Sarah had made possible for the Lincolns was in some jeopardy if Thomas's farm could not profitably sustain it.

At times during the 1820s Thomas not only insisted that Abraham lay his books aside and work from sunup to sundown on the farm, but also rented him out to neighboring farmers, who often complained of his distractedness and indolence. Until he was twenty-one, Abraham had to turn over every penny he made to his father. Current suggests that "a real estrangement between the two" took place during this time. Reportedly, at the age of nineteen or so Abraham even considered running away. Dennis Hanks, who lived with the Lincolns until his marriage, confirms how much Abraham hated all the chores of "farming, grubbing, hoeing, making fences." If he wasn't reading or meditating, he was always talking and cracking jokes. Some were at his father's expense. When a stranger or neighbor came by, Abraham would invariably intrude into the conversation—or even correct some comment from his father. At work, Abraham might stop, inducing everyone else to do so as well, and tell stories from a tree stump. When his parents joined the local Baptist church, Abraham did not, but he was not above satirizing the parson's sermons the following week, when he should have been working. Normally well behaved, Abraham simply couldn't resist such rhetorical recreation.

Tom Lincoln was not a cruel man. Yet he could become so momentarily angry at his son that, in Dennis Hanks's words, "Sometimes a blow from the old man's fist would hurl the boy a rod." There was no enduring hatred between the two, only the growing impossibility of mutual understanding. By this time, Tom had no fixed purpose in life, if he ever had, only a sort of aimless ambition to settle somewhere. Abraham was not so much insolent as impatient to move on.

Still, there was at least a glimmer of communication, and on the father's part a kind of suppressed pride. Despite Thomas's problems, Sarah recalled, "I induced my husband to permit Abe to read and study at home, as well as at school. At first he was not easily reconciled to it, but finally he too seemed willing to encourage him." Whatever his shortcomings, Thomas Lincoln was the unquestioned head of his household. Even if he only tolerated his son's reading and learning, it made a considerable difference in Abraham's preparation for a better life.

Although he worked many odd jobs in his teens, woodcutting and rail-splitting as well as planting and harvesting, Lincoln learned far more of the wider world working on a ferryboat on the Ohio River and particularly as a deckhand on two adventurous trips on flatboats going down the Mississippi to New Orleans. On the first trip, when he was only nineteen, hired by a local merchant, Abraham was part of a crew conveying meat, corn, and wheat to the Crescent City. In New Orleans he also saw for the first time the brutal face of slavery, a memory he carried vividly into his public life. All his wages still went to his father.

In 1830, having moved three times since his first marriage but no better off financially than he had been at the outset, Thomas Lincoln, that "roving, melancholy spirit," set out for the brighter prospects of Illinois. He sold most of what he and Sarah possessed and moved to an area near Decatur. In the last twenty years of his life Thomas would move three more times within the state, finally settling on a modest homestead in Coles County called "Goosenest Prairie." His family and goods were transported on ox-drawn wagons. Perhaps symbolically, Thomas gave Abraham the ox whip and told him to lead the procession. By then past his twenty-first birthday, he would stay with them only a year. First he went on another flatboat trip to New Orleans, but this time he could keep what he earned. Then Abraham moved to New Salem, Illinois, working a variety of jobs before settling into his legal and political careers. In miles it was not so far away from his parents' new home, but in independence it was a world apart. Although he would visit his parents when legal business took him to Coles County, he had left home for good. The death of his sister, Sarah, in childbirth deepened his melancholy and separation from his roots.

Abraham's stepbrother, John Johnston, turned out to be the more authentic reflection of Thomas Lincoln—imprudent, unsuccessfully ambitious, then increasingly inactive. Johnston directed constant entreaties for assistance to Abraham, who, now settled in Springfield, was increasingly busy with his flourishing law practice and his own family. He responded with more than money. Hearing from Johnston that Thomas was sinking fast, and "He Craves to See you all the time," in the spring of 1849 Abraham delayed an important trip to Washington so that he could visit with his father, who indeed was quite ill. It was a three-day trip each way. Thomas recovered, and so when throughout 1850 Johnston's letters continued, Abraham ultimately replied through correspondence rather than with another journey. He wrote, "I sincerely hope that Father may yet recover his health; but at all events tell him to call upon and confide in, our great, and good, and merciful Maker." Abraham never saw his father again.

Thomas Lincoln died at seventy-three in January 1851. Nine years later, two railroad ties were presented at the Republican National Convention that nominated his son for president, purportedly "made by Thomas Hanks and Abraham Lincoln, whose father was the first pioneer of Macon County." Shortly before his death in 1865, Lincoln expressed the desire to place a marker on his father's gravesite. It was finally done in 1880, by Robert Todd Lincoln, Abraham's only surviving son. There is no papering over the alienation between Abraham and Thomas Lincoln. It remains sad, however, that the noble sentiments President Lincoln later expressed of "malice toward none, with charity for all" might not have been extended more fully to his father.

# 6

## AMBITION'S STERNER STUFF

### Jacob Johnson • Jesse Root Grant
### Rutherford Hayes Jr. • Abram Garfield
### William Arthur

IN MANY GUISES—from humble, heroic Jacob Johnson to ambitious, irre-pressible Jesse Grant; through the parishes of Parson William Arthur, the fields of Abram Garfield, the enterprises of "Ruddy" Hayes—initiative has been the hallmark of America's first fathers.

## Jacob Johnson

Jacob Johnson was the most tragically heroic of all first fathers. He saved two men from drowning, and the exertion killed him. He was only thirty-three. Because one of the men was the publisher of the local news-paper, Jacob's posthumous reward was an obituary of uncommon promi-nence for one of his humble station in life. Jacob was praised "for his honesty, sobriety, industry, and his humane, friendly disposition." His hard-pressed widow, Mary, had little time to dwell on such qualities—she couldn't read, in any case—or even the luxury to mourn. Only the older of her two sons had been afforded much of an opportunity to know his father. The younger son, Andrew, was just three when Jacob Johnson died.

Energy and ambition are not necessarily synonymous. A congenial man of all work, Jacob Johnson was undoubtedly industrious, but his ambitions were limited to simply earning a settled sort of life some-where. He had emigrated from England around the end of the eigh-teenth century. Wandering aimlessly around the countryside, Jacob found Raleigh, North Carolina, to his liking. The capital of a state only recently admitted to the Union, Raleigh bustled with lawyers, legislators, and those seeking their services. There was already an acquisitive aristocracy of sorts in place, with the means to employ anyone willing to work.

That suited Jacob. Before long he was serving as everything from county constable and church sexton to porter of the state bank. He even tolled the town bell, announcing major events to the community. He quickly established a reputation for availability, reliability, and honesty. He was popular enough to be elected captain of a company of militia composed of workingmen like himself. Much of his time was spent helping out at a lively new inn and tavern called "Casso's," opposite the bank.

Here he met and fell in love with a pretty eighteen-year-old chambermaid named Mary McDonough, known to all as "Polly." As industrious as Jacob Johnson, Polly was also a skilled seamstress. They married in 1801, their union signified by making their marks in the town registry, and moved into a small log house adjacent to the inn. Polly took in washing and mending to supplement Jacob's modest income. Their first child, a girl, died in infancy. Their second—sturdy, fair-haired William— was born in 1803.

It would be six years before the arrival of their next child, fated to be their last. During the festive Christmas season of 1808, on December 29, Polly Johnson gave birth to a second son. Biographer Lately Thomas writes, "The boy was as dark as the other was light, and he, too, gave the promise of being strong and hearty." His first cries were accompanied by fiddles from the tavern next door. The news spread to the jolly revelers at Casso's, some of whom were from Tennessee. Reportedly they invaded the Johnsons' cabin and insisted that the boy be named for Andrew Jackson. True story or not, the adult Andrew Johnson would adopt at least Old Hickory's temperament.

He would have no memory of his father. The prominent local citizens who planned their fishing outing for one of the coldest December days of 1811 hired Jacob to accompany them, probably to clean their catch and to bring along the food and drink. Some of those spirits must have been consumed early, because one of the men, Colonel Thomas Henderson, owner of the *Raleigh Star,* began to rock a canoe he had boarded with two others. All three fell overboard. One made it back to shore; another, who could not swim, frantically clung to Henderson, taking both down to the icy depths. Jacob promptly dived in, and with immense effort managed to get both men back to safety. He probably contracted pneumonia. Still, he was at his post some days later, ringing the town bell for another's funeral, when he collapsed and died. There would be no marker on the grave of this "humane" man for fifty-five years, until the unlikely presidency of his younger son.

Jacob's admirers did what they could to assist the family, but it was never quite sufficient. Polly finally settled for the sole solution readily available in those times to one in her dire circumstances—she married again. Had it been to someone with the energy of Jacob Johnson, there might have been some hope for the future. Instead, she wed shiftless Turner Dougherty (or Doughtry), who possessed neither skills nor the inclination to use them. If possible, conditions got worse.

To relieve some of the pressure, both sons were apprenticed to a Raleigh tailor. When, having at least learned a trade, Andrew Johnson set out to establish his own tailoring shop in Tennessee, he still wasn't quite on his own. As biographer Lloyd Stryker notes, young Andrew not only lacked education and influential friends, "His mother was wholly dependent on him for his support." Andrew's older brother, William, fled to Texas, where he would stay. At eighteen, Andrew was already head of a household—and its sole breadwinner. He cared for his mother and step-father for the rest of their lives, finally settling them on a farm he purchased.

Of all the American presidents, the most thoroughly self-made was Andrew Johnson. He was not the son of the customarily struggling pioneer family—a hardscrabble farmer and his resourceful wife—but of a porter and a chambermaid, equal in illiteracy. Andrew's mother would have liked to help him, but she lacked the means. Her first husband was a good man who died too soon, her second a wastrel who lived too long. When Johnson was selected to run with Lincoln on their ticket of national unity in the extraordinary wartime election of 1864, much was made of their similarly humble origins—the rail-splitter and the tailor. They were born six weeks apart in genuine log cabins and grew up in Southern border states. In all, Lincoln had perhaps one year of formal schooling; Johnson had not a single day. Thomas notes, "A childhood friend said of his remarkable rise, 'I reckon he started underground.'"

During an especially bitter reelection campaign for Congress, Johnson was opposed by William "Parson" Brownlow, a man no more noted for political restraint than Johnson. How was it possible, Brownlow queried, for someone of such undeniable consequence as Andrew Johnson to have been the son of an "illiterate loafer" like Jacob Johnson? (Well, at least he got it half right.) Was not Johnson in fact the spitting image of the nephew of a prominent Raleigh judge? Surprisingly, Johnson, whose mother was still alive, did not respond by physically assaulting Brownlow. Instead, he went back to North Carolina, carefully gathered the legal affidavits regarding his birth, and detailed them in an open letter to the voters, characterizing Brownlow as a "hyena," "vandal," "devil," "coward," and other less moderate epithets. Political discourse was not notably more elevated in the nineteenth century than in the twenty-first. Johnson won. His combative temperament did little to diminish controversy during his tumultuous political career, although the issues he faced after the Civil War would have tried the talents of a Lincoln.

Taught to read and write largely by the devoted wife he met and wed in Tennessee, and immaculately attired in clothes of his own cut, Johnson was anything but embarrassed by his origins. Once, on the floor of the Senate, he reminded a colleague, "Sir, I do not forget that I am a mechanic, neither do I forget that Adam was a tailor . . . or that our Savior was the son of a carpenter." Johnson himself was the son of a man of many humble vocations who was also a hero. He may have been unlettered and more energetic than ambitious, but Jacob Johnson was much mourned, having died as the result of saving the lives of others.

## Jesse Root Grant

Ambition can be a motivation not only to justify the expectations of others, but also to prove them wrong. As Ulysses S. Grant, upon becoming a major general in the United States Army, wrote to his wife, Julia, "Is Father afraid yet that I will not be able to sustain myself?" It would be less than fair to Jesse Root Grant, among the most successfully self-made of all the first fathers, to suggest that he did not rejoice in the ultimate attainments of his son. On the contrary, he rejoiced in them excessively. But before, as biographer William McFeeley puts it, "the obscene exhilaration of war" brought about so dramatic a change in Ulysses' fortunes, Jesse was hardly alone in regarding his oldest son as a perplexing failure.

As Jesse noted, Ulysses mirrored his devout mother, with whom he shared a sort of silent communion. "He rarely ever laughs, never sheds a tear or becomes excited . . . never says a profane word, or indulges in jokes." How could his oldest son, always his favorite among his children, "my Ulyss," be so utterly unlike him? It was sometimes just so hard to acknowledge the credit Jesse craved. Yet when Jesse Root Grant died, Ulysses was inconsolable. Characteristically, he couldn't find words to express his grief.

Jesse Root Grant

Long after both his parents were gone and just before his own death, Ulysses S. Grant completed his memoirs. He had fought to preserve a Union his forebears had helped to create. At the outset he observed, "My family is American, and has been for generations, in all its branches, direct and collateral." Matthew and Priscilla Grant, from Dorsetshire in England, arrived at Plymouth, in the Massachusetts Bay Colony, on the *John and Mary* in 1630, only ten years after the *Mayflower.* By the time of the Revolution, the Grants were established as a prosperous farm family throughout Connecticut, active in community affairs.

Something went wrong with the advent of "Captain" Noah Grant, Jesse's father. Noah, born in 1748, claimed to have fought gallantly in the Revolution, but there are no records to support it. What is certain is that he found time in the midst of war to marry Anne Richardson, who bore him two sons but died before the end of the conflict. A cobbler and land speculator as well as a farmer, but addicted to strong spirits, Noah managed to lose all of his inheritance, and set out on foot to find a fresh start to the west, in Pennsylvania. The local economy was based not only on agriculture but also on brewing cider, beer, and whiskey, and shipping them downriver to Ohio and Kentucky. Noah began to trade in animal skins, another much-needed frontier commodity, and married a young widow named Rachel Kelley, who bore him seven children. The fourth, Jesse Root Grant, was born on January 23, 1794.

Rachel's death in 1804 seems to have destroyed any sense of responsibility in Noah Grant. He dispersed his family. Jesse, only ten, had the good fortune to be sent to work on the farm of Ohio Supreme Court judge George Tod. The judge took a liking to the boy. He taught Jesse to read, made sure he was better clothed, and sent him to the local school for six months. At the Tod residence Jesse Grant glimpsed a new life—laid out before him not only in its comparative opulence, with china, silverware, fine furniture, and all the books of Tod's library, but also in a close-knit family. Encouraged by Tod, Jesse, at sixteen, devised a plan for his own life, the foundation of which was to be as unlike the father who had abandoned him as possible. When the time came, he would be a true father to his children.

But what calling could he pursue? He knew something of only farming and selling animal skins. His half-brother Peter was already a successful tanner. There was nothing remotely appealing about this bloody business of working with animal hides, but leather in all its forms was absolutely essential to western expansion. It had about it the odor of wealth, and on the frontier, wealth—whatever its source—led to social acceptance. Jesse thoroughly learned the business until he finally had his own tanning yard in Point Pleasant, Ohio.

The plan for his life was set—to be financially secure by twenty-five, to marry well and build a fine home, to improve his education and become a community leader, to raise a loving family in comfortable circumstances, and then to retire by sixty. Only an attack of malaria set him back a year.

And so he was twenty-six when he met Hannah Simpson and her family. At her father's six hundred–acre farm, not far from Cincinnati, Jesse witnessed just the kind of life he had in mind for his own future family. The Simpsons, devout Scottish Presbyterians, had come to Philadelphia in 1762, established a fertile farm in Berks County, fought in the Revolutionary War, and like so many others moved farther west after the War of 1812. They were a loving, close-knit family, if not particularly demonstrative, devoted to learning. Into this household swept brash Jesse Grant, whose background could hardly have been more different. This, however, did not put off Hannah's father, John Simpson, who saw instead the young man's yearning for knowledge and his ambition.

Hannah, in her restrained fashion, was also impressed. Jesse Grant was hardly handsome, with a long face, his sandy brown hair slicked to one side. Later he would grow chin whiskers and sideburns, in the fashion of the Pennsylvania Dutch, and read with the small, wire-rimmed spectacles Hannah also favored. But he had a keen look in his blue eyes, a healthy glow, an energetic manner, and a sturdy frame almost six feet in height. Hannah is described by biographer Jean Edward Smith as "slim, above medium height, handsome but not pretty, serious, steadfast, and supremely reserved." Dark-haired and neatly groomed, she had been to school in Pennsylvania, but was too shy to show off her knowledge. Jesse had little fault to find with her. He could talk enough for both of them.

Although Hannah and Jesse were polar opposites in demeanor, they got along well. They were married on June 24, 1821, and moved to the small frame house Jesse had built at Point Pleasant. It represented only a way station on his road to respectability. Here, ten months after their wedding, on April 27, 1822, their first child was born, a large healthy son weighing almost eleven pounds.

For six weeks he had no name. To Jesse, his first son merited something special. Why not Ulysses, after the powerful Greek hero from antiquity he was reading about? Hannah's pious father was partial to Hiram, the Phoenician king from the Old Testament, who helped King Solomon build his temple. Eventually they settled on Hiram Ulysses Grant. Jesse never called him anything but Ulysses, or preferably Ulyss. His strong son, "my Ulyss," Jesse boasted to anyone who would listen, "is a most beautiful child." Biographer Geoffrey Perret writes, "With his russet hair, blue eyes, and pink complexion, Ulysses Grant looked in childhood like a glowing miniature of his robust energetic father." Before long, the name Hiram was simply dropped by everyone.

By the time the boy was eighteen months old, Jesse moved his family to a larger brick home, a tangible symbol of his prosperity, in Georgetown, Ohio, the new county seat, on the White Oak River. The town was surrounded by a hardwood forest of oak trees, the prime source of tanbark, an essential ingredient in the tanning process. As McFeely writes, "In one way or another, Jesse Grant was always struggling to establish himself." In Point Pleasant he had taken classes to improve his grammar.

He wrote letters to newspapers on every conceivable subject. In Georgetown they tended to be political pieces for an abolitionist publication. He befriended prominent men, his treasured library grew, he became master of the local Masonic lodge, and for one term he was even elected mayor of Georgetown. A contentious Democrat, if he was not quite beloved throughout his community, at least he was admired for his up-by-the-bootstraps success. He and Hannah had two more boys and three girls, who were given more normal names—Samuel Simpson, Clara, Virginia, Orvil, and Mary.

Young Ulysses didn't feel very heroic, nor did he look very robust. Throughout his childhood he was undersized for his age, and given to colds and other ailments. Even when he went off to West Point at seventeen, Ulysses weighed no more than 117 pounds and stood only five foot one. He would grow broader and taller there, but he would never rise to the height of his father. Yet, coughing or not, he was always strong physically. Other children probably knew it or at least sensed it, although Ulysses felt no need to demonstrate it. His father later remarked, "He never had a personal controversy with man or boy in his life." Ulysses Grant rarely felt the need to raise his voice, either with people or with the horses he learned to train. Nor did his parents argue or berate their young. It seems a subdued setting for someone as voluble as Jesse Grant, but it was the kind of home he had longed for.

However little he discussed it, Jesse clearly hoped that his sons would come into the business with him, and eventually take it over. Two of them did, but his oldest son, Ulysses, hated everything about the tannery. Not that he didn't help, but Ulysses tried to distance his tasks as much as possible from the tannery's premises. As he later wrote, "When I was seven or eight I began hauling all the wood used in the house and shops." He did everything related to horses and tried to avoid everything else. He also worked on his father's small farm and enjoyed the cleaner labor of plowing in the country air. Ulysses was not completely withdrawn as a child. He entered into games and enjoyed fishing and swimming. But, like the young Abraham Lincoln, he had no use for hunting. He loved all animals, not horses alone, and abhorred cruelty of any kind. He felt revulsion at the very sight of blood, a peculiar aversion for one who would see so much of it. How could he envision a career, however prosperous, in the tanning trade?

Jesse continued to praise his son extravagantly, but he felt increasing concern at why so little of his instinctive shrewdness had been inherited by the boy. Sent to buy a colt, for example, young Ulyss was instructed to offer twenty-two and a half dollars but was told that he could go as high as twenty-five if necessary. At the outset, he revealed everything to the seller—and of course paid the higher price. Was this laudable honesty or simply naïveté? In the hardheaded world of frontier commerce, it seemed softheaded. Ulysses was becoming viewed in the community as a bit slow-witted. Behind his back, some of his contemporaries called him "Useless" Grant.

Despite his relative freedom at home, Ulysses loved to travel. He often rode the fifteen miles to the warmer environment of his Simpson grandparents, or drove his neighbors on their trips, often far out of town, in his two-horse carriage. No one questioned his skill at the reins. Precisely where, his father wondered, was Ulysses himself headed? He had been given the best education available, first at the local school in Georgetown, then at well-regarded Maysville Seminary in Kentucky, and finally at Presbyterian Academy in Ridley, Ohio. Ulysses was a dutiful student but hardly outstanding. He talked vaguely about farming or becoming a "down the river" trader. Of one thing he was certain. Once he became twenty-one, only four years away, he would leave the tannery for good.

Jesse had a more specific plan. He told his startled son that he was about to receive an appointment to the United States Military Academy at West Point. "But I won't go," Ulysses blurted out. The response he heard from his father, in a tone uncommonly assertive, settled the matter. "I think you *will* go," Jesse said, adding that it was for Ulysses' own good. West Point offered a free, high-quality, structured education to help direct the boy to make something of himself. McFeely writes, "Ulysses spent his life alternately repudiating Jesse Grant's bleak world and trying to prove himself worthy of it." His father's attitude would prove similarly cyclical. At any hint of accomplishment, Jesse would praise "my Ulyss" excessively, making subsequent disappointments even harder to accept and leaving his son embittered. Despite his apprehension, Ulysses felt undeniable excitement. For one thing, West Point represented a trip beyond anything he had imagined. In his haste, the local congressman, assuming that Ulysses' middle name was Simpson, submitted his appointment for a "Ulysses S. Grant." So it would remain. Ulysses' neighbors gave him a tearful sendoff, but the farewells at home were predictably less emotional. "They don't cry at our house," Ulysses explained.

Grant grew at the academy, both physically and in confidence. During his first return home, even his undemonstrative mother noted that he was standing straighter, although the customary Grant slouch would return later in his life. Academically he did better than anyone had expected. His friendship with his senior class roommate, Frederick Dent of St. Louis, was one of a number he formed with classmates, despite his residual diffidence. Grant was commissioned a second lieutenant in the infantry, not quite the glamorous cavalry appointment he had coveted, but his first posting, and Dent's, at Jefferson Barracks, Missouri, carried an unexpected bonus. He met Dent's sister, Julia, and fell in love.

Seventeen-year-old Julia Dent was rather plain and plump, suffering in comparison with her graceful, aristocratic mother. But Julia had two qualities that were immensely appealing to Ulysses S. Grant. She, too, loved to ride, and her sociable nature brought the lonely, still rather shy young lieutenant out of his shell. The Dents lived in a Missouri imitation of a Southern plantation. Its proprietor, self-styled "Colonel" Frederick Dent the elder, was a boorish, slave-owning businessman turned country squire, whose fortunes fluctuated more than his limited energies. He was as opinionated as Jesse Grant, but of entirely opposite convictions. When they finally met, the antipathy was immediate, mutual, and enduring.

Ulysses' focus was only on Julia. For her part, although Ulysses cared little about his appearance, her sandy-haired, blue-eyed Northern suitor was not only handsome, but she also sensed in him a kind of inner resolve. They would not marry until the summer of 1848, over five years after they met. Grant's regiment was sent to Louisiana, as tensions with Mexico escalated, and then to Texas. Like many Americans, both in and out of the military, Grant opposed the Mexican War as a shamelessly unequal struggle, but as he later put it, "With a soldier the flag is paramount." There is no denying that the conflict gave the officer corps opportunities for distinction unimaginable in the glacial peacetime army. Lieutenant Grant's regiment was awarded ten battle honors. His personal heroism and cool leadership under fire were much praised. When he and Julia were finally wed in August 1848, all of Grant's groomsmen would be future officers of the Confederacy.

Grant's postwar postings were hardly stimulating. Despite the vast new territory to be defended, the size of the army was reduced. Grant, still only a lieutenant, was sent to Detroit, to Sackets Harbor, New York, and then back to Michigan to be, of all things, a quartermaster. Julia loyally accompanied him, but in the fall of 1849 she became pregnant and went home to have their first child. A boy, he was named Frederick Dent Grant—after Julia's father, not Ulysses'. (One can imagine Jesse's reaction.) It was at about this time, bored and lonely, that Ulysses turned to the solace of alcohol. Perret writes that he had previously been a moderate drinker but in Michigan began imbibing whiskey so excessively that he joined the Sons of Temperance to try to overcome it.

It didn't work. Pregnant with a second child, who would be named Ulysses Jr., Julia couldn't accompany her husband as he moved to one dismal assignment after another—from the unhealthful climate of Panama to the one bright interlude in San Francisco, to Fort Vancouver, Oregon, to Fort Humboldt, California. By then, under a commander he particularly disliked, Ulysses was drinking in earnest. "How forsaken I feel here," he wrote Julia. He hadn't the means to bring his family to be with him. In 1854 he was finally commissioned a permanent captain. After sending his letter of acceptance, assured of the rank, Grant resigned from the United States Army.

When the news reached Jesse in Covington, Kentucky, where he had moved, he was thunderstruck. He wrote to his local congressman to intervene and then, with an irony that would only be appreciated in future years, directly to Secretary of War Jefferson Davis, himself a West Point graduate. In Jesse's view, Ulysses, after "spending so many years in the servis [sic] . . . will be poorly qualified for the pursuits of private life." Davis responded that a resignation, once tendered, could not be reconsidered. Ulysses arrived home dejected and penniless but anxious to make a fresh start, together with his family. The month he returned, Julia became pregnant with their third child, Nellie, their only girl.

In 1854 Jesse Grant turned sixty, the age he had settled on for his retirement so many years earlier. By any measure he was wealthy. His children were well settled, all but Ulysses. At an awkward meeting with his oldest son, Jesse offered him a job in his Galena, Illinois, store. However, Jesse decreed, Julia and their children could not accompany him, at least not initially. Ulysses indignantly refused. He had a two-year-old son he had just seen for the first time. It is likely that Jesse's motivation for this harsh condition was most of all his fear of Julia's potential profligacy, but it marked the lowest point in his relationship with Ulysses.

Instead Ulysses decided to go into farming. However reduced financially, Julia's father had given her a modest farm as a wedding gift. It must be said to Jesse's credit that, however intrusive, he never ceased trying to help Ulysses. He put up most of the money his son needed to buy stock and build a house. At first the farm, which Ulysses called "Hardscrabble," seemed to prosper. Julia, whose surprising strength belied her image of

Southern gentility, was particularly helpful. Ulysses wrote his father around the end of 1856, "Every day I like farming better." Only a few months later, however, reduced by the Depression of 1857, Ulysses was asking Jesse for a five-hundred-dollar loan. In 1858 his fourth and last child was born, finally another Jesse Grant. By the end of the year, disappointed and ailing, Ulysses gave up farming for good.

Perhaps Julia's performance in the ill-fated enterprise had impressed Jesse. He renewed his offer to employ Ulysses at Galena, but this time with his entire family in residence. It was the summer of 1860. Ulysses was not merely to be a clerk at the store; he was also a buyer of hides—which must have struck him as ironic—traveling as far as Iowa and Wisconsin. He would eventually be a partner. He made an honest effort, but his heart was never in it.

In the election of 1860, Grant voted for Stephen A. Douglas, one of two Democratic candidates for president. The party's suicidal divisiveness helped assure the election of Republican Abraham Lincoln, the enthusiastic choice of Jesse Grant. Ulysses understood what it meant. "The South will fight," he calmly predicted. When his prediction came true, Grant—the only man in Galena to have commanded troops—declined to lead a regiment of local militia but agreed to help train it. He wanted a command in the regular army. He realized he had left the army under a cloud. For once, he would have to promote himself.

Ulysses wrote his father, whom he feared might be in some peril living in a slaveholding state like Kentucky, informing him of the obvious—that as a trained military man he must answer the call of his country. His feelings were conflicted. Now he could finally validate his worth, but he had no enthusiasm for the bloody carnage he knew was coming. Grant finally obtained command of a notoriously undisciplined regiment of volunteers from Ohio, and was named a colonel. His father no longer controlled his future—but never gave up trying. For the last twelve years of his life, Jesse Grant was little less a trial to Ulysses than his military and political opponents. The positions of father and son were reversed. It would not be Jesse urging Ulysses to become more ambitious, but Ulysses remonstrating with his father for restraint. One acquaintance remarked that Grant "could remain silent in several languages." His father couldn't remain silent in any.

When rumors began to circulate that a military leader might be chosen to oppose embattled Abraham Lincoln in the presidential election of 1864, Grant, increasingly in the spotlight, denied such ambitions, writing his father, "Nothing personal could ever induce me to accept a political office." His victories helped assure Lincoln's triumph in 1864 over politically minded General George B. McClellan. As commander of the Army of the Potomac, now a full general, Grant accepted General Robert E. Lee's surrender at Appomattox Court House.

Just as victory was at hand in 1865, an assassin's bullet denied the nation Lincoln's leadership. Ulysses had narrowly escaped Lincoln's tragic fate. General and Mrs. Grant had other plans that evening. Named secretary of war in the traumatic, transitional administration of Andrew Johnson, Grant tried to stay above the partisan turmoil. Since the cessation of hostilities, despite the fearsome toll of casualties under his command, he had been anointed the greatest of national heroes. Converted to at least nominal Republicanism during the war, he seemed to many Americans the natural successor to the Great Emancipator in 1868, a candidate of national unity. A steady stream of influential visitors asked Grant to have his name placed in nomination at the Republican National Convention in Chicago. He told Julia that he harbored no ambition to be president, but were he nominated, he could not refuse. His personal platform was no more specific than "Let us have peace."

His father harbored no doubts. He tirelessly planted "inside accounts" in major newspapers, written by journalists he had befriended, with titles such as "The Early Life of General Grant by His Father." When the patriotic procession opening the Republican convention was led in by one-legged General Dan Sickles, there was Jesse Root Grant, "the man who has a boy," seated prominently among the dignitaries on the stage waiting to welcome the delegates. Grant was nominated on the first ballot. The election, against Democrat Horatio Seymour, was surprisingly close, at least in the popular vote. Seymour won Kentucky. Perhaps garrulous Jesse was campaigning too vigorously. Grant's reelection in 1872 was by a wider margin.

Despite his good intentions, Grant was not among the more successful of American presidents. The scandals that plagued his two terms, however, failed to diminish his personal popularity. A subsequent tour around the world was a triumph. But the failure of Grant and Ward, a New York brokerage firm to which he lent his name but paid little heed, ruined thousands, among them Grant himself. Jesse was right—Ulysses had no head for business. His final act of quiet heroism, under the auspices of Mark Twain—completing the memoirs that sold so successfully that they saved his family—also completed his life.

Although it took his grandson to find him accommodations for the inaugural in 1869, Jesse wasn't offended. He attended both inaugurations and came, invited or not, to the White House several times a year, always avoiding old Colonel Dent, similarly addicted to publicity, who had taken up residence there. Reclusive Hannah was nowhere to be seen in Washington, although she lived until 1883. As McFeely writes, Jesse could always be counted on "to the delight of reporters"—and the embarrassment of his son—"for outlandish comments." Jesse was even appointed to his own public office as postmaster of Covington.

At the inauguration ceremonies of 1873, Jesse slipped on some ice and fell. He died in Covington three months later, on June 29, 1873, at the age of seventy-nine. The fall only weakened the tough old tanner. The real cause of death was cancer, from which Jesse had been suffering for a year. Informed that his father was failing, Ulysses boarded a special train for Kentucky. He did not get there in time but was among the mourners. Perret writes that Grant "was so prostrated by grief he couldn't utter a word in reply" to a friend's attempts to console him. McFeely writes, "We can only speculate about the sense of relief, mingled with guilt that Grant must have felt at being at last not beholden to a father."

Relief or grief? Perhaps something of both. As he grew older, Ulysses S. Grant reflected fondly about his years at West Point. He wrote a cousin, "If a man graduates from here, he is safe for life." Historian James Barber considers that West Point, "the most formative experience" of Grant's youth, "did not necessarily guarantee him a start in the world, but it did give him a direction to pursue and an education to build upon." It was his father's doing. If Ulysses longed to prove Jesse wrong, he finally proved him right. An uncertain youth, an unhappy adult, Ulysses at thirty-eight could only have seemed a disappointing failure to so ambitious a father as Jesse Root Grant. When, by forty, Ulysses was well on his way to becoming a national hero, the original decision, against his will, that had made it all possible turned out finally to be Jesse's triumph as well.

# Rutherford Hayes Jr.

It is little wonder that Sophia Birchard Hayes ceaselessly urged her son Rud to emulate his father's example in every way possible. Rutherford Hayes Jr., known to everyone as "Ruddy," was among the most attractive and admired of the men who fathered future American presidents. His mother, Chloe, hardly the easiest person to please, considered Ruddy "the glory and pride of our family." He was also handsome, energetic, strong, good-natured, uncommonly tolerant of others, and—until the last few years of his life—an inveterate optimist.

Rutherford was originally a last name (like Millard) from the maternal side of the Hayes family. Ruddy's father, Rutherford Hayes Sr., followed the multiple careers common in the American colonies, if not with excessive zeal. He was a blacksmith, a farmer, and eventually an innkeeper. From a Scottish family originally named Haie, renowned for their valor, Hayes eschewed his Highland heritage. He avoided fighting in the Revolutionary War by moving to Vermont, where there was no conscription, and was one of the relieved signers of the subsequent "Plea of Conciliation" settling subsequent disputes between Vermont and New York. He simply wanted to live his life in peace. His popular Brattleboro tavern was really run by his more practical wife, Chloe.

Their second son, Rutherford Hayes Jr., or Ruddy, was born on January 4, 1787. He was frail as a child and would always be slender, but by his teens was strong-bodied. What struck everyone about Ruddy, beyond his flaming red hair, was an unusual combination of energy and amiability, an amalgam of both his parents. He was sent across the river to New Hampshire to attend the select school at Atkinson and did well, winning academic awards. The Hayeses might have sent him on to Dartmouth, but whether by their preference or his, he went instead into retailing, as a clerk for John Noyes's growing firm of Noyes & Mann. Noyes had married Ruddy's sister, Polly. Biographer Harry Barnard writes that Ruddy dreamed of one day running a mercantile establishment of his own, "and he was in 1804 the happiest youth in the valley."

Noyes and his partner, Jonas Mann, had decided to expand their business. Chain stores came early to Vermont. First Noyes & Mann went to Putney, and then opened a store in Wilmington, sending young Ruddy Hayes to manage it. He made his customarily favorable impression, particularly on one Sophia Birchard. Sophia was a striking young woman, as Barnard puts it, "attractive in a clean and chaste way," with rather a long "Yankee face" but a trim, slender figure, "tightly combed brown hair, and piercing blue eyes." She had extremely rosy cheeks, which caused her no end of embarrassment, implying artificial embellishment. Later Ruddy would write her, in the florid fashion of the time, that "the lass with the roseate cheeks shall not be long forgotten by the lad with the rubicund hair." Despite her aversion to crimson, when Sophia glimpsed Ruddy behind the counter of his store, the sparks between them were simultaneous.

Young Sophia was serious and studious, excelling at the district school. She was outgoing, however, and loved to converse in an animated fashion. She read endlessly, her tastes running to such weighty works as *Pilgrim's Progress.* If she sometimes seemed somber beyond her years, it was because she'd had an early acquaintance with grief. Her father, a farmer and merchant, had died when she was thirteen. Her mother, who remarried and then was divorced—a scandalous circumstance in those times—died of spotted fever a few years after Sophia met Ruddy. No region of the North American continent was impervious to such epidemics. Spotted fever cost Sophia not only her mother but also a young brother and sister and many other relatives. By 1813 she was already a surrogate mother to her three surviving brothers.

Through it all, Ruddy was her solace and support. He had been transferred back to the main Brattleboro store, but saw Sophia on weekends and sent letters through friends. Fortunately, neither was stricken as the epidemic ran its course. Their correspondence resounds with the sort of playful ardor epitomized by Abigail and John Adams: "My Dear—I am not fond of far-fetched sentiment. But do not think I mean to throw all Ceremony out of the Question and by a careless indifference alienate your affections and weaken the bonds of friendship . . . I subscribe in full truth the name of RUTHERFORD HAYES, JR. P.S. Pardon me, I love you, Sophia." On September 13, 1813, Sophia and Ruddy were married. He was twenty-six, she, twenty-one.

After the festivities, they went off to live in the bustling Vermont town of Dummerston, where Ruddy was now not only a manager but had been made a part owner—Noyes, Mann & Hayes. Two of Sophia's brothers went to live with relatives; the third, twelve-year-old Sardis, came to live with them. Good-hearted Ruddy adopted the boy, who would more than reciprocate his generosity in the next generation of Hayeses. Although Ruddy was a militia captain, he saw no action in the War of 1812. The conflict, "Mr. Madison's War," was profoundly unpopular in New England. Moreover, it hurt the local economy. With products imported from England no longer available, sales on the high end of Noyes, Mann & Hayes's merchandise declined. It was a precursor of more serious problems to come.

Still, to Sophia, her Ruddy remained unfailingly upbeat, "cheerful and kind." In August 1814, their first child was born. He was to have been named Rutherford Birchard Hayes, but he lived for only a matter of minutes. For the first time, Sophia witnessed a terrible melancholia in her husband. Undoubtedly, she shared in his grief, but she demonstrated a quality later noted by her daughter, Fanny. When things were going well, Sophia feared for the future. In times of tragedy, she had an uncommon capacity to cheer everyone up, "thus preserving the equilibrium of our family." Gradually she brought Ruddy out of his depression. In 1815 Sophia gave birth to another son. Thankfully, this one was healthy, his hair as bright red as his father's. They named him Lorenzo.

It was a different sort of depression that determined Ruddy to take his family west. In 1814 John Noyes, who had lost previously, finally won a race for Congress. Jonas Mann, who strenuously opposed Noyes's staunch Federalism, withdrew from the partnership. With Noyes gone, at least for a time, and Mann gone permanently, could a Hayes & Company be far off? There was only one problem. The end of the war had brought not only rejoicing but also a severe economic depression. Retailing was as hard-hit as manufacturing and farming. With agricultural prices plummeting, farmers could no longer afford to patronize the local merchants as they had in the past. In 1816 the coldest winter anyone could remember seemed almost a sign of divine dissatisfaction.

Ruddy had heard of "golden opportunities" in Ohio. Although many of their friends and relatives had already caught "the western fever," Sophia was particularly reluctant to abandon all she had ever known. Nor was Ruddy anxious to leave, but he had to see these new lands for himself. He was far too prudent to simply pick up stakes and uproot his family, however bleak the immediate prospects seemed in worn-out Vermont. And Sophia was pregnant again.

Ruddy set out alone on horseback, riding throughout Ohio. Following a new stagecoach route, he found a large tract of land to his liking in the settled town of Delaware. It already had some four hundred residents, many of them fellow Vermonters, who were committed to the importance of churches and schools in their community. He came home to tell Sophia that there really was a more abundant life awaiting them out west. She had already given birth to a daughter, whom they named Sarah Sophia. Reluctantly or not, Sophia agreed.

In 1817 the firm of Noyes & Hayes was dissolved. That fall, the business sold, Sophia, Ruddy, and their two children set out for what Ruddy's mother called "a distant land," a trip that would take forty days, their belongings in three wagons. They stopped first to visit with Ruddy's parents in Brattleboro. On the day of her son's departure, Chloe Hayes wrote in her diary: "Sept. 10, 1817. With tender emotions and feelings which cannot be erased from my mind I will reckon the transactions of this day. . . . I hope a kind Providence will protect them thru all the dangers they may have to pass." She knew she would never see her son again.

From the day he arrived in Delaware, as Sophia recalled, Ruddy was "always busy." He had a fine house built in the town and bought up other farmland surrounding it. Unlike many newcomers, Ruddy had the means not only to work but also to invest. He brought in imported merchandise to sell, as he had in Vermont. His most promising venture was distilling whiskey, in partnership with a local physician. That particular business was probably not to Sophia's liking, but after less than five years in Ohio, she had reason to feel satisfaction in having supported her husband's enterprising decision. She enjoyed a handsome home, abundant fruit orchards, the company of many transplanted New Englanders, fulfilling work in community activities, a loving husband, and a growing family. Sophia had given birth to a second daughter, Fanny, a delightful child, and she was pregnant yet again. Naturally, she feared it must be time for things to go bad.

For all his success, Ruddy had failed to find the immense wealth he had sought in Ohio. Reproaching himself for an excessive "spirit of speculation," he sought a higher purpose for his life by joining his wife's Presbyterian church. Forty-two days later he was gone. In the summer of 1822 a pervasive epidemic of typhoid fever swept through Ohio. First little Sarah Sophia died. Then her father was stricken while working in his fields. In three days, Rutherford Hayes Jr., too, was dead, at only thirty-five. Everyone else in the household was terribly sick. On October 4, a still-feverish Sophia gave birth to a frail little boy. With undaunted hope she named him Rutherford Birchard Hayes—for the father and older brother he would never know—and simply willed him to live. The boy's father, Rutherford Hayes Jr., was mourned by the largest assemblage of residents who had yet attended a funeral in Delaware, Ohio. Sophia mourned him the rest of her life.

Rud Hayes grew up with so vivid an image of his father that he could describe him as being of "medium height—about five feet, nine inches, straight, slender, healthy and active." Of course, it was really his mother's description, but almost a living reality to the boy. As Barnard writes, "Indeed, from the way Ruddy Hayes was remembered in Delaware, Rud felt at times that he was more favored with his dead father than his friends with their live fathers." It was quite a legacy, living up to the example of Ruddy Hayes.

## Abram Garfield

"Your father was five feet and eleven inches high, large head, broad shoulders and chest, high forehead, brown hair, blue eyes, light complexion, as beautiful a set of teeth as any man ever had . . . cheeks very red, lips tolerably full, but to me very handsome. . . . His bearing noble and brave, his . . . benevolence was fully developed, fond of his friends, everybody liked him, his judgment very good." It is not a reconstruction by a son, as with young Rud Hayes, but a depiction from life *for* her son by Eliza Ballou Garfield, three decades after the death of her beloved husband, Abram Garfield. In his ambition and the admiration of others, he very much resembled Ruddy Hayes. Unfortunately, Abram left his widow with much less, rendering Eliza's subsequent struggles even more heroic than those of Sophia Hayes.

In her "brief sketch of my early life for the gratification of my Children after I am laid in the Grave," Eliza wanted particularly the youngest and brightest of them, rambunctious James, to be inspired by the enterprising example of his father. In many ways James was like Abram. If only he could be induced to harness all that unbridled, unfocused energy. It became the goal of Eliza's life, and when she finally succeeded, her grown son acknowledging the "golden thread" of his mother's influence, Eliza understood how much it was also an inheritance from Abram. In the thirteen years of their marriage, they had given so much to each other that any reflection of it in their children was a beneficence from both parents.

The Garfields and the Ballous seemed to have followed each other across the American frontier, but they were very different families, even in their physical appearance. The Garfields, as historian Theodore Smith writes, were "typical New England stock," of Norman English extraction, among the earliest settlers of Massachusetts, arriving in 1630. Garfields tended to be tall and sturdy, given to action and evincing little in the way of intellectual curiosity. They enjoyed a reputation for enterprise, generosity, and great skill with tools. Following the Revolutionary War, in which Garfields had fought, Abram's grandfather left New England for Worcester, in central New York. Abram was born there on December 28, 1799. He was christened Abraham but always went by the name of Abram. Shortly thereafter, his father, Thomas, died, and his mother married a similarly solid man named Caleb Boynton. As a youth, Abram, described by biographers Margaret Leech and Harry Brown as "a warm, open-hearted boy, stamped with the Garfield pattern of exceptional muscular strength and little interest in book learning," was as typical a representation of his family as diminutive Eliza Ballou was of hers.

The Ballous, who settled in Rhode Island in the seventeenth century and then moved throughout New England, were noted for their small size and quick wit, described by a contemporary as a sort of "French pony breed." Many were creative and intellectual—educators and clergymen. A Ballou founded Universalism. Eliza's colorful father, James, known locally as "Ole Conjurer Blue" or "James the Astrologer," was not only a New Hampshire farmer but also a mathematician who was renowned for having an uncanny facility for telling fortunes. Unfortunately, his own fortunes flagged before he died in 1808, leaving his widow in dire straits. However, she was a skilled weaver and put her talents to use. As Eliza later pointedly put it, "In those days it was not a disgrace to work." Her mother sold the farm and took her five children to New York State, where she had relatives near the town of Worcester. There Eliza first met Abram Garfield. He was fourteen, she was twelve, and she didn't like him very much, considering him a "green boy."

Eliza, a true Ballou, is described by biographer Allan Peskin as having rather sharp features but also duplicating "her mother's bright coloring as well as her fine hands. . . . Her fine singing voice made her welcome in any gathering. . . . She was small and quick . . . fond of company and chatter." Historian Hendrick Booraem adds that although Eliza was short in stature, her wit, energy, and perception were already viewed as remarkable by her friends. Abram Garfield may have hoped someday to be numbered among them, but it was her prettier, older sister Mehetabel, called "Hitty," with whom he fell in love. When, in 1814, the Ballous, along with thousands of others, moved west to Ohio, Hitty promised in the fashion of teenage lovers to be eternally faithful. Alas, she married another. In 1819 Abram set out for Ohio and rediscovered Eliza Ballou. After glimpsing the strapping young Garfield, a neighbor assured Eliza that she would be married within three months. Eliza ridiculed his prediction until she took in the confident young man Abram had become. They *were* married within three months, on February 3, 1820. He was twenty, she only eighteen.

They set out with high spirits to seek their fortune in the Western Reserve, Ohio's northwestern frontier. Abram had learned no specific trade, but he knew something of farming and had demonstrated a skill for woodworking. Moreover, he seemed to possess an instinctive ability to win the regard of others. Neither he nor Eliza had much in the way of education, but she loved books as much as Abram avoided them. Perhaps in time she could win him over to a greater regard for learning.

Settling on forty acres of land, before Abram could even set about building a house, both became terribly ill of that common frontier ailment, the "ague," probably a form of malaria. Fortunately a number of Boynton relatives lived nearby and readily provided them with refuge. Despite everything, in the years before they had their own home, Eliza gave birth to four children, two boys and two girls. When Abram was finally up to working full-time, he used all of his Garfield charm to talk two other men into taking on a contract to construct part of the new Ohio Canal. The two helpers grew to twenty, and overcoming his inexperience, Abram completed the work and did it profitably. Unfortunately, a second, larger contract was compromised by rising costs and wiped out all his profits from the first. After eight years of marriage, he was back where he started, but now with a family to support, his strength and his wife's undiminished confidence his only assets. Abram concluded that farming, their original objective, was still the best option. Eliza helped to keep them going by doing weaving for others. It was no disgrace to work.

Before long the Boyntons were helping a renewed Abram raise the roof of a log house, crafted with his own skill. Just constructing it buoyed his spirits. He cleared additional acres and planted wheat and other crops. Things seemed to be looking up. It remained in Eliza's memory as "a golden time." By the third year in their new house, she recalled, "We lived as well as our neighbors." Food of all kinds was abundant. "Your father would do as much work in one day as any man would do in two. . . . Our family circle was unbroken. We enjoyed ourselves with our little children."

Then tragedy struck, without warning, as it so often did on the frontier. Their two-year-old son, Jimmy, their favorite, died suddenly in his mother's arms. Speechless with grief but searching for any semblance of solace, Eliza and Abram eventually turned to the fundamentalist faith of a visiting preacher from the Disciples of Christ. They prayed for another son, a sign of God's grace—and indeed Eliza soon became pregnant again.

James Abram Garfield, in his mother's words, "the largest Babe I ever had," was born in a log cabin on a farm in the township of Orange, in Cuyahoga County, Ohio, on November 19, 1831. Named for both his father and his departed brother, a not uncommon practice in those times, James looked "like a red Irishman" to his mother. He had a "very large Head and Shoulders [but] He was a very good natured Child." With dimensions appropriate for a Garfield, arriving as the answer to his parents' prayers, was he not meant to do great and good things? Unlike so many presidential parents who favored their oldest sons, the Garfields saw something special in their youngest.

He would have no recollection of his father, only his mother's account of Abram's legendary strength and good heart. James was eighteen months old when, in the dry, dangerous spring of 1833, a fire broke out in the woods surrounding the Garfield home and the new acres Abram had cleared. To keep it from spreading, he fought the blaze all day. Coming home drenched and exhausted, Abram caught a violent cold, probably pneumonia. A friend treated his throat with a frontier remedy, but his condition worsened. In two days he was dead, at the age of only thirty-three. Realizing the end was near, Abram is reputed to have said to his wife, "Eliza, I have brought you four young saplings into these woods. Take care of them." That she did, despite the odds.

If, as Allan Peskin concludes, President James Garfield "would be more remembered for what he was than for what he did," that only enhances the influence of his parents. He matured through the strenuous efforts of a mother he knew, but also, as Leech and Brown put it, "in the reflected light and legend of a father he could not remember."

## William Arthur

William Arthur was born twice, first in Ulster in 1796. Then he was "born again," as it is put today, in Vermont in 1827, and called to preach the gospel. The first of the three first fathers who became ministers, Arthur turned to religion in his thirties, after pursuing very different careers. His life encompassed the heritage of many denominations. Born a Presbyterian, he was reportedly also a lay reader in the Episcopal Church, and he married a Methodist. But it was as a Baptist that he preached to parishioners in a succession of pulpits. He and his equally devout wife, Malvina, also sought to impart the certainty of their faith to their children, particularly to their conspicuously worldly son, Chester.

William Arthur

The Arthurs were from Scotland, tracing their lineage as far back as MacArthurs (likely a warlike tribe) in the fifteenth century and to the Campbell clan. Like many Scots they ultimately found their way to the north of Ireland. William Arthur was born to a farming family in 1796—located, in the mellifluous words of leading Arthur biographer Thomas Reeves, "in the townland of Dreen, across the bridge from the village of Cullybackey in County Antrim." A childhood accident helped determine William's future. A brick wall fell on one of his feet, giving him a life-long limp. It directed him away from both games and labor on the family farm to an emphasis on schoolwork that his devoted parents were already encouraging. At eighteen he graduated from Belfast College. In 1818 or 1819, with prosperity receding in Ulster, he emigrated to Canada to enhance his prospects.

To get started, he worked at a series of jobs in Quebec, notably teaching in Dunham, fifteen miles north of the Vermont border. He also discovered eighteen-year-old Malvina Stone. Her family's English fore-bears had settled in northern New Hampshire in the seventeenth century. As biographer George Howe writes, the Stones were "typical frontier Yankees, frugal, God-fearing, and industrious." However, the family lived on both sides of the border. Malvina's father, despite being named George Washington Stone, moved his family to Quebec. Here Malvina met William. They fell in love, eloped in 1821, and had a daughter, after which William determined to move south, to Vermont, and study law. It must have been getting rather confusing for Malvina. Which country did she belong in?

In Burlington, William readily found a clerkship in a lawyer's office, taught school to help support his family, and looked forward to an eventually prosperous career. Always interested in religion, he happened to attend a Baptist revival meeting in Waterville and had an epiphany. The emotional preacher seemed to be talking directly to him. William decided on the spot that *his* life, too, must be devoted to saving souls for the Lord. He was licensed as a "free will" Baptist preacher in 1827 and, after a rigorous clerical examination, was ordained in the regular Baptist clergy in 1828. William Arthur brought eloquence and energy to his new calling, but his spellbinding sermons were to bring him more converts than comfort, and his uncompromising nature led him, over the next three decades, to eleven different congregations.

The first of them was in the small farming community of Fairfield, Vermont. Already in his thirties, William and his perpetually supportive wife now had four daughters to provide for. With an annual salary of only $250, to come even reasonably close to making ends meet, William was obliged to teach school, fulfill his pastoral duties in Fairfield, and serve as a visiting preacher at other small congregations on both sides of the Canadian border. Whether he liked it or not, for his congregation to grow, he had to compete with other Baptist churches.

On the night of October 5, 1830, the Arthurs finally had a son, a healthy nine-pound boy they named Chester Alan Arthur. Or was it October 5, 1829? The loss of Chester Arthur's private papers in a fire made the date and place of his birth uncertain, fueling later speculation by his political opponents that he was actually born in Canada, making him ineligible for the presidency of the United States. What is indisputable is that parishioners of Elder William Arthur, as he was called, were astonished to witness him actually dancing for joy when he received the news of Chester's birth. The hard-pressed parson did not view his son as an extra mouth to feed but rather as the heir to a legacy of faith more precious than riches. Eventually the Arthurs had nine children.

Moving from parish to parish in Vermont and New York may have given him the aspect of an itinerant preacher, but William possessed a formidable intellect. During his uncommonly lengthy tenure, for five years in Greenwich, New York, Arthur was so renowned for scholarship that he was awarded an honorary master of arts degree from Union College. In Schenectady he edited for four years a magazine of "popular knowledge" called *The Antiquarian and General Review.* He spoke Greek, Latin, and Hebrew. As time allowed, he took in students to tutor and prepare for college, augmenting his always meager income.

Reeves describes William as "of medium size," clean-shaven, with a thatch of dark hair and "a keen, penetrating eye." He was a man who left a strong impression—articulate, witty, passionate, whose "sarcasms, when used, were cutting." He never lost his thick Irish accent. Although a man of the cloth (even if sometimes threadbare), he also retained a rather unclerical temper and argumentative spirit. Sometimes it seemed almost as if he enjoyed shocking his parishioners with hard truths about what leading a Christian life really entailed. His uncompromising attitude led to frequent disputes with the deacons and trustees of his churches. It is little wonder that he was obliged to move so frequently. True, he was a great preacher, but should a parson not also be a man of peace?

To someone of William's convictions, one had not only to espouse the literal lessons of the Bible but, whether comfortable or not, to live them. He viewed slavery as an abomination no Christian could possibly sanction—and he didn't mind saying so in his sermons. He is believed to have co-founded the New York Anti-Slavery Society in 1835, before such abolitionist views were widely shared, even in the North.

He and Malvina suffered many sorrows. Two of their children died young, a son at two and a favorite daughter at eighteen. Financial problems dogged the devout couple, but they denied themselves even some of the necessities of life to help their remaining children, none more than Chester. Always an amiable child, "Chet," as he was called, started school at the Union Village Academy, went on to the local lyceum, where he edited the student newspaper, and finally entered Union College as a sophomore. He pursued a demanding classical curriculum. Although more sociable than scholarly, he graduated in 1848 Phi Beta Kappa, near the top of his class. A paper he wrote denouncing the practice of slavery as "disgraceful" particularly pleased his father.

They had some physical similarities, although the mature Chester favored fashionable sideburns and a mustache. He stood six foot two, taller than his father, was slender but quite strong physically, and is often described as "strikingly handsome." An early teacher referred to Chester's "dark and brilliant eyes," much like his father's, but also noted a profound difference in their temperaments. Chester "was frank and open in his manners and genial in his disposition." William may have been similarly frank and open, but he was genial only if you agreed with him. It was on the basis of that geniality, and his adaptability, that Chester launched his political career. After his college graduation, Chester taught for a time, at one point in his own modest academy in the basement of his father's church, now located in North Pownal, Vermont. Then he went on to study law. He was admitted to the bar in 1854 and within two years had his own firm, successful from the start.

These were also relatively promising years for his father. Need piety always be accompanied by privation? Contemplating retirement from his peripatetic ministry, its final location at the Calvary Baptist Church in Albany, William settled in nearby Newtonville, New York. He anticipated expanding his boarding school for college-bound students and perhaps even attaining a modest measure of profitability, but the Civil War intervened. As Chester went off to serve, although his preferential assignment would be no more dangerous than as inspector general and quartermaster general of New York (ever after he liked to be called "General"), his father's advice followed him. "Pray daily," William urged, "for you know not, when called to meet the enemy, you may fall in Battle. . . . Do, my son, ask God that whether you live or die [you] may be the Lord's." Chester had become increasingly sophisticated in his urban environment and—in the fashion of the times—quite skeptical of the literal Christianity epitomized by what seemed the simple country faith of his parents. However, it never diminished Chester's appreciation of how much they had sacrificed for him.

Chester Alan Arthur went on to a political career characterized by the titles of his two major biographies—*A Quarter Century of Machine Politics* and *Gentleman Boss*. Arthur became renowned for his luxurious lifestyle—attired fashionably, even elegantly, residing in a handsome brownstone and employing Irish maids little removed from the humble dwellings of his father's family in the old country. He managed all this opulence through a troubling alliance with the venal political machine of New York's Republican Party. Yet when he became president upon the death of James Garfield, Arthur surprised both his friends and his critics. As he explained in refusing to grant political favors to an incredulous visitor, "Since I came here I have learned that Chester A. Arthur is one man and the president of the United States is another."

William Arthur had died of stomach cancer nearly six years before, on October 27, 1875, at the age of seventy-nine. His oldest son visited him near the end, to his evident delight. Perhaps Chester took something away from that final meeting, a renewed appreciation of his father's values. As Howe testifies, despite Chester Arthur's attainment of a lifestyle light-years removed from his childhood, ingrained habits of generosity and kindness remained to sustain him. When granted for a time the greatest power he would ever possess, President Arthur finally rediscovered another inherited quality, his father's honesty.

# 7

## "TELL THE TRUTH"

### Richard Falley Cleveland • John Scott Harrison
### William McKinley Sr.

CHARACTER IN THE FACE OF ADVERSITY unites conscientious Richard Cleveland, a better teacher than preacher; land-loving John Harrison, burdened by his prominent family name; and William McKinley Sr., who sacrificed his own ease to secure his children's education.

### Richard Falley Cleveland

The Reverend Richard Falley Cleveland simply ran out of time. Time was a precious commodity, not to be wasted, a tenet he impressed on all nine of his children. Perhaps the most promising, if not the most intellectual, was his fifth child and third son, Grover. When he was only nine, the boy wrote this reflection of his father's precepts: "If we expect to become great and good men and be respected and esteemed by our friends we must improve our time when we are young." But more than time was lacking. There was never enough money. Worn out by cares and commitments before he was fifty, Reverend Cleveland simply lacked the means to provide the college education Grover clearly merited.

If this made Grover resentful, he never revealed it. On the contrary, he felt fortunate to have had such an inspiring father whose lessons were timeless and to whom he owed so much. Only months before he died, Cleveland reflected: "Looking back over my life, nothing seems to me to have in it more both of pathos and interest than the spectacle of my father, a hard-working country clergyman, bringing up acceptably a family of nine children, educating each member so that, in afterlife, none suffered any deprivation in this respect, and that, too, upon a salary which at no time exceeded a thousand dollars a year. It would be impossible to exaggerate the strength of character thus revealed."

Richard Falley
Cleveland

There was little doubt that Richard Cleveland would be a clergy-man. Generations of Clevelands had committed sons to the Protestant clergy, on both sides of the Atlantic. Their family name was derived from the rocky "cleves" of England. Born on June 18, 1804, Richard was a most conscientious student. He graduated from Yale with high honors in 1824 and began studying for the ministry in Baltimore, prior to going on to Princeton Theological Seminary. To support himself he also worked as a tutor in a private academy.

In Baltimore he met lively, fun-loving Ann Neal. Daughter of a pros-perous law-book publisher and his socially prominent wife, Ann loved luxury almost to the point of ostentation. Her collection of jewelry and her stylish wardrobe were the talk of her wide circle of friends. Yet some-how she fell in love with this Yankee divinity student—spare, serious, somber Richard Falley Cleveland. Of course, stereotypes don't always stand up. Biographer H. Paul Jeffers notes that Cleveland was rather handsome and hardly devoid of charm. His "genial blue eyes," prominent Roman nose, and firm mouth gave him an aspect both aristocratic and kindly.

In September 1829, after his return from Princeton, Richard Cleveland and Ann Neal were wed. He had already secured a position, as minister to the First Congregational Church in Windham, Connecticut. Well prepared, well married, surely he had the makings of a distinguished divine. He was only twenty-five, Ann twenty-three. Perhaps Richard simply overlooked the trunks and trunks of clothes and adornments, not to mention Ann's black maid, who accompanied them by coach and canal up to Connecticut. When they finally arrived, the reaction of the good women of Windham was hardly surprising. Richard's new parishioners were appalled by having a slave in their midst, let alone one who was the servant of their parson's wife. They were equally aghast when they witnessed the costly embellishments of Mrs. Cleveland's person. She seemed to be a pleasant enough young woman, but had she no knowledge of the scriptural admonitions against vanity and display? Quickly the maid was dispatched back to Maryland. Ann Neal Cleveland, in the first weeks of her marriage, determined at least in terms of appearance to be more Puritan than the Puritans.

She would need to be. Despite his earnest efforts and his undeniable talents, Richard never quite achieved his potential in the pulpit. No collection of his sermons was ever published. His family's circumstances sometimes verged on destitution. Perhaps his true calling was more in academia—a better teacher than preacher. Yet his churches prospered, even if the Clevelands did not. Biographer Alyn Brodsky writes that the young couple were "poor only in goods. They had culture, congeniality, and spiritual wealth." That is true enough, but they also soon had children to nurture and support. Four arrived during the first five years of their marriage. Richard's health was already showing signs of stress, and in 1832 he accepted a call to become acting minister of a Presbyterian church in warmer Portsmouth, Virginia. Within two years, however, he returned to the north, to become pastor of the Presbyterian church in Caldwell, New Jersey.

It was here that Richard enjoyed his most sustained success. He added seventy-five new members to his congregation and raised a substantial sum to remodel and repair the church structure. Cleveland's salary, of course, was anything but substantial, but perhaps Jeffers puts his finger on why he failed to rise higher in the church hierarchy. He had no single outstanding quality. "His flocks found him kindly, expansive and somewhat of a charmer who was serious but not brilliant." According to a colleague, Richard was noted for "the happy union and equal development of his virtues," combining the "tastes and habits of the Christian scholar with practical wisdom and efficiency." He meant this to be complimentary, but the quality Cleveland lacked, despite such equanimity, was the ability to stand out, to fire a congregation. He was the absolute reverse of a William Arthur.

In the Caldwell manse Ann gave birth on March 18, 1837, to the couple's fifth child, a healthy boy who would earn a special place in her heart. He was named Stephen Grover Cleveland for William's predecessor, who had founded the church in 1787. Although he would be later be called "Big Steve" (and "Uncle Jimbo") by his playmates, Grover discarded his first name as soon as he could—officially when he came of age—and no one seems to have ever used it very much.

Despite his relative success in Caldwell, Reverend Cleveland moved on to the Presbyterian church in Fayetteville, New York. Here he would enjoy his longest tenure—nine years. It was Fayetteville, "this pretty village," that Grover would always view as his childhood home. The pleasures of Grover's childhood were within a framework of pervasive piety and genteel poverty—worship and work. As he grew, Grover supplemented the family income by such muscle-building jobs as hauling rock lime and directing barges on the Erie Canal to where they could be loaded. Grover's education started in the home, then at the district schoolhouse, and finally at Fayetteville Academy, where at the age of nine he wrote his essay on the use of time. However critical that commodity, after the obligations of each day were completed, time was made for healthful outdoor play. Family games involved everyone, including the parents. Grover particularly loved fishing and swimming and taking long hikes. He was also fond of rather nonmalicious pranks. His sister Susan recalled "a little round-faced, blue-eyed boy . . . chuck full of fun."

When Grover was thirteen, in 1850, his father faced the harsh reality that, however much they all scrimped and saved, he simply could not support a family of eleven on a small-church parson's scant stipend. He accepted a position as district secretary of the American Home Missionary Society. It meant traveling throughout central New York but paid the munificent sum of $1,000 a year. The family moved to the handsome town of Clinton, New York. Clinton had a particular attraction for Grover, because it was the home of Hamilton College, which he hoped to attend. He plunged into his studies at the Clinton Liberal Institute.

But all the travel, over rudimentary roads and in all sorts of weather, was taking a terrible toll on his father. With great reluctance Richard finally resigned and took a position at half the salary as minister of the Presbyterian church at Holland Patent, a quiet village ten miles from Utica on the Black River. Richard's first sermon at Holland Patent in September 1853 was also his last. He had been diagnosed with gastric ulcers, and the affliction left him too weak to even get out of bed. Grover looked in on his father each morning. On October 1, seeing Richard sleeping peacefully, he drove one of his sisters into Utica in their carriage to do some shopping. She was to be married soon. Their father died that day. The cause of death was "acute peritonitis"; he was forty-nine.

Although Grover's dream of going to college was buried with Richard Falley Cleveland on October 4, 1853, he never blamed his father or ceased extolling the virtues of higher education. His postpresidential career included heading the board of trustees at Princeton, where he had profound differences with the college's president, Woodrow Wilson, but even Cleveland's cherished Sigma Chi badge was honorary.

In their maturity, father and son had many similarities. Physically, Richard's frame had thickened over the years. Brodsky writes, "In the son we see the father's generous height and portly figure, blue eyes, balding brow, and their most distinctive shared trait, the prominent Roman nose," although Grover would add an equally prominent mustache. In addition, both had a "charming manner and a studiousness that stopped short of brilliance." More important, "Richard had been the primary influence during Grover's formative years." As Cleveland reflected after his presidency, the struggling parson's life epitomized "the qualities of pluck and endurance which have made the American people what they are."

After all, it was values that counted. Grover's brother William, the Presbyterian minister in his generation, officiated at his White House wedding to the lovely Frances Folsom, forty years his junior, the daughter of his late law partner. Eyebrows were surely raised, but it was a prior event that caused a greater stir. It is ironic that as scrupulously honest a man as Cleveland is so vividly remembered for an indiscretion. He may have fathered an illegitimate child. Although the woman in question had other admirers, making Cleveland's paternity less than certain, as the only bachelor involved he stepped forward as the father and agreed to support both mother and child. To his anxious campaign workers in 1884 who asked how they should handle such a situation, Cleveland issued a simple directive: "Tell the truth." Cleveland went on to win the presidency. In fact, he won it twice, losing to Benjamin Harrison in between, the only occupant of the office to serve noncontiguous terms. The incident is recalled, however, by a famous cartoon and accompanying doggerel, "Ma! Ma! Where's my Pa? Gone to the White House, Ha! Ha! Ha!"

Even Cleveland's political opponents rarely questioned his honesty. He had hired a substitute to serve in his stead in the Civil War not because he feared to fight but because his continuing financial support was absolutely essential to the welfare of his mother and his siblings. Literary legend H. L. Mencken, more noted for his acerbic estimation of politicians, may have put it best: "We have had more brilliant presidents than Cleveland . . . but we have never had one, at least since Washington, whose fundamental character was solider and more admirable."

From "we must improve our time" to "Tell the truth." In the span of his lifetime Grover Cleveland never ceased to reflect the earnest admonitions of the "hard-working country clergyman" who was his father.

## John Scott Harrison

John Scott Harrison was a man in the middle. Both the father and son of American presidents, a unique distinction, Harrison really only wanted three things for his life: to be a successful farmer, to be a good husband and father, and to be left alone. The first, for whatever reasons, did not happen, and the third was impossible; the Harrisons were too prominent a family. Only in the second objective was John Harrison successful. To the only one of his thirteen children who pursued a career in public service, "Little Ben" Harrison, he poured out a stream of advice, much of it of impressive clarity and common sense.

Grandson of the colorful signer of the Declaration of Independence, Benjamin Harrison V, and third son of President William Henry Harrison, John was born on October 4, 1804, in Vincennes, Indiana. His ambitious father, then governor of the territory of Indiana and later to be renowned as "the hero of Tippecanoe," had some difficulty supporting his ten children after resigning his army commission in 1814. John, the only son still alive to witness his father's brief tenure as president, would be of some practical help in enabling General Harrison to get there.

Conscientious and dutiful, John Scott Harrison graduated at the top of his class at Cincinnati College and went on to study law. But he always preferred the lure of the land. When his father was named minister to Colombia in 1828, John was left in charge of the Harrison's six-

John Scott Harrison

hundred-acre farm near North Bend, Ohio, called "The Point." In good times and bad it would remain John's home for the rest of his life.

More than John's acreage was fertile. He had three children by his first wife, Lucretia, before she died in 1830. He had ten more by his second wife, Elizabeth, who died giving birth to her last child in 1850. Although only seven of his thirteen children survived to maturity, with so many mouths to feed, Harrison faced increasing challenges to make ends meet. The vagaries of nature and man, whether floods or low prices for his crops, seemed always to inhibit his success. For all his hard work and seeming good sense, John had a soft heart, often signing notes for friends with no firm guarantees of repayment. Eventually it all combined to do him in.

John's second child, and second son, Benjamin, was born at The Point on August 20, 1833. Technically he was Benjamin Harrison VI or even VII, but he went simply by the name of Benjamin. His earliest instruction was on the grounds of his father's farm, the small log school-house John had constructed between the Ohio River and the family's large brick home. So small that he was already called "Little Ben," Benjamin showed promise as a student but much preferred the outdoors.

He failed, however, to find any charm in such chores as planting, harvesting, carrying wood and water, and feeding the horses, cattle, hogs, and sheep daily. His future would not be in farming. Biographer Elizabeth Myers notes that John Harrison talked with his children in an admirably honest way, on equal terms, almost as adults. It was probably in his teens that Ben had his earliest intimations of his father's financial difficulties. Still, he and his brother Irwin went off to an excellent preparatory school, staying with relatives. Unable to afford an elite college in New England, in 1850 John sent Benjamin to the best alternative in the area, Miami University of Ohio. He entered as a junior, graduated in 1852, fell in love with Caroline Livinia Scott, the daughter of a local educator, and decided he wanted to be a lawyer.

By the time he returned home to inform his widower father of his professional plans, it was clear that John simply could not afford law school. Over the next two years, father and son did each other a notable service. John obtained for Ben a clerkship in a prominent Cincinnati law firm, a viable alternative to law school. The next year Ben married Carrie Scott, and in 1854 he established his own legal practice in Indianapolis. Prior to this, however, he had filled in for his father, living for a time at The Point. John's neighbors, although they appreciated his disinclination to trade on his family's name, had asked him to stand for Congress. With young children still at home, John demurred. Ben's decision enabled him to run, and he won.

Although keenly interested in politics, John had never viewed it as a career for himself. Perhaps the prospect of a regular salary was particularly enticing at that time. Characteristically, in Congress he said little, meditated much, and voted his conscience—all but guaranteeing a short tenure in office. Given his antislavery views, Harrison opposed the Kansas-Nebraska Bill that exacerbated tensions on both sides, but with equal conviction he denounced "the disruptive effects of abolitionist agitation." The Union must be preserved.

Although he wrote home in plaintive tones, "My thoughts are continually wandering from the hall of legislation to my children and my home," when his two years were up, he chose to run again, and was reelected. Then he ran for a third term—and was defeated only because of his stubborn insistence on following his convictions. When in 1856 Senator Charles Sumner of Massachusetts was beaten senseless by Representative Preston Brooks of South Carolina, Harrison joined in the denunciation of Brooks but opposed his expulsion from the House, telling his colleagues, "I dare do anything I think right; and when my constituencies seek to deprive me of that privilege, I will say to them: 'Take back this bauble of office which I did not seek.'" They did. Harrison never ran for office again.

The money he earned was not nearly enough. As the notes he had so imprudently signed for his friends came due and they were unable to pay, Harrison was obliged to sell off piece after piece of the land he had inherited, until only a few precious acres were left. Eventually he was bankrupted, enabled to continue living in his lifelong home only through the charity of his sons. Despite all his efforts, as biographer Harry Sievers writes, "John Scott Harrison was a poor manager and, like his father, General William Henry Harrison, seemed to draw more than his share of bad luck both in farming and property speculation." As his father's short-lived political career waned, Ben's took off. When introduced to the Republican National Convention in 1856 as "Young Tippecanoe," Ben stated, "I do not wish to be acclaimed as the grandson of anyone. I think every man should stand on his own merits."

That didn't inhibit his father's advice. As the two major political parties emerged, John insisted that it was the Democrats who would be dominant in the 1860s. Benjamin, however, went his own way, affiliating with the newly formed Republican Party, and was elected city attorney of Indianapolis under its auspices. However they differed—and to John Harrison politics under any banner tended to be a "crooked and devious" business—he was extremely proud of his son. Ben's heroic services in the Civil War—he emerged as a brigadier general—cemented his father's admiration. As historian Stephen Hess points out, within one month Benjamin Harrison fought in more battles than had William Henry Harrison or Andrew Jackson in their entire lives.

Little Ben, barely five and a half feet tall, was neither a typical politician nor a typical Harrison. He came, as Hess writes, "from a tribe of giants [and] congenial hail fellows." Although hardly a congenial hail fellow, tall John Scott Harrison, with his lean, long face, at least looked like his father and prior Harrisons. Moreover, Hess describes Benjamin as "curt to the point of incivility." Famed American editor William Allen

White is more charitable, picturing Benjamin Harrison as "bearded, soft-voiced, gentle-eyed, meticulous in dress and manners, in speech and thought . . . shy, most diffident and unassertive." Yet his oratory could sway an audience, whether they were seated in a jury box or an auditorium. He took to wearing a silk hat everywhere, perhaps to look more imposing, although it became a rather patrician trademark. Whether he liked it or not, when he finally ran for president, Harrison was nominated at the 1888 Republican convention as the bearer of a name "woven into the very fabric of American history." Democrats proclaimed, "Grandpa's pants won't fit Benny." Republicans replied, "Yes, but grandfather's hat fits Ben!"

As with James Buchanan Sr., John Harrison seems to have been most impressed by his son's skill as a lawyer. After a particularly spectacular courtroom victory, John wrote Ben: "I congratulate you, my dear son, on your success in the case and hope your client was in every way worthy of your powerful and effective 'defense.' . . . I can hardly express to you the pleasure that these triumphs of yours at the Bar afford me. I feel much prouder of them than I would of your success in politics. Any demagogue may obtain office, but it takes brains and learning to sway a judge and jury." Yet, should the time come that high office came calling, John urged, "Forget self for country."

Time was running out for John Harrison. Still strong in his seventies, the white-bearded patriarch remained in the North Bend home that his son's contributions had secured for his old age. To help support himself, he turned to a most surprising avocation—he became a public speaker. Had his name been John Scott, no one would have paid much attention. As John Scott Harrison, however, bankrupt farmer or not, he was at least a modest success on the lecture circuit. The family name could be useful after all. Ironically, and there had been a good deal of irony in his life, his most popular talk was on "The World's Race for Wealth." He was against it.

On the evening of May 25, 1878, John Scott Harrison quietly passed away at the age of seventy-three. The last son of President William Henry Harrison and the father of future president Benjamin Harrison was laid to rest on May 29. At the small Presbyterian church known as The Little Church on the Hill, the services, modest as the man, were simple and brief. One of two eulogies aptly extolled John Scott Harrison not as a successful farmer or political figure but as a "consistent Christian, a faithful husband and a kind and just father." As the mourners watched the casket lowered into the earth, some were distressed to observe that a neighboring gravesite had been recently disturbed. What had happened?

Their grim suspicions were confirmed in what has been called the "Harrison Horror." Within twenty-four hours of his burial, Harrison's body was discovered in a shaft at the Ohio Medical College, likely in preparation for dissection. Its dean had made a ghoulish agreement with grave robbers to bring him fresh cadavers for the edification of his students. It was a not uncommon practice, but the resulting national furor spurred legislation to bring it to an end. It represents a posthumous contribution by Harrison, but a horrific postscript to his life. Many people, even in Ohio, had been previously unaware of his passing. The *Cincinnati Daily Enquirer* noted rather insensitively, "Most of those who will hear of the death did not know that he was living," but later the paper added that Harrison had been "an honored citizen of the Ohio Valley and beloved member of society."

After Ben and his young wife had set up housekeeping in Indianapolis, every year they received an immense supply of everything edible that the Harrison farm produced. In later years the son more than reciprocated by caring for his father. At nineteen Ben had reflected, "An utterly selfish man can find no happiness in heaven because he carries hell in his heart." John Scott Harrison, a man in the middle, uncomfortable with the famous name he bore and its implications for his life, was successful, as we measure success, only as a husband and father. In that alone, however, he found more satisfaction than have many others in prominent families, before or since.

# William McKinley Sr.

William McKinley Sr. always carried three books with him, even as he tended his blast furnaces—the Bible and the works of Dante and Shakespeare. His education may have been limited to grammar school, but his neighbors noted that he had worn the pages thin on every book he owned. So committed was McKinley to educating his children that he had his wife take them to another Ohio town ten miles away because it had a more advanced school.

As McKinley biographer H. Wayne Morgan writes, "The man who was to father a president was not extraordinary except in the force of his character." He did not live to see the son who bore his name become president, but in the year William McKinley Sr. died, William McKinley

William
McKinley Sr.

Jr. was already governor of Ohio. Not surprisingly, the word the younger McKinley used most frequently to describe his father was also "character." One might add, as historian Margaret Leech does, a few additional words: "William was proud of his father's obstinate industry and upright, independent character."

When in 1743 the first McKinley, as the name emerged after a customarily convoluted series of spellings, came to America, his heritage, from Scotland and Ulster, not only encompassed strength, hard work, high spirits, and independence, but also a profound respect for learning. He was called "David the Weaver," although the primitive nature of his new land required that he undertake multiple tasks—not only weaving but also farming and, most significantly for the future of his family, working with iron. The trade had already occupied members of his family in the old country. David settled on over three hundred acres in York County in Pennsylvania, near the Susquehanna River and the border with Maryland. McKinleys were not particularly prominent in colonial politics but accepted their share of the burdens of administering their county's affairs—serving on juries and in the local militia, helping administer the law and collect taxes. Notably industrious, David set the tone for the future of his family.

In America, the McKinleys—Pennsylvania's equivalent of Augustine Washington—became more and more immersed in the mining and manufacturing of pig iron. True to their Highland heritage and their independent inclinations, McKinleys fought extensively under the command of Augustine's son, George, throughout the American Revolution. Some of them left the line of battle only to cast lead bullets and cannon, a task even more crucial to the Continental Army's success than leveling a musket at the enemy.

After the War of 1812, in which the family also participated, David's son James joined the western migration, moving with his wife, Rose, to New Lisbon, Ohio, in search of better opportunities. The iron foundry business, in which Rose's family also had deep roots, moved with him. As the nation expanded, metalworking promised fortune to those enterprising enough to turn one hand-worked furnace into many. Just as Jesse Grant grasped the need for leather goods on the frontier, James McKinley, although he remained a part-time farmer, knew that everything the westward wagons contained moved on wheels of iron.

His son William, born on November 15, 1807, in New Lisbon, was strong of physique and extremely taciturn, hardworking yet fun-loving, conditioned to rising and retiring early, and adaptable to many tasks. Morgan writes, "He could forge iron, mend fences, paint, plow, tend animals, build houses, work wood, and occasionally invent things." In his teens he already had the firm jaw and "keen eyes" that reflected his determination to succeed in the harsh environment of the American frontier. Despite an education limited to the local grammar school, enhanced by his own scattered reading, he loved books—another McKinley trait—and had shown some talent for figuring.

By the time enterprising William was sixteen, he was already operating three charcoal furnaces of his own, in partnership with his brother. It was either in the local schoolhouse or at the Methodist church that he met bright, strong-minded, capable Nancy Allison. She attended both regularly, committed to learning and so religious that had she been a man, the ministry would likely have been her calling. If, as Morgan writes, McKinley was extraordinary only in the force of his character, that is what counted to Nancy. The two were wed on June 6, 1829, their union symbolized by venturing to a spring where they shared a drink of cool water from a gourd dipper.

They settled in the small Ohio town of Niles, surrounded by hills that contained deposits of coal and iron ore. Despite such promising possibilities and his energetic efforts, William never quite found the success he sought. His family's fortunes ranged from just above to just below adequate, and he was constantly on the road seeking business for his foundry. That left his wife largely in charge of the household, but there was little if any discord. They were very much of one mind in terms of how their children should be raised.

There would be nine, four boys and five girls. Remarkably for such times, only one child, a girl who would have been their tenth offspring, died in infancy. It was their seventh child, not the firstborn male, who was named for his father. William McKinley Jr. was born on January 29, 1843, in the long, low clapboard house attached to the town's general store that would be his home for his first nine years. In later years, his mother—who would be popularly known as "Mother McKinley"—denied that she had particularly doted on any one of her children. However, both parents early recognized unusual qualities in young William. He was as quiet as his father, but he seemed to be measuring things in a rather adult, reflective way. Like all the children, he had his chores to perform. Among his memories was the warmth on his bare feet of the places where milk cows had lain before he drove them to a new pasture. It was hardly a life of ease, but it was a most secure childhood, marred only by the frequent absences of a father William knew to be stronger than other men. Until the day of the senior William McKinley's death, his son would write his name "William McKinley Jr."

As biographer Eva Higgins points out, discipline in the McKinley home was evenhanded and firm, but it was applied with an affection that need not be expressed with excessive hugging or kissing. There was no card playing, drinking, or very much levity in the household, but this did not prevent William from enjoying a normal, happy childhood he would always recall fondly. He enjoyed games and sports of all kinds—marbles, baseball, archery, and swimming.

William's first formal instruction in the rudiments of learning (although he had been enrolled in Sunday School even earlier) was in the already well-worn frame schoolhouse in Niles. In 1852, as he neared his tenth birthday, his parents came to a significant decision. Niles was a pleasant but rather isolated community, with limited educational opportunities. In the larger nearby town of Poland there was a more advanced academy, Union Seminary. The three older children, who were all but ready to make their way in the world, were sent to live with relatives. Nancy and the six remaining children went to live in Poland.

It was an enormous sacrifice for their father, but one he firmly believed was necessary. Not only would his business keep him in Niles, but he had to establish a new home for his family. For years he would only see them on weekends, riding horseback each way, but the education of his children came first. Somehow McKinley managed to settle his family in a far larger, more attractive house, with an immense kitchen for his wife, surrounded by handsome maple trees and a white picket fence. Years later President McKinley recalled the whole town with great nostalgia, "the trim neat little village on the yellow creek, with its . . . white frame dwellings, its dear old academy and the village store from which we got our political inspiration." Poland was also a way station on the Underground Railroad. Both William McKinleys hated slavery.

By the time young William graduated from Poland's Union Seminary at seventeen, Morgan describes him as "a handsome boy, with ample dark hair, a somewhat slight but muscular build, and penetrating eyes. His courtesy and kindness enhanced his physical attractiveness." After commencement he went on to Allegheny College in Meadville, Pennsylvania. His father's immense pride was tempered with apprehension. The financial panic of 1857 had already impelled belt-tightening. The McKinley children worked any jobs that were available to help pay for their tuition at the seminary. Their father's liquidity, never very secure, had taken a major blow when his imprudent brother, Benjamin, left for California, leaving William responsible for his debts as well.

Young William stayed only a year at Allegheny. He fell ill at the end of his first semester, and mounting financial problems at home made his return impossible. For a time he taught school and worked in the post office, but a more serious crisis was coming. With the advent of the Civil War in 1861, McKinley enlisted as a private in the 23rd Ohio Volunteer Regiment, under the command of Rutherford B. Hayes. By the end of the war McKinley was a twenty-two-year-old major who had been decorated for bravery in several engagements. In 1864 he cast his first vote, for Abraham Lincoln. He, too, would be a Republican.

William had already completed law school in Canton, Ohio, when his parents in 1867 chose to settle there, uniting all of their family who remained in the area. Never given to inactivity, William McKinley Sr. invested in a blast furnace in Michigan and oversaw it for the next seven years. By 1869 William Jr., already active in politics, was elected prosecuting attorney of Stark County. In 1871 he married Ida Saxton, of a leading local family. Only a decade after he had served under Hayes in the war, McKinley, a newly elected congressman, joined President Rutherford B. Hayes in Washington. A bit thicker around the waist, his hair receding, William McKinley Jr. was still strikingly handsome.

William McKinley Sr. passed away on November 24, 1892, at the age of eighty-five. Perhaps only his character was "extraordinary," but it never ceased to inspire the son who bore his name and was by his side on the day he died.

# 8

# "ONE MUST LIVE
# FOR THE LIVING"

## Theodore Roosevelt Sr.

AMONG THE MOST ADMIRABLE of first fathers, "Thee" Roosevelt combined what one contemporary characterized as "maniacal benevolence"
with love of life and devotion to family that induced his "Teedie" to call
him "the best man I ever knew."

Flags throughout the city were at half-staff. Over two thousand people
packed the Fifth Avenue Presbyterian Church for the funeral service.
Many more could not get in. Over the preceding few days, hundreds had
kept a vigil at the home of the stricken man. The eminent left their
cards. Outside, in the winter chill, the poor paid their silent tribute. At
the service, the elder of the two presiding ministers was so overwhelmed
with emotion during his eulogy that he could complete it only with difficulty. Few pulpits that Sunday did not extol the virtues of the deceased.

Every newspaper in New York, and many elsewhere, detailed his life
not only in obituaries but also on the editorial pages and even their front
pages. Perhaps the *New York World* put it best, celebrating one "who was
eyes to the blind, feet to the lame, good to all." The *New York Times*
praised his example of public-spirited moral purpose, as one who used
"great opportunity for the best end." Later, *The Nation* considered his life
in the context of the times: "We believe that the mere fact that New
York could even in these later evil years, produce him and hold his love
and devotion, has been for hundreds of those who knew him and
watched his career a reason for not despairing of the future of the city."

The deceased was no head of state, or even of his own municipality.
He never held or sought to hold public office. Yet, although he had
always avoided publicity, he was esteemed when he died at the age of

Theodore
Roosevelt Sr.

only forty-seven, just before midnight on February 9, 1878, as the first citizen of New York. His name was Theodore Roosevelt. Only many years later would he be remembered as Theodore Roosevelt Sr.

His son, the other Theodore, was at Harvard when he received the urgent summons to come home on the next train. Only a few days before, he had written home, "Am very uneasy about Father. Does the Doctor think it is something serious?" His son's education was a subject of some importance to Theodore Sr., although he had characteristically cautioned him to "take care of your morals first, your health next and finally your studies." The son had written home early in his freshman year, "Not another boy in college has a family who loves him as you all do me, and I am *sure* there is no one who has a Father who is also his best and most intimate friend, as you are mine."

The train took all night. His father was already dead when young Theodore arrived home. Grief-stricken, all he could write in his diary that night was "My dear Father. Born September 23, 1831 . . ."

What had made Theodore Roosevelt Sr. so beloved a figure? The progression of seven previous generations of Roosevelts in America had achieved distinction and wealth, and had demonstrated generosity. But no previous Roosevelt had ever exhibited anything remotely approaching Theodore's relentless commitment to helping others. Perhaps, as many of his contemporaries believed, it was motivated by a "troublesome conscience." What had he done to deserve so much when only a few blocks down Broadway were so many who had next to nothing?

That Claes (or Klaes) Martenszen van Rosenvelt had chosen in 1649 to make the arduous journey to the New World is evidence of his ambition. There were abundant opportunities at home, but overseas trade was essential to a world power. With eminent practicality the Dutch settled only one colony in North America, crowned by the finest natural harbor they could find. They called it New Netherlands, and the city that would develop around its harbor, New Amsterdam. In less than forty years it would be New York. Claes was both a farmer and a merchant. His sons, their family name now anglicized to Roosevelt, established its two notable branches. The most prominent of what became the Hyde Park line was the first Isaac Roosevelt, a sugar planter and American patriot who helped secure the adoption of the Constitution. The most prominent of the Manhattan line was the formidable Cornelius Van Schaak Roosevelt, who turned what had become essentially a hardware business in other directions, importing glass, selling real estate, and eventually establishing a private bank. Known as "C. V. S.," he became the family's first millionaire and was the father of the first Theodore Roosevelt.

Theodore, the youngest of the five sons C. V. S. sired, was born in 1831 into a lively household ensconced in a sizable redbrick house, with a staff of servants, on bustling Fourteenth Street. Biographer Allen Churchill notes that even as a child Theodore exhibited a balanced, cheerful personality. Perhaps because he was the youngest of their boys, both parents doted on their "Thee." C. V. S. was the last of his family to speak Dutch at the dinner table, few words of which his children understood. Like his predecessors, he was more stimulated by the challenge of commerce than by simply accumulating wealth. Unlike them, his wife was not Dutch. Margaret Barnhill Roosevelt's Quaker forebears had come over with William Penn. Thee enjoyed the influence of more than one tradition.

A thoroughly outgoing youth, Thee loved animals of all kinds, especially horses. As he grew, he delighted in riding his favorite mount and even more in recklessly driving his four-in-hand through the still-rural environs of upper Manhattan. Education in the Roosevelt household was still largely conducted by tutors. Only one son went to college, his Columbia degree a specific preparation for the law. Yet when Thee was nineteen, his parents decided to send him on a grand tour of Europe. He made the customary rounds of cathedrals and castles, but his letters home dwelt more on incidents that reveal a growing social conscience. He was struck by the extremes of public squalor and private splendor.

Still, when he arrived home he went directly into the family business on Maiden Lane, soon becoming a partner in what was really Roosevelt and Sons. His income was enhanced by a hefty inheritance after his father died. But, try as he might, business was never Thee's true calling. It simply couldn't challenge him as it did other Roosevelts. His thoughts were already focused on the attainment of loftier pursuits.

One of them, the most enchanting girl in the world, lived on a plantation in Roswell, Georgia. Thee's travels had taken him not only to Europe but also to the American South. Through relatives he met captivating, diminutive, dark-haired Martha Bulloch—and was enthralled. "Mittie" Bulloch was also smitten. Roosevelt biographer Edmund Morris refers to Thee's "leonine features, and big sloping shoulders." Biographer David McCullough describes Thee as a "fine figure" of a man, "physically imposing, athletic, with china blue eyes, chestnut hair . . . and a good, square Dutch jaw." There seems to have been the antebellum equivalent of a spontaneous Sicilian "thunderbolt." Although their actual wedding would not take place for three years, Thee and Mittie pledged themselves to each other at Roswell.

On the surface, beyond attractiveness and affluence, the two seemed such opposites: Mittie—slight, humorous, creative, emotional, and very Southern; Thee—large, serious, motivated, self-contained, and very Northern. Yet the mutual affection of Martha Bullock and Theodore Roosevelt, so quickly kindled, would never wane, an example of constancy that would inspire their children. Mittie wrote after his departure, "I feel dear Thee—as though you were part of my existence, and that I can only live in your being." When he received this letter, Thee, "feeling the blood rush to my temple," uncharacteristically pushed his work aside and responded, "Oh, Mittie, how deeply, how devotedly I love you!"

Their wedding at Bulloch Hall in Roswell at the end of December 1853 was followed by a week of festivities. After a brief honeymoon, the couple arrived at their new home in New York City—a compact, four-story brownstone on Twentieth Street, near fashionable Gramercy Park.

Its chaste façade fronted a dark interior filled with the heavy furnishings of the time, although Thee had the rear opened onto a spacious, airy piazza. Here was a staff waiting to do Mittie's bidding. At eighteen, Mittie had never been obliged to run anything. Moreover, she found the immense city "bewildering." Although Mittie brought in light and laughter, it was not until three years later, when her mother and sister, Anna, moved up to New York, that she finally felt a secure mistress of this somber household.

In less than a year, Mittie was pregnant. Their first child, a girl, was named for Mittie's much-loved sister, Anna, and nicknamed "Bamie," short for the Italian "bambina." Bamie was a joy to both her parents, but also a challenge and a precursor of problems to come. She was born with curvature of the spine, from which she was never entirely to recover, despite the constant attention of doctors using the latest techniques and apparatuses. Most of all she was patiently nursed and exercised by her parents, only strengthening the bond between them. Thee always felt a special tenderness for her and resolved to do something for others similarly afflicted. He helped to found and fund the New York Orthopedic Dispensary and Hospital, turning ever more to the concerns that would consume him.

On October 27, 1858, they had a second child, their first son. It was a most difficult delivery. They called the eight-pound boy Theodore. He was promptly dubbed "Teedie" (he would always hate Teddy) to differentiate him from his father. Mittie thought him the homeliest child she had ever laid eyes on, and loved him all the more. Young Theodore Roosevelt would be the first American president to be born in a great city.

The Roosevelts had two more children—Elliott, called "Ellie," in 1860, and Corinne, called "Conie," in 1861. None was entirely healthy. Bamie might have been crippled for life, but for young Teedie it would be a question of life itself. Almost from birth, he had difficulty breathing. His asthma became so severe that he could sleep only when propped up in bed or wrapped in blankets in a chair. Both parents attended to him around the clock.

"My really great father," Teedie recalled, "saved my life. . . . I remember . . . him carrying me . . . in my battles for breath, up and down a room all night. . . . I could breathe, I could sleep when he had me in his arms. . . . He got me breath, he got me lungs, strength, life." Even on blustery winter nights, Thee would have the carriage brought around and bundle his son in rugs, holding him tight, while they raced through the silent streets to catch the air. Still, Thee must sometimes have pondered what terrible fate had brought so beautiful a mother as Mittie such homely children, and so vigorous a father as himself such debilitating sickness in his offspring.

As Teedie grew, in Churchill's words, "into a wan wistful child, with a wide mouth, large teeth, unruly hair, and spindly legs," it was believed by physicians that if he exerted himself as little as possible he might somehow outgrow the asthma. His father suspected otherwise. Might not a more active, stronger body provide the best antidote to any ailment? Of the quality of Teedie's mind there was soon no doubt. From an early age he demonstrated curiosity and creativity. Like his father, he loved the outdoors, whatever the doctors might advise. He was particularly interested in everything relating to the natural world, perhaps birds most of all. He loved to talk, inheriting his mother's volubility. His bursts of nervous energy amazed and sometimes perplexed his parents, although he tired quickly.

He came to view his older sister as almost an adult. He felt closer to Conie and Ellie, defining them as "we three" against the world. Teedie learned to read and write early and easily and, despite the weakness of his eyes, started keeping a diary of his observations by the time he was ten. He would read any book he could find, and books were abundant in his home. If only Teedie were strong enough, Thee vowed, the boy must go to college. His father early settled on Harvard.

By the time Teedie arrived, Thee was well launched on his true vocation. His personal commitment to philanthropy became less an avocation than an obsession. His friend John Hay referred to Roosevelt's "maniacal benevolence." Others, seeing him approach with his great strides, the glint in his eyes, would simply ask, "How much this time, Theodore?" Thee restlessly roamed the city. Seeing shivering newsboys on street corners, he founded a Newsboys Lodging House. He would spend every Sunday evening there, encouraging the boys without a trace of condescension. Monday nights Thee set aside for visiting families in New York's rapidly expanding slums. He often picked up stray kittens on his rounds. Naturally, he helped to found the Society for the Prevention of Cruelty to Animals, as he had the Young Men's Christian Association. Seeing so many homeless children on the city's streets, he initiated the Children's Aid Society. He served on every charitable board he could induce the city and state of New York to set up, never taking a salary.

"One must live for the living," Thee would insist. Thee's politics were largely an amalgam of well-intentioned reforms. Labels mattered little. Originally a Democrat, Thee would become, to his wife's consternation, a Lincoln Republican. His hope, as McCullough points out, was for what New York might become—a melting-pot symbol for the nation, as the nation should be for the world. In his view, "no other city offered such opportunity for those wishing to do something for the good of mankind." He nurtured institutions that aided the blind and the deaf as well as schools for immigrant children. He helped to found the Metropolitan Museum of Art and the American Museum of Natural History. He seemed, he said, never to tire.

But Thee was hardly one-dimensional. As his friend Louisa Lee Schuyler remembered, "His sense of enjoyment was great; his love . . . of riding and driving and boating was as strong at forty-six as at sixteen. Who more than he enjoyed a four-in-hand drive in the park, or a waltz in the ballroom? . . . I can see him now, in full evening dress, serving a most generous supper to his newsboys in the Lodging House, and later dashing off to an evening party in Fifth Avenue." It was a charmed life, interrupted only by the drums of war.

In 1861 Thee had a most agonizing decision to make. Although he had helped organize a massive antiwar rally in New York after Fort Sumter, there could be no doubt of his loyalties. Yet he could not bring himself to fight against his wife's kin. Instead, he risked his life in other ways, helping to form an Allotment Commission and traveling from one army camp to another, often on the front lines, to convince Union soldiers to send a portion of their paychecks home. He also supported the Sanitary Commission, predecessor of the Red Cross, and the Freedmans Bureau. If Teedie later viewed Thee's decision not to fight in the Civil War as his exemplary father's single blemish, there is no record of it.

However fastidious he was about his attire and appearance, Thee enjoyed nothing more than roughhousing with his children. He taught them how to climb trees, ride, and sail, how to appreciate nature in all its forms. What he provided, as his younger son Ellie put it, was the gift of sympathy, his great heart, "the sunshine of his affection." In the family prayers that started each day, the children would gather around their father in the library, their most cherished place the "cubbyhole" next to him on the sofa. Afterward, he would often send Teedie out to buy fresh strawberries from a nearby market for breakfast. The signs, sounds, and smells of the city were not foreign to these privileged children. Nor was affection. Mittie referred to the sessions of hugging her children as "family melts."

By the time Teedie was ten, his bedroom had been transformed into his own personal Roosevelt natural history museum, although live turtles and stuffed woodchucks sometimes found their way all over the house. Despite such activity, both parents were alarmed by Teedie's pallor and the lack of development in his frail physique, as well as the generally poor health of their other children. Mittie suggested a bracing tour of Europe. Thee worked out the itinerary. The children preferred the more leisurely summers they had enjoyed, most recently in Oyster Bay, Long Island—an "enchanting" place of "special delights," as Conie Roosevelt recalled it.

In 1869, like it or not, the full Roosevelt family embarked on their tour. For Teedie the trip was a revelation. Tirelessly touring museums, Teedie protested, "If only Raphael had painted landscapes instead of church things." A highlight was the festive celebration of his eleventh birthday in Cologne. His parents attended in full dinner dress. Having seen them dance with such effortless ease only heightened Teedie's resolve to join "the fellowship of the doers." He yearned to become stronger.

His father concurred. Thee took his son aside and gave him the advice that would shape his life. "You have the mind," Thee said, "but not the body. Without the help of the body the mind cannot go as far as it should. You must *make* your body. It is hard drudgery ... but I know you will do it." Thee transformed the second-floor piazza into a fully furnished gym. It may have been intended for all his children, but it became Teedie's haunt. Hour after hour he lifted dumbbells, worked with horizontal bars, and punched a large bag. The gym was not drudgery to Teedie, it was salvation. He gloried in any modestly measurable improvement in his body.

By the time Teedie returned from a second family trip to Europe, this one extending to the Near East and Africa, he was all but physically transformed. So vast a fresh territory also offered opportunities for endless explorations and specimens to add to his collections. After a hike along the Nile delta, his exhausted but obviously pleased father remarked, "I walked through the bogs with him at the risk of sinking hopelessly and helplessly for hours. . . . I felt that I must keep up with Teedie."

Thee returned home some months before the rest of his family. When they finally arrived back in October 1873, he had a staggering surprise waiting for them. He had secretly supervised the construction of an immense new home, more a mansion, on West Fifty-seventh Street, near the green expanse of Central Park. Thee told Mittie, "We have now probably one abiding resting place for the rest of our days."

With the aid of an excellent tutor, Teedie was accepted at Harvard in the class of 1880. In October of his freshman year, he wrote his father, "I have kept the first letter you wrote me and shall do my best to deserve your trust." By the fall of his sophomore year, Teedie knew that his father was sick with an undetermined ailment and likely tried to cheer him up when he wrote home on December 8, 1877, "I am anticipating the most glorious fun during the holidays."

Always reform-minded but politically naïve, Thee was surprised to hear from President Rutherford B. Hayes that he would be nominated as collector of customs for the port of New York. Political bosses Roscoe Conkling and Thomas Platt weren't about to let such a plum fall into scrupulously honest hands. They delayed Roosevelt's confirmation by the United States Senate until it could be narrowly rejected. Thee was relieved but distraught. He wrote "Dear Old Theodore" on December 16, 1877, "A great weight has been taken off my shoulders. . . . I feel sorry for the country, however, as it shows the power of the politicians who think only of their own interests." He did not mention his illness.

Thee seemed better when Teedie returned from college for his much-awaited Christmas vacation. Perhaps his son's arrival served as a tonic. Teedie proudly wrote in his diary his father's pronouncement "that after all I was the dearest of his children to him." Now, even more, he must prove worthy of "the best and most loving of men." After Teedie had returned to Cambridge, his family finally learned the truth about Thee's illness. There had been only a brief period of remission. What had been initially diagnosed as "peritonitis" was in fact inoperable cancer of the bowel. The urgent telegram went to young Theodore on February 9 to come home as quickly as possible.

"He was everything to me," Teedie wrote three days after his father died, "the one I loved dearest on earth." When he had finally recovered from "the first sharpness of grief," Teedie wrote his mother on March 24, 1878, "Darling Little Motherling, I have just been looking over a letter of my dear Father's. I do not even think I *could* do anything wrong while I have his letters."

"My father . . . was the best man I ever knew," Teedie recalled. "He combined strength and courage with gentleness, tenderness and great unselfishness." Yet Thee had insisted, "One must live for the living."

His admonitions had been simple and direct: "Get action!" "Seize the moment!" "Whatever you do, enjoy it." Six years later Teedie's mother and his young wife would die within hours of each other in the same house, which his brother Elliott now viewed as "cursed." Young Theodore Roosevelt went on to rebuild his life, follow a career far removed from ornithology, marry a second supportive wife, father six children, and try to emulate every cherished detail of a childhood marred only by sickness.

As it turned out, his tenure as president began on his father's birthday. His sisters happened to be visiting. "It is a good omen," he told them. "I feel as if my father's hand were on my shoulder and as if there were a special blessing on the life I should lead here."

# 9

# "My Will Is the Better Man"

## Alphonso Taft

ALTHOUGH GENERALLY A KINDLY MODEL of rectitude, Alphonso Taft prodded his genial, "lazy" son, Will, "foremost in talents," to excel—only belatedly appreciating that the boy's deliberative nature represented a judicial temperament much like his own.

After feeling the biceps of heavyweight boxing champion John L. Sullivan, Judge Alphonso Taft of Cincinnati is reputed to have said, probably with at least a slight smile, "My Will is the better man." Certainly powerful William Howard Taft was the bigger man. By the time he became president he weighed more than 325 pounds, considerably more than any other chief executive in history. Alphonso's regard for his son was hardly limited to his strength. He encouraged—one might say more than encouraged—all his children, but for whatever reasons, he early decided that Will was "foremost" in talents among them. It would prove quite a burden for the boy—and for the man he became.

Alphonso Taft was most frequently described by those who knew him as "kindly" and "gentle." His son Will declared, "A man never had . . . a dearer, kinder, more considerate father." Will's wife, Nellie, described her father-in-law as "gentle beyond anything I ever knew." True, Alphonso's demeanor could seem as austere as the granite hills of his native Vermont, but as Henry Pringle, the leading Taft biographer, writes, "The austerity of Alphonso Taft masked a gentleness and sweetness far more familiar to the children than the austerity itself."

Yet one of his sons, who had been first in his class at Yale, had a nervous breakdown and died in a sanitarium at the age of forty-three. Another, who was probably in fact the brightest of Taft's children, defied his father's

150

Alphonso Taft

intention that he practice law (all the sons studied law, although not all practiced it) in order to found a school, a plan that Alphonso viewed as "fanciful." Even Will, the repository of the most sustained parental pressures, wrote back rather plaintively from Yale, "You expect great things from me, but you mustn't be disappointed if I don't come up to your expectations." Of course, his father, and his mother as well, *would* be disappointed were that to happen. To his classmates at Yale, who envied Will's receipt of so many letters from home, he explained that letter-writing was viewed as "a recreation" by his father.

If such stress made John Quincy Adams lose weight, it had the opposite effect on William Howard Taft. His immense size may have been originally due to a glandular condition, but it was probably increased through overeating. To Alphonso Taft, parents were measured by their children's achievements and their character. Will Taft was not lazy, although eventually even he came to believe it. He was deliberative, his judicial temperament very much like his father's. What he craved even more than food was his parents' approval.

Born on November 5, 1810, at his family's farm near Townshend in the Vermont uplands, Alphonso Taft was in the fifth generation of his family to reside in New England. Alphonso's father, Peter Rawson Taft, a good-natured but unsuccessful farmer, was also a self-educated lawyer who became a judge. He managed well enough to send Alphonso to college, first to Amherst and then to Yale. Both frugal and energetic, Alphonso is reputed to have walked all the way to New Haven.

By the time he was twenty, Alphonso weighed a strapping two hundred pounds. He remained clean-shaven throughout his life, and was quite handsome, with a thatch of dark hair, penetrating eyes, and a firm mouth, but a rather prominent nose. In every photograph of Alphonso that survives, his gaze is set and serious. After graduating Phi Beta Kappa in 1833, he taught school for a time in Connecticut and then went back to Yale to earn his law degree in 1838. Alphonso may have enjoyed his childhood, but as a place to prosper he viewed Vermont much as a contemporary characterized New Hampshire: "It is a noble state to emigrate from."

He looked to establish his practice in a major city. Traveling as far west as Ohio, by canal boat, stage, and railroad, he was impressed by Cincinnati. Already called "the Queen City," it was growing rapidly, with over 40,000 inhabitants. There was a good deal of legal business and, as he wrote his parents, "very few men of the Bar of much talent." He settled there, and never had cause to regret it. He then set about renewing his acquaintance with pretty Fanny Phelps, daughter of a Vermont judge. Fanny and Alphonso were married on August 29, 1841. She was only eighteen; he was thirty.

Alphonso prospered in Cincinnati. His careful preparation of cases and dignified courtroom bearing belied his age. He became active in politics, later helping to form the new Republican Party. In Fanny he found an ideal helpmate. Immersed in charitable and church activities, she considered their life together an "unbroken sea of happiness." Unfortunately, it lasted only eleven years. Fanny was very delicate, and she died of what was probably tuberculosis in 1852, at the age of only twenty-nine. She left Alphonso with two young sons, Charles Phelps and Peter Rawson Taft.

It is no reflection on his fond memories of Fanny that within a year Alphonso was back in New England seeking a new wife and a mother for his boys. In Massachusetts he met charming, spirited, dark-haired twenty-five-year-old Louisa Marie Torrey, whom everyone called "Louise."

Encouraged by their progressive parents, Louise and her older sister, Delia, had set out to lead independent lives. Unfortunately, it was getting a bit expensive for their father. Alphonso pronounced Louise "a splendid woman—one of whom a man might be proud." Unfortunately, he was seventeen years her senior, and seemingly so stolid.

It took some persistence, but Alphonso finally won Louise's heart by appealing to her head, convincing her that he respected her ideas and would grant her what today would be called her "space." They were married at the home of her parents on December 26, 1853. Alphonso was forty-three, Louise twenty-six. By any measure the marriage was a success. True to his word, Alphonso encouraged his wife's interests. Her ebullience brought him out in a manner not unlike Mittie Roosevelt's effect on Theodore Sr.

Louise's endless activities—her charities, book clubs, art lessons, musicales, foreign language classes—never interfered with her husband's career or with her primary role as a wife, and later as a mother. She turned herself from a free spirit into a highly capable manager, always referring to her husband as "Mr. Taft," and maintaining a Victorian respectability in their large Mt. Auburn house. There was no drinking, smoking, or swearing in the Taft home. To the social elite of Cincinnati, the Tafts were less a fashionable family than a highly respected one. They represented a kind of paradox—open-minded and progressive in their ideas, old-fashioned and conformist in their family structure. In religion they were Unitarians.

To her sister, Delia, Louise confided, "I delight in large families." She hoped to have as many children as possible but feared she had started too late. Her joy with the birth of her first child, "Sammie," was dashed when he died of whooping cough shortly after his first birthday. Alphonso could commiserate; he had lost children in infancy during his first marriage. Perhaps that is what made the birth of William Howard Taft even more special to both his parents. Their first child together—that is, their first surviving son—was born at home on September 15, 1857. There would be two more boys, and a girl, to join Alphonso's two sons by his first wife. High achievement would be expected of each of them, but the burden fell hardest on William.

That he was such a pleasant child seemed a promising presentiment to Louise. Little Sammie had been so passive. His parents called their son "Willie" at first, a name he came to profoundly dislike (as his friend Theodore Roosevelt disdained "Teddy"). Perhaps it seemed too suited to a jolly fat man. He would much prefer "Will" or "Bill." His mother gushed, "He is very large for his age and grows fat every day. . . . He has such a large waist that he cannot wear any of the dresses made with belts." When Will was only seven weeks old, Louise observed, "He spreads his hands to anyone who will take him and his face is wreathed in smiles at the slightest provocation." Could there be a more charming, cherubic child, with his flaxen curls and eyes of a light cerulean blue? Louise wrote to Delia, "I feel as if my hands and feet were tied to this baby," and to her mother, "I do not believe we can love our children too much."

Certainly Will was spoiled in his early years. His parents showered attention and affection on him. When Will was eight, Louise insisted, "I have more pride in Willie than in all the rest." Alphonso concurred in terms of his "noble, healthy, fast-growing boy." When Will turned fifteen, his father anointed him "the foremost" of his children, and added, "I am inclined to think he always will be." Affection had already turned to pressure.

Given his congenial nature, is it any wonder that throughout his life William Howard Taft would strive to please others, to satisfy their expectations of him? First it was his parents', then his wife's, then Theodore Roosevelt's, finally the Republican Party's and the nation's. Even as president, as Pringle writes, Taft was "a large, good-natured body, entirely surrounded by people who know exactly what they want."

It is not quite true that Alphonso Taft's ambitions for himself were limited to the legal and local. They were, however, subordinated to his standards. He would not promote himself or stoop to expediency. How could he preach ethical conduct to his children if he compromised for his own advancement? It would cost him his highest career aspirations. As an independent-minded city councilman, Alphonso voted his conscience. He was never a party regular, even as he attended conventions as a delegate of the Republican Party he had helped to form. Alphonso supported the Union cause throughout the Civil War, although he had expressed to Southern friends his hopes that the conflict might have been averted. Always opposed to slavery, Alphonso had taken Louise to an abolitionist convention in 1854, where they heard Frederick Douglass. As a three-term judge of Cincinnati's superior court, Alphonso was so praised for his probity that friends promoted him for high elective office. He failed twice, however, to win the Republican nomination for governor of Ohio. Nor would he be appointed to the United States Supreme Court, his logical goal. He ran early and unsuccessfully for Congress and never caught on as a potential national candidate.

Taft did serve, however, for a short time in Washington in 1876 as President Grant's secretary of war and later as attorney general. In this capacity he was obliged to establish the electoral commission that settled the controversial Hayes-Tilden presidential election of 1876. Somehow Taft escaped any taint of involvement in this period's pervasive political controversy and corruption. He was probably relieved to return home, Louise less so—although she was disappointed in official and social Washington. Most hostesses along the Potomac were little more literate than the provincial matrons of Cincinnati.

"To be the founders of a family," Alphonso wrote, "is a great matter." Even in grammar school, Will worked harder than other children, anxious to gratify his parents. He *was* bright. His father was right about that. But he was hardly brilliant—he was a plodder, not a plunger. His anxiety was also evident through all the good cheer. So was his bulk. Called "Lub" or "Lubbers" or even "Roly-Poly Boy" by his classmates, he was more teased than ridiculed. It was hard to dislike earnest Will Taft. Will loved sports. He was an excellent hitter in baseball but—not surprisingly—couldn't run very fast. Later in his life, despite his size, he would enjoy horseback riding and golf. By the time he entered high school, Will was certain he wanted to be a lawyer—and, he hoped, one day a judge, like his father. Graduating second in his class at Woodward High School in 1874 at the age of sixteen, at commencement Will spoke on the importance of woman's suffrage. If his parents were disappointed in his standing (why not first?), they can't have opposed his stand.

Emulating his father again, Will went off to Yale, probably feeling both apprehension and anticipation. Pressure even came from Will's half-brothers. Peter Taft wrote him, "We expect you younger boys, who have had the benefits of our experience in education, to do great things. Never be content until you have done the very best you could have done. . . . Work hard and do your part in building up the reputation of the family."

Pringle describes Will during his years at Yale as, naturally enough, "big and heavy," with "fair skin, blue eyes, and light hair. He was good-natured, but authority marked his bigness and integrity his personality." In his twenties he had already started to grow his trademark flowing mustache and looked much as he would throughout his life. Historian Stephen Hess describes Will in later years as appearing to have legs too short for his torso. "His face was ruddy with a blondish mustache and dark hair. Despite his great bulk he was light on his feet and a great dancer." Unlike pictures of his father, photographs of the mature William Howard Taft frequently show him smiling, and almost invariably looking benign.

By all accounts Will became the most admired man in his class at Yale. He exuded, at least on the surface, calm and confidence, and was an acknowledged leader. He neither smoked nor drank, except for an occasional beer. He joked about his weight, but, as later in his life, could be tough as well as gentle. Competition was keener at Yale. Taft had to work even harder, and his prodigious cramming for exams became almost legendary. His analytical mind was not ideally suited to the constraints of a collegiate calendar. Good-humored at most times, generous and helpful to others, Will was not to be bothered when he was studying—the image of his demanding father almost a physical presence to him.

Alphonso would not permit Will to row or play football, viewing both activities as a waste of valuable time. For that matter, could he have even fitted into a racing shell? Alphonso also suggested that Will decline a coveted bid to Skull and Bones, Yale's most selective secret society, even though Alphonso had helped to found it. For once Will disobeyed his father. Alphonso even questioned the value of having too many friends, writing, "I doubt that such popularity is consistent with scholarship." By dint of effort no less immense than his size, in a class of 132 Taft came in second in the final academic evaluation, as he had in high school. His senior oration was on "The Professional and Political Prospects of the College Graduate." Will pondered his own. Had he let his parents down?

Taft went on in 1878 to relatively slow-paced Cincinnati Law School, which allowed him to lapse into at least a measure of recreational lethargy that had been impossible at Yale. He read law in his father's office, enjoyed an active social life, and passed the bar, but worked for a time as a newspaper reporter covering the law courts. In 1880 he finally settled into public life, with his appointment as assistant prosecutor of Hamilton County.

Defeated in his final quest for the Republican nomination for governor of Ohio, Alphonso withdrew from private practice, the end of Alphonso Taft and Sons. Will's future preoccupied him ever more. "I do not think you have accomplished this year as much as you ought," Alphonso wrote him. "Our anxiety for your success is very great and I know that there is but one way to attain it, and that is by self-denial and enthusiastic hard work in the profession. . . . This gratifying your fondness for society is fruitless." But nonetheless such "fondness" was enjoyable to Will, and he wasn't about to give it up. In 1886 he married bright, strong-willed Helen Herron, whom everyone called "Nellie." He had pursued her for years. If possible, she was even more ambitious for Will's success, reflecting her own, than were his parents.

From 1880 on, Will Taft was employed in public service of one kind or another for most of the next thirty-two years. In 1887, Will was made a judge on the superior court of Ohio, as his father had been. In 1890 President Benjamin Harrison appointed him solicitor general of the United States. Two years later Will was named a judge of the United States Circuit Court of Appeals. Perhaps he was "foremost" after all. "I like judicial life," he confided to his father, who by now must have recognized his son's similar temperament. Will was less comfortable as a practicing attorney, particularly pleading cases in a courtroom.

When he was seventy-two, his own career seemingly coming to a close, Alphonso received astonishing news. He had been named American minister to the court of Austria-Hungary. Why? Alphonso had no prior diplomatic experience, nor had he expressed interest in such a posting. He understood that its requirements were largely ceremonial and sensed that Louise might be behind it. He was right. She had quietly influenced President Chester Arthur to name her husband. At last she would have the opportunity to preside over festive social events and mingle with people of the highest quality and taste. Alphonso could not disappoint her. After all, her life for nearly thirty years had been circumscribed by caring for her husband and family.

In regal Vienna, Louise blossomed, her grasp of languages and enduring vivacity an immense asset in diplomatic and social circles. Alphonso became a rather bewildered appendage in her wake, but he was happy for her. He was subsequently named ambassador to Imperial Russia, and Louise similarly dazzled official St. Petersburg. Will came over to see them. He was now married and the father of Robert Alphonso Taft, born in 1889. Nellie was pregnant with the second of their three children. "I am very happy in your prospects," Alphonso told Will.

After a particularly severe Russian winter, Alphonso's health began to fail. He and Louise returned not to Cincinnati but to lengthen their final days together in the warm California sun. Louise wrote Will from San Diego with perceptive reflection, "What a resource is a cultivated mind. What can people do when old and sick without intellectual resources?" They still had much to talk about—the hallmark of a good marriage. Alphonso wrote Will with wry poignancy, asking that he consider "the fate of an old man who has to be across the continent from the best children in the world." Finally, in the spring of 1891, sitting by Alphonso's bed, Will saw his father, who had been drifting in and out of consciousness, look up at him, "and in the sweetest way imaginable" smile and say, "Will, I love you beyond expression." It was all he had ever hoped to hear. Alphonso died peacefully shortly thereafter, on May 21, 1891, at the age of eighty. His body was brought back to Cincinnati, as he had directed. Funeral services were in his Mt. Auburn home, and then he was borne by his sons to burial in Spring Grove Cemetery. In tangible form he had little to leave his family after a lifetime of labor—a good name, their home, and $482.80.

As Alphonso once said, the Tafts bred "men who knew how to get rich and men who dared to be poor." He had spent his substance bringing up his family. Will had written him in appreciation of the education and travel he had afforded them, "Certainly that is something for you to be proud of and for us to be thankful to you for."

Anticipating the end, Will had told his wife, "I have a kind of presentiment that Father has been a kind of guardian angel to me in that his wishes for my success have been so strong and intense as to bring it, and as his life ebbs away and ends I shall cease to have the luck that has followed me thus far." Will went on, "It is some satisfaction" that his own judicial career had been launched "at a time when it added to Father's happiness."

Louise had come to understand that Will, like his father, was simply too guileless to scheme and plot a successful political career. Alphonso had always told Will, "To be chief justice is more than to be president." Differing with Nellie Taft's ambitions, Louise stated publicly, "I do not want my son to be president. . . . His is a judicial mind, and he loves the law." It was too late, or perhaps too early. With Theodore Roosevelt's blessing, William Howard Taft was elected president, a most unhappy one, in 1908, and was defeated for reelection in 1912. Nine years later, at the age of sixty-four, he finally satisfied himself—and proved his parents right. President Harding named him Chief Justice of the United States.

No one would have appreciated better than Alphonso Taft this exchange between Supreme Court Justice Louis Brandeis and future Justice Felix Frankfurter. "It's very difficult for me to understand," Brandeis said, "why a man who is so good as chief justice . . . could have been so bad as president." Frankfurter replied, "The explanation is very simple. He loathed being president and being chief justice was all happiness for him." William Howard Taft would leave an estate a thousand times larger than his father's, but they shared the same values.

When, in 1907, his mother's health was failing and Will hesitated to go on an around-the-world tour because of her condition, she intervened. The trip was intended by his friend (and future foe), Theodore Roosevelt, to enhance Taft's prepresidential stature. Although she opposed its purpose, Louise was as firm with Will at fifty as she had been when he was fifteen. She told her son, "No Taft, to my knowledge, has ever neglected a public duty for the sake of gratifying a private desire." Alphonso Taft couldn't have said it better.

# 10

## "You Have Only to Persevere"

### Joseph Ruggles Wilson

THE PRESBYTERIAN COVENANTER FAITH shared by the learned Reverend Doctor Joseph Ruggles Wilson and his son Woodrow guided both to the conviction that the youth was destined for greatness, leading him to a remarkable career culminating in universal prophecy.

For a short time between 1917 and 1920, Woodrow Wilson would be admired, even loved, to an extent few statesmen in history have experienced. But throughout his life, in private as well as in public, he seemed to require constant reassurance. Seemingly so austere and cerebral, Wilson actually enjoyed it when someone in a crowd would yell "Woody" at him, implying at least a measure of the public affection regularly showered on his ebullient competitor, "Teddy" Roosevelt, a more natural politician.

Yet affection was hardly lacking in Wilson's childhood. Unlike William Howard Taft, who wore his heart on his sleeve but whose praise from his parents could be conditional, Thomas Woodrow Wilson enjoyed effusive expressions of affection from both his parents. To his mother, Jessie, he could do no wrong. "You have never been anything but a comfort to me all your life!" she wrote him late in her own. "God bless you, darling boy." To the boy's more demanding father, the imposing Reverend Doctor Joseph Ruggles Wilson, "Tommy" *could* do wrong, but only if he went against his nature or compromised his standards. He was destined for greatness.

It is impossible to overestimate the importance of the certainty of his father's Covenanter faith to Woodrow Wilson. As he informed incredulous political associates in 1912, "I am a Presbyterian and believe in pre-

Joseph Ruggles Wilson (center), Woodrow Wilson (extreme left), members of the family, and servants

destination. . . . God ordained that I be the next president of the United States." Wilson intoned to the United States Senate in 1919, seeking their unqualified approval of the Treaty of Versailles and his vision for a League of Nations, "The stage is set, the destiny disclosed . . . the light streams upon the path ahead, and nowhere else." One doesn't compromise with destiny. Given the enduring influence of his father, it is not surprising that Wilson ultimately set out to redeem the world, finally giving up any semblance of policy for prophecy.

The fervid correspondence between father and son reads almost like love letters. Even when critical of his "precious son" for some perceived lapse, Joseph Wilson would conclude, "*You* have only to persevere. . . . It is just because of my love for you that I have always tried to be faithful in telling you the truth about yourself." Or, on a happier occasion, "My dearest boy—How much we all love you cannot be put into words, and we are proud of you besides." If Wilson felt the pressure of such intimidating expectations, he also came to believe that happiness could result only from high achievement.

The Wilsons had been Americans for only a generation when they became Southerners by choice. Woodrow's father was born in Ohio, his

Joseph Ruggles
Wilson

mother in England. All four of his grandparents had been born abroad. In 1807, at the age of twenty, Woodrow's paternal grandfather, the gregarious, enterprising James Wilson, arrived in Philadelphia from Scotland by way of Ireland, driven more by ambition than destitution. After marrying a devout young lady named Anne Adams, whom he had met aboard ship, and learning the printer's trade, James set out for Ohio in 1815. He settled in Steubenville and rose quickly to both affluence and prominence, eventually becoming the proprietor of newspapers in both Ohio and Pennsylvania. Wilson was named a justice of the peace, was elected to the state legislature, and became an elder of the Presbyterian church. The Wilsons had ten children. Joseph Ruggles Wilson, their last child and seventh son, was born in Steubenville on February 28, 1822. Within only a few years it became clear to his parents that this last of their progeny was probably also their brightest and best. Joseph was dutiful and studious, excelling at the local Male Academy, religious like his mother, and outgoing and forceful, like his father. He was also strikingly good-looking. As Woodrow Wilson would later say of him, "If I had my father's face and figure, it wouldn't make any difference what I said."

James was intent that this son must have a college education. Joseph didn't disappoint him, graduating in 1844 as valedictorian of his class at Jefferson College (later Washington and Jefferson) in Canonsburg, Pennsylvania. He became a schoolmaster for a time, studied at a Pennsylvania seminary, and then went on to graduate from Princeton Theological Seminary, as had Richard Cleveland. Before being ordained, Joseph returned to teach at his old school in Steubenville.

There was also a companion Female Academy in town. One of its students was nineteen-year-old Janet Woodrow, whom everyone called "Jessie." She was almost painfully shy, but her keen intelligence had so impressed her father, the Reverend Thomas Woodrow, that he determined to enhance her education. Described by writer Doris Faber as slender, "whispy-haired," and "possessing an ethereal quality that substituted quite effectively for mere earthly beauty," Jessie made the acquaintance of young Joseph Wilson. He was already regarded as a preacher of promise and a teacher of uncommon ability. He was also, at a sturdy six feet, with his thick brown hair, regular features, and penetrating gaze, quite the handsomest man she had ever laid eyes on.

The attraction was mutual. On June 7, 1849, only a few weeks before his ordination by the Presbytery of Ohio, twenty-seven-year-old Joseph Ruggles Wilson married twenty-two-year-old Jessie Woodrow in Chillicothe, Ohio. Jessie's father, who performed the nuptials, could not have been more delighted. It seemed a promising merger as well as a marriage. As biographer John Mulder writes, the Woodrows were a more distinguished family than the Wilsons, "tracing their ancestry back to prominent Scottish divines across six generations." The family of Woodrow Wilson was the most ecclesiastical of any American president. His earliest political heroes were English, particularly the great Liberal prime minister William Gladstone.

Joseph Wilson would always feel most fulfilled when he was enabled to both teach and preach. After his wedding, he served as an instructor in rhetoric at his old college and at the same time was pastor of a small Pennsylvania church. Word of his erudition spread. In 1853 he was offered a promising professorship at Hampden-Sydney College in Virginia. A measure of the breadth of his knowledge was that he taught chemistry as well as natural science. For the remainder of their lives together, Joseph and Jessie Wilson resided in the South, and their children would think of themselves as Southerners. Distinguished Wilson scholar Arthur Link notes that when news reports surfaced that President Wilson was the son of an old Virginia family, he replied, "I wish I could say it were true."

The Wilsons had four children, the first two girls. Marian was born in 1851. Two years later Annie arrived. In 1855, the Reverend Wilson was called to the pastorate of the First Presbyterian Church in the lovely Virginia town of Staunton, nestled in the Shenandoah Valley. Here, in the spacious manse that still stands, on December 28, 1856, the Wilsons' first son was born. He was not named Joseph Ruggles Wilson Jr. but Thomas Woodrow Wilson, for his mother's favorite brother even more than for her father. "Junior" would be the Wilsons' second son and final child, born almost a decade later. "Little Tommy," as his mother almost immediately called him, was "a fine, healthy fellow," she announced with uncommon enthusiasm, "just as fat as he can be . . . [and] as little trouble as it is possible for a baby to be."

Wilson grew up with the Civil War. His first recollection, at the age of four, was standing at the gate of his parents' home, hearing passersby talk about the election of Abraham Lincoln. "This means war," one said, and he was right. The gateway was to a new home, deeper in the South. In 1857, the same year he received his doctor of divinity degree, Wilson ventured down to the larger community of Augusta, Georgia, to officiate at the wedding of his brother-in-law, Thomas Woodrow. While in town, he was asked to preach at the First Presbyterian Church, whose prominent pulpit had recently become vacant. Wilson's eloquence made so strong an impression that he was invited to become their minister. The offer was enhanced by the construction of a handsome new brick manse. He and his family would spend the next twelve years in Augusta, the most productive of the Reverend Doctor Wilson's career.

Woodrow Wilson observed, "A boy never gets over his boyhood." The Civil War ended when he was not yet nine. It not only delayed his formal education, but his father's decision to side with the South colored Woodrow's later views in many areas. Through prayer and reflection, Joseph Wilson decided that God's will ordained the preservation of the established order in the South, even if that resulted in secession, war, and the continuation of slavery. The First General Assembly of the Confederate States of America was held in Wilson's church in Augusta, and he was elected its permanent clerk. Aside from the sadness of separation from their Northern brethren, it was an extraordinary distinction for so young a clergyman.

Despite Augusta's status as a major supply center for the Confederacy and a good deal of fighting in the vicinity, tangibly the Wilson family suffered surprisingly little in the Civil War. The church building itself was damaged. Later its sanctuary served as an emergency hospital and its grounds as a stockade for Union prisoners. It must have been an exciting time for a young boy, but Woodrow tended to be rather removed from it all, a dreamy and solitary child. He liked to play with his armada of toy ships, working out complicated maneuvers. During the war years, the family drew even closer together.

Daily devotions and Sunday school continued even as regular school was interrupted. It was followed on every Lord's Day, as in peacetime, by two church services, highlighted by the Reverend Doctor Wilson's sermons and by singing hymns at home in the evening. Woodrow loved the music, and praying aloud. He would always prefer the simplicity of the Presbyterian service to all others, but he believed in being demonstrative in one's worship. He also began to try to emulate his father's eloquence. Gladstone had a competitor.

Woodrow's mother and his sisters were his first teachers, reading aloud to him, but his father became his closest companion. Biographer George Osborn stresses that Woodrow and Joseph were inseparable, playing everything from tag to chess and walking everywhere together, the father instructing the son in the significance of everything they observed. Their relationship developed even more fully after the war. Woodrow found in his father his most informative teacher, particularly in the use of language, spoken and written. Rhetoric was the key to success. Even after he started taking lessons from a former Confederate officer in a small school in Augusta, Woodrow still looked to his father for inspiration. Finally going to a school, however, brought the boy out a bit. He learned to play with others and found he loved baseball—and even more enjoyed organizing the games.

Yet why did he have such difficulty learning to read? Even after the dislocations of war, it was a perplexing question. Tommy Woodrow Wilson had what today would be called a learning disability. It was probably dyslexia, and it took a great deal of effort to overcome. It is likely that Woodrow couldn't fully comprehend what he read until he was eleven or twelve years old. One result was his interest in shorthand, which he could understand more readily than Greek or Latin—or English.

In 1870, the Reverend Doctor Wilson received an appointment, actually two appointments, that seemed the capstone of his career. He had become "stated clerk" of the Southern Presbyterians and was reluctant to leave his congregation in Augusta, but he had been called to a greater challenge, as minister of the much larger First Presbyterian Church in Columbia, South Carolina. At the same time, Wilson was asked to accept a professorship in pastoral theology at Columbia Theological Seminary. Wilson fully expected to remain in these dual capacities for the remainder of his career, but his tenure would last for only four turbulent years.

Woodrow went off, at his parents' behest, in 1873 to leafy Davidson College in North Carolina, then as now the leading liberal arts college in the South and closely affiliated with the Presbyterian church. It was his intention to become a distinguished divine like his father. But being on his own for the first time opened new vistas for reflection. To win the world one must be *in* the world. By all accounts, Wilson did well at Davidson, both in its demanding curriculum and outside the classroom. Not surprisingly, given his father's influence, he was particularly interested in debating and literary pursuits. He dropped the name Tommy as not quite mature enough for a grown man. He played baseball and other sports. He made fast friends and developed an affection for the college that never dimmed. But around the end of his freshman year, he suffered the first of his rather mysterious breakdowns—physical, emotional, or both—which it took him over a year of recuperation at home to recover from. He did not return to Davidson for his sophomore year.

Meanwhile, Joseph Wilson's difficulties in Columbia were mounting. They stemmed initially from his church congregation's desire to have a full-time minister. Someone less stubborn might have dealt with and disposed of such understandable concerns quickly and equitably. Wilson could not. In this, as in other ways, father and son surely were similar. Both suffered from bleak periods of depression throughout their lives that could be overcome only by sustained work. Neither ever developed a capacity for compromise. Wilson once advised his son, "I would rather have you think too much of yourself than too little." In personality the Reverend Doctor Wilson could be most agreeable. He was worldly enough to play billiards as well as chess, to banter with his parishioners and students, and even to take an occasional nip of scotch. He believed in such enlightened measures as higher education for women, but he sometimes magnified even trivial disagreements into questions of conscience.

After insisting "I know that I have done right," he left both his positions in Columbia. In 1874 he accepted the prestigious pulpit of the First Presbyterian Church of Wilmington, North Carolina, but he was embittered and discouraged. Despite staying there for eleven years, he was never quite the same. Even more, he urged Woodrow on to greater heights— "Let the esteem you have won be only a stimulant to fresh exertions"— but this was still accompanied by reassuring affection, should his son, too, face inevitable disappointments. "I am not in the least blaming you. . . . I could not do so, my precious son, my precious friend." When they met, they embraced.

Despite his fragile constitution, Woodrow had considered applying to the naval academy, but he never regretted following his father's advice in 1875 to return to college at Princeton (it became Princeton University in 1896). He flourished there, not only in academics, which were not so rigorous as Davidson's, but in a variety of activities, from debating and baseball to editing the new college newspaper and joining a convivial eating club. Most important, before graduating in 1879, he resolved the general outline of his future. He would do the Lord's work outside of the ministry, hopefully eventuating in public service. If his father mourned the loss of a potentially great cleric, he voiced little regret. His son might do more good for humankind as a great statesman than confined to the clergy.

Woodrow decided to start by going to law school at the University of Virginia, entering in the fall of 1879. He found the study dry and didactic, but he persevered. His father remained his constant correspondent and mentor, editing and refining every written effort sent to him by his son. In a typical example, he wrote to Woodrow, "I return to you the mss. containing your discussion of cabinet government. I have read it and re-read it, and have ventured to make a few verbal corrections. . . . It might, with advantage, be made to *glow* a little more," but, of course, adding, "As it is, I feel proud of you and send you thanks for the pleasure this essay has given both your dear mother and myself." Sometimes Joseph Wilson would lapse back into self-justification. During Woodrow's first semester at Charlottesville, his father wrote him, "I am disposed that . . . half the battle of professional life . . . is won by first a manful declaration of independence as to surrounding circumstances, especially where . . . *duty* requires us to stand and fight."

The closest to a crisis in their relationship came when Woodrow pondered the possibility of withdrawing or even being dismissed from his legal studies at the University of Virginia. From his aggrieved father: "June 5, 1880, My dear son—Your pain-giving letter has just been received. I have all along had fear lest your frequent absences . . . end in grief, and tried to warn you but then I will add this—that come what may *you possess our confidence,* because we well know your character."

Woodrow fell sick again. At the behest of his parents, he came home. Doctors in Wilmington feared that if Woodrow stayed in Charlottesville, he might suffer damage to his digestive tract. He was permitted to complete his law studies at home, passed his examinations, and graduated in 1882. The following year he was admitted to the bar and set up a practice with a friend in Atlanta, but Woodrow's heart was never really in it. It was smitten, however, during his brief legal career when, visiting in Rome, Georgia, he met the bright-eyed, auburn-haired, demure Ellen Louise Axton, daughter of the local Presbyterian minister. He was married to his "Ellie Lou" two years later, in Savannah, on June 24, 1885, by his father and her grandfather.

The same year, the Reverend Doctor Wilson, admitting that "discouragement knocks at my door and, all too often, I let him . . . in," went back to teaching. It was hardly a Davidson or Princeton, but the relative backwater of Southwestern Presbyterian University in Clarksville, Tennessee. As his father's career receded, Woodrow told his bride, "I am more eager than I can tell you to be at my life's work." His drive to excel, implanted by his father, now came from within.

He would become a scholar and teacher, particularly of government, and then go on to a career of "effectual public service," ultimately to its highest level. Perhaps he had left Davidson, Charlottesville, and Atlanta prematurely, but in only seven focused years, Wilson rose to the heights of academia. Despite diminished financial resources, his father supported him unreservedly, financing his graduate studies. Between 1883 and 1890 Woodrow Wilson earned his Ph.D. at Johns Hopkins University, taught at Bryn Mawr and Wesleyan colleges, and finally joined the faculty of Princeton University itself. In 1902 he was named Princeton's president. In 1910 he was elected governor of New Jersey, and in the dramatic three-way race of 1912 was elected president of the United States—the only (and likely the last) professional academic to win the nation's highest office.

By 1885 Wilson had written his first major work, *Congressional Government,* to much acclaim. It was dedicated to his father, "the patient guide of his youth, the gracious companion of his manhood, and his best instructor and his most lenient critic." Well, perhaps not all that lenient. The Reverend Doctor Wilson was surely pleased but would never admit to being surprised. It was only the start.

Jessie Wilson died in 1888. Now lonely as well as depressed, his own health in decline, Joseph quit his final post and traveled from place to place, often serving as a guest preacher on Sundays. Back in Wilmington he was pleased to be remembered so fondly by his old parishioners. He had loved all four of his children; his oldest, Marian, died too young. Only sharing in Woodrow's growing renown provided the old man with a reason to go on living. In 1901 Wilson finally gave up his wanderings and his lifelong fight for faith and went to stay in Princeton with Woodrow and his family. He lived long enough to witness his son's ascension to a presidency, even if it was only of the university.

It would be pleasant to relate that the patriarch's final days were filled with joy. But in truth, they were difficult for everyone. Wilson's three daughters tired of hearing endlessly from this intrusive, ailing interloper that "your father is a very great man." A terribly painful gall bladder obstruction finally, mercifully, took his life. The Reverend Doctor Joseph Ruggles Wilson died at "Prospect," the Princeton president's home, on January 21, 1903, at the age of eighty. His body was taken to Columbia, South Carolina, where he was buried in the churchyard of his most prominent parish, next to his wife—both Southern by preference in life and death.

Wilson aptly memorialized his father as "a master of serious eloquence, a thinker of singular power and penetration, a thoughtful student of life and God's purpose, a lover and servant of his fellow man, a man of God." As biographer August Heckscher notes, Joseph "had instructed the boy in his youth, counseled him with rugged good sense, until without envy he had seen his son surpass him in worldly success." He need not witness it all. Only Woodrow Wilson's greatness had been foreseen by his father, not its final fulfillment. Few prophets die fulfilled.

# 11

# "I Hate to Go Away"

## George Tryon Harding II • John Calvin Coolidge
## Jesse Clark Hoover

GEORGE HARDING, JOHN COOLIDGE, AND JESSE HOOVER each provided his children with a strong sense of place—Ohio, Vermont, Iowa—but it was the generous Coolidge who left the most enduring imprint on his son, encouraging shy Calvin without pressure.

## George Tryon Harding II

Warren Gamaliel Harding really *looked* like a president: chiseled features, noble bearing, silver hair. His appearance, his amiability, and his availability constituted the bulk of his qualifications for high office. Harding found it so hard to say no that his father suggested that had he been born a girl, he would always be in the family way. His distinctive middle name, Gamaliel, after the teacher of Saint Paul, was not conferred on him by his devout mother but by his ambitious father, George Tryon Harding II, after a Methodist clergyman in his family.

Tryon, as he liked to be called, bore rather a noble-sounding name himself, but little else about him seems very notable. If favorable appraisals of Warren Harding are rare, positive accounts of his father are virtually nonexistent. Tryon, according to Harding biographer Francis Russell, was "unstable, with a slackness that was both inward and outward. . . . He would play out his life on the fringes of small towns, usually in debt, never accepted by the 'better people' anywhere." Physically, Tryon "was small for his age—his height at maturity would be below average—dark-complexioned, with dark curly hair and over-large ears. Some would call him ferret-faced." Biographer Charles Mee's description is equally merciless. Harding "was a small, idle, shiftless, impractical, lazy, day-dreaming, cat-napping fellow whose eye was always on the main chance."

Phoebe and George
Tryon Harding II

If, as he aged, Tryon did become "shiftless," perhaps it was because his gaze had been shifting for so long. He tried just about everything. His pursuit of happiness led him in a dozen different directions, although all within two counties in Ohio, and only three towns. Unlike many restless first fathers, Tryon was more anxious to move up than to move on.

The first American Harding was a Puritan fisherman and farmer who crossed the Atlantic in 1623 and settled in that favored locale of future presidential families, Braintree, in the Massachusetts Bay Colony. Following the customary progression from New England to Pennsylvania to Ohio, the first George Tryon Harding was born in the "Harding Settlement" around the attractively named town of Blooming Grove. Two generations later George Tryon Harding II was born nearby on June 12, 1843. Although smaller than prior Hardings, Tryon resembled them in his swarthy complexion. There had been recurring rumors that the family had Negro blood, perhaps from their early seafaring days in the West Indies. Intimations of black antecedents became particularly virulent during Warren Harding's political career, and—if it matters—have never been resolved. He once told a writer friend, "How do I know, Jim? One of my ancestors may have jumped the fence." In the end, it did not inhibit his success, but such slurs probably heightened both his sensitivity and his opposition to racial and religious bigotry.

Tryon would be the last of the farming Hardings. Fortunately it was still possible to "read" any profession—teaching, law, even medicine—so long as some education preceded it. Starting at the local schoolhouse, Tryon went on to the more advanced subscription school of his Aunt Clara. There, Tryon couldn't take his eyes off one of the girls. Slender Phoebe Elizabeth Dickerson, still in pigtails, who excelled at recitations, was becoming a self-assured young woman. In 1858, at the age of fourteen, Tryon entered Iberia College (later Central Ohio College), a few miles from home. In three years he earned a bachelor's degree, completing at least a foundation for his future. Teaching, notoriously low-paying then as now, was the easiest profession in which to get a start. He and Phoebe were secretly engaged. Now, however, the nation was embroiled in civil war. Despite his short stature, Tryon longed to fight for the Union. Despite his youth, he also longed to get married.

He was able to do both, but his military career, such as it was, turned out to be more musical than martial. He enlisted as a "fifer" in the 96th Ohio Volunteer Infantry and later as a "drummer boy" in the Ohio National Guard. In both instances he was mustered out due to illness. The highlight of his military service was meeting President Abraham Lincoln, who told Tryon and a friend that they could return to Ohio satisfied that they had seen "the handsomest man in the United States." In between, Tryon managed to elope with Phoebe.

Their first child, a son, was born on November 2, 1865. Warren Gamaliel Harding, the first president of the United States born after the Civil War, was a large, healthy, happy baby (few future presidents seem to have been small, unhealthy, unhappy babies). His mother called him "Winnie," had him blessed by the local Methodist minister, made special clothes for him, and almost at once started relating to others his exceptional qualities. Phoebe would have seven more children, but none who fueled her expectations as Winnie did.

Tryon moved ahead to his now firmly fixed career goal—to be a successful country doctor. He bought a secondhand set of medical books and convinced a well-respected practitioner named Joseph McFarland to take him on his rounds. Phoebe, too, became interested in medicine. Somehow, between babies, she found it possible, as a practical nurse and midwife, to assist her neighbors in birthing theirs. After completing two semesters at the Homeopathic Hospital College in Cleveland, Tryon was entitled officially to put out his shingle as an M.D. It would not be in Blooming Grove, however, but in Caledonia, Ohio, fourteen miles distant.

Tryon's practice flourished, although his rural clientele often paid him in produce instead of money. But, as Warren ruefully observed many years later, there was another problem. "My father has always been a benefactor to his fellow man, and successful, too, as long as you could keep him to doctoring. But he did like to trade a bit on the side."

Tryon's addiction to "swapping" became obsessive, eating up any profits from his medical practice. He would buy, sell, or swap almost anything—horses, cows, carts, carriages, farm implements—but it went further than that. One of the founders of the local building and loan association, Tryon bought land and laid out what he projected as an entirely new residential neighborhood. He bought and sold retail stores. But it was his purchase of the town's struggling newspaper, the *Caledonia Argus*, that would mean the most to young Warren. While still in school, he became a "printer's devil," learning to set type, washing down the press, delivering newspapers, even cleaning the floors—mastering the business literally from the ground up. He kept a tiny steel makeup ruler, a gift from the paper's editor, as a sort of lucky talisman for the rest of his life.

Warren's first seven years in Blooming Grove, and his later years in Caledonia, prefigured his later dilemma. He longed to fit in, yet also wanted to stand out. He excelled without seeming to exert much effort. Outside of school, a typical country boy, he performed all the farm chores, swam in the local creek, and played sandlot baseball. But there was a difference. Perhaps because of all the taunts of his classmates about his olive skin and dark hair, supporting the rumors about his ancestry, he was particularly considerate of others. More than anything, he wanted to win people over. He was such a good-natured child, adults noted, so well-mannered and handsome, despite his rather oversized head and his dark coloring, that Warren Harding was hard to resist. But the inner tension of his childhood never left him. At Caledonia Warren attended a larger school and continued to do well, reading more advanced literature and winning oratorical contests. His father gave him a cornet, which he learned to play proficiently. Robust and already six feet tall by the age of fourteen, he towered over Tryon.

His land deals gone bad, his swapping unproductive, Tryon was forced to give up his family's Caledonia home and reluctantly moved to a forty-acre farm nearby, where he tended to do more brooding than planting. By now, despite her many domestic responsibilities, the steadier Phoebe Harding had taken obstetrics courses and expanded her own practice in treating women's and children's ailments, keeping the family afloat, however precariously. After graduating from Iberia College, where he continued to do well, Warren dabbled in various professions, but most of all seemed to enjoy "bloviating"—or simply hanging out with his friends. As Mee writes, Harding's real genius lay in "ingratiating himself with people." Consciously or not, Tryon gave his son focus.

Reinvigorated by a small inheritance from his father, who had died in 1878, Dr. George Tryon Harding II moved a few miles to the west, to larger Marion, the county seat, where his services might even be compensated in cash rather than cucumbers. Among his many ventures was a half-interest in the local *Marion Star.* As its new editor he installed his nineteen-year-old son, Warren. There were subsequent ups and downs in the local three-paper newspaper wars, but for Warren journalism proved to be the bridge to his political career. After he married formidable Florence Kling, daughter of the richest man in Marion, his career really took off. "The Duchess," as he called her, five years older than Warren, kept him on the track his father had at least laid down.

Warren started attending Republican conventions. After some early defeats, he was elected to the state senate in 1898 and, except for one instance, never lost an election again. In 1910, after her wonderful Winnie had already served as lieutenant governor of Ohio, Phoebe Dickerson Harding died at the age of sixty-six. Her death hit Warren hard. Every Sunday he had either taken flowers to her or had had them delivered. Had Woodrow Wilson not already made Mother's Day a national holiday, President Warren Harding surely would have.

Her death was even more devastating to Tryon. She had held the family together in three locations while he tore about the countryside seeking new schemes for success that always proved elusive. The financial panic of 1907 had exacerbated his problems. As his practice floundered, he finally became the indifferent, untidy, and indolent figure his son's biographers later pictured, often simply napping in his back office. From 1910 on he was largely supported by Warren. In 1911 he could not be dissuaded from marrying an attractive widow from Indiana named Eudora Kelly Luvisi. He saw her as a new lease on life. She viewed him, with astonishing inaccuracy, as a potential meal ticket. When both expectations went unrealized, they were divorced in 1916. Undeterred, in 1921, at the age of seventy-eight, Tryon eloped with buxom, thirtyish Alice Severns. "I was lonesome, simply unbearably lonesome," he explained to reporters.

Father and son shared a weakness for what used to be called a trim ankle. Warren's romances, so luridly publicized after his death, were with comely Carrie Phillips, the true love of his life, who was also married at the time, and fetching young Nan Britton, who might be called the great lust of his life. They had a child together, Elizabeth Ann, as described in Nan Britton's book *The President's Daughter,* published four years after Harding's death. It was doubtful, however, that he would ever have left the Duchess. He needed her in practical terms even more than Tryon had needed Phoebe.

The passion that most sustained Tryon in his old age was sharing in his son's success. He became almost as intrusive as Jesse Grant had been over half a century earlier. Human-interest articles were written under Tryon's name about "My Boy Warren." He took to wearing a replica of his old Civil War uniform, haunting reunions of the Grand Army of the Republic. When none was upcoming, an equal-opportunity veteran, Tryon attended a reunion of the United Confederate Veterans. He was treated so well that he suggested that he might be inclined to vote for a local Democrat, causing Warren no end of embarrassment. To Tryon's delight, the press rediscovered him when Warren ran for the presidency in 1920, "bloviating" to a receptive nation that what it needed was "not nostrums but normalcy." There was old Tryon in the photographs, in his suspenders, ceremonially spreading gravel from a wheelbarrow to make a smooth limestone yard for the multitudes who would come to visit during his son's front-porch campaign, reminiscent of McKinley's.

Harding, like McKinley, would win, swept along on a wave of good feelings, a genuinely modest man who, to paraphrase Winston Churchill, perhaps had much to be modest about. As Harding later wrote to one of his many friends, "Frankly, being President is rather an unattractive business unless one relishes the exercise of power. That is a thing that has never greatly appealed to me."

Later it was some of those friends who kept him awake nights. He appointed too many of them, and—like Grant—supervised them too little. From Teapot Dome to the Veterans Bureau, Harding's "Ohio Gang" formed probably the most corrupt administration in American history, leading to indictments and suicides. It took a terrible toll on the president.

Yet, despite his personal and political lapses, Warren Harding was a man of honorable instincts. It was his august secretary of state whose treaty reduced the navies of the great powers. It was Harding who expressed his belief in free speech by releasing the Socialist Eugene Debs from jail. It was Harding who promoted an eight-hour workday. It was Harding, not the segregation-supporting Woodrow Wilson, who spoke in the South in favor of full legal equality for all the nation's citizens, black as well as white, not because of his complexion but his convictions.

Near the end he sought to overcome the sordid deals of his old cronies, most of which had not yet been made public, by embarking on his own "Journey of Understanding" across the nation. He wanted to go out and see more people personally to talk in favor of the World Court, perhaps even in preparation for a reelection campaign in 1924. However, many noted that he seemed terribly worn out. On the West Coast he contracted what appeared to be indigestion or food poisoning from some tainted seafood. Physicians insisted that he rest completely. After a few days he said he felt better but was still "so tired, so tired."

On the evening of August 2, 1923, after his wife, who had been reading to him, went to her own compartment, Harding's nurse left his side momentarily to bring a glass of water for his medicine. He was sitting up. She arrived back just in time to see him twitch and slump over suddenly, his mouth open. The cause of death was probably a cerebral hemorrhage, but Florence Harding, for whatever reason, did not permit an autopsy. Warren Gamaliel Harding was only fifty-seven.

Tryon, the first father of an American president to outlive his son, for once was silent, mute with grief. Wearing his GAR uniform, with his great white mustache and dignified bearing, he looked every inch an honored, aged veteran of real battles. His son's coffin was carried with great care into his parlor after its long journey across the country to Washington and back again to Ohio. The railings of his front doorway had to be removed for it to pass through. For hour after hour the public silently filed past, until two the next morning. The final of four funeral services took place in the stifling midsummer heat of Marion Cemetery, as taps sounded and Tryon stiffened to a twenty-one-gun salute.

George Tryon Harding II died at the age of eighty-five, in desired obscurity, on November 19, 1928, in Santa Ana, California. His prior life had been limited to a small portion of Ohio, but his dreams were not defined by its dimensions. His grand schemes came to nothing, but something in them must have sparked the imagination of his son, the twenty-eighth president of the United States, and the seventh from the Buckeye State.

# John Calvin Coolidge

The knocking on his front door grew louder. What could this insistent visitor want? It was after midnight, August 3, 1923. John Calvin Coolidge had been sleeping soundly since 9:00 P.M., his normal time to retire, in the small first-floor bedroom of his modest farmhouse. After determining who was at the door and reading the telegram he brought, Coolidge called upstairs to wake his son. Calvin and his wife, Grace, had been visiting, a pleasant escape from Washington's humidity. The next morning they were to leave for a friend's mansion, quite a contrast with this humble homestead. They dressed quietly, said a brief prayer, and came downstairs; Calvin had learned the news, in a more tremulous voice than he had ever heard from his father. John Coolidge was also the first person to address his son as "Mr. President."

Later that morning, at precisely 2:47, by the light of an oil lamp, the senior Coolidge, a notary public, using the family Bible, administered a hastily typed oath of office to his son. Observed by only six others, the ceremony took place in the cottage's well-worn fourteen-by-seventeen-foot sitting room. Grace Coolidge was overcome with emotion. Her husband's first reaction was a customarily calm "I think I can swing it." Everyone had believed that President Warren G. Harding was on the way to recovery from his recent illness, but he had died quite suddenly the preceding day in San Francisco. The Coolidges of Plymouth Notch, in Plymouth Township, one of the remoter regions of Vermont, were among the last Americans to learn of it. Although his son was vice president of the United States, John Coolidge had not previously felt any necessity to have a telephone installed in his home. Intrusiveness, either incoming or outgoing, was never in his nature.

Nor in his son's. For a man immersed in public life for almost thirty years, "Silent Cal" Coolidge seemed taciturn even by the standards of rural New England. Yet there was nothing reserved in Calvin's appreciation of his father, recognizing all that he owed the man everyone in the region called Colonel Coolidge. (He had earned the title in 1900 as an

Calvin and John
Coolidge

aide to the governor of Vermont and had just enough ego not to mind being addressed by it.)

Of course, other presidents similarly esteemed their fathers. Calvin Coolidge went a step further. "My father," he wrote, "had qualities greater than any I possess." Given their emotional attachment, it is not surprising that Woodrow Wilson and his father embraced upon encountering each other, even in public. Given their customary reserve, that Calvin and John Coolidge would kiss whenever *they* met was viewed with astonishment by reporters and onlookers alike.

The quality, however, that most separates John Coolidge from other memorable first fathers is entirely consonant with Coolidge's character—restraint. He did not pressure his son. John understood that Calvin would do his best. He patiently supported his son into his thirties. Sensitive, shy, and uncertain, but ambitious nonetheless, Calvin needed no spur to find his way and cherished his father all the more for understanding.

The two were often described similarly. After his father died, Calvin reflected, "He was a man of untiring industry and great tenacity of purpose. . . . He always stuck to the truth. It always seemed possible for him to form an unerring judgment of men and things. I cannot recall that I ever knew of his doing a wrong thing. He would be classed as decidedly a man of character." Although few might refer to Calvin Coolidge's "untiring industry," his seeming somnolence as president becoming the stuff of satire, a contemporary journalist commented: "People liked him because he kept his word and was scrupulously honest. He inherited from his Vermont ancestors their character of plain living and high thinking, thrift, taciturnity, and humor. . . . He was . . . sparing in his words, [but] had a mind of his own."

If the words were spare, in describing what mattered most to him—his family and the soil that shaped them—Coolidge was capable of eloquence. In his autobiography—not surprisingly, the shortest of any twentieth-century president—Coolidge begins almost lyrically: "The town of Plymouth lies on the easterly slope of the Green Mountains, about twenty miles west of the Connecticut River. . . . Vermont is my birthright. Here one gets close to nature . . . fields tilled not by machinery but by the brain and hand of man. . . . Folks are happy and contented. They belong to themselves, live within their means, and fear no man."

As for his childhood, still so vivid in his memory, it seems idyllic: "Even when I try to divest it of that halo which I know always surrounds the past, I am unable to create any other impression but that it was fresh and clean. . . . It would be hard to imagine better surroundings for a boy than those which I had. . . . Country life does not always have breadth, but it has depth. It is neither artificial nor superficial, but is kept close to the realities."

In Calvin's case, it also had continuity. The hardy, homogeneous character of the scattered homesteads of rural Vermont's hills and valleys was not all that different from the Massachusetts Bay Colony that the first American John Coolidge found in 1630. Calvin Coolidge's living connections with his Yankee forebears were his colorful grandparents, Calvin Galusha and Sarah Almeda Coolidge. Both were cherished companions of his childhood. The spare six-foot "Galoosh" was an anomaly, a garrulous Coolidge. He loved farming and the outdoors, raising and trading horses, animals of all kinds, practical jokes, and politics. When Calvin was not yet four his grandfather took him up to the legislature in Montpelier and rather prophetically placed him in the governor's chair to see how he liked it. Galusha's death little more than two years later was the first great blow of Calvin's life.

Sarah and Galusha had only two children, both sons. John Calvin Coolidge was born in Plymouth Notch on March 31, 1845, and seems to have come into the world running. His younger brother, rather surprisingly named Julius Caesar Coolidge, died at the age of twenty in 1870. John's education, beyond that provided by his parents, was limited to the local schoolhouse and a few terms at the boarding school of Black River Academy in nearby Ludlow. When home, he was always working. His earliest recollection of gainful employment was "burning out" some of the diminishing supply of local lime. In addition to helping on his father's farm, he worked for the village wheelwright and learned carpentry, bricklaying, masonry, and carriage making. Calvin wrote of his father, "If there was any physical requirement of country life which he could not perform, I do not know what it was." Biographer Claude Fuess adds, "He pitched the hay onto the oxcart; he owned and knew how to use the tools for mending water pipes and tinware; he could even help a blacksmith at the forge." When a visitor suggested that John seemed to serve his community as everything but an undertaker, he replied that, yes, he had also made coffins. He even taught school for a time, at nearby Pinney Hollow, and parents there vied to put up the popular young man.

By the time he reached his teens, John was nearly the height of his father, with an impressive physique hardened by physical labor—as biographer Robert Sobel writes, "a powerfully built man with an impressive square face." On May 6, 1868, twenty-three-year-old John Calvin Coolidge married lovely but delicate twenty-two-year-old Victoria Josephine Moor, whom he had met at school. Although named for a queen and an empress, ethereal Victoria Moor came from a family as Puritan as the Coolidges. Despite the disapproval of his land-loving father, John decided to supplement farming by operating the local general store, which initially he rented and, of course, ran profitably. In addition, he managed the post office. Later he would be involved in insurance, real estate, and even credit reports. It was to his relatively spacious five-room cottage, adjoining the store and post office, that John brought his bride.

Their first child, a boy they named yet another John Calvin Coolidge, was born there on a date that would always bear a special significance to him—July 4, 1872. By the time, three years later, that his sole sibling, his sister Abigail, dear "Abbie," arrived, the family had moved to a larger house across the street on two acres of land, with several out-buildings, including a blacksmith's shop—and Calvin's mother had become an invalid. She died of tuberculosis on her thirty-ninth birthday, March 14, 1885. Calvin was twelve. "It always seemed to me that the boy I lost was her image," he wrote. He would carry her image with him every day for the rest of his life.

His mother lived in memory, but it was his father, a sustaining phys-ical presence, whom Calvin wrote most about in his autobiography. It was almost in awe. The Colonel could do just about anything. Calvin eventually gave up his first name, as had Stephen Grover Cleveland and Thomas Woodrow Wilson, but perhaps for a different reason. He would be plain "Calvin Coolidge," not a junior version of his formidable father. Calvin wrote: "My fundamental idea of both private and public business came from my father. He was a generous and charitable man, but regarded waste as a moral wrong. . . . I was accustomed to carry apples and popcorn balls to town meetings to sell, mainly because my grand-mother had said my father had done so when he was a boy, and I was exceedingly anxious to grow up to be like him."

Unfortunately Calvin was not at all like his robust father physically. He grew to be as tall, but his frail-looking, slender frame was more like that of his mother's family than the heartier Coolidges. He was fre-quently and alarmingly ill with severe colds and asthma. His father feared that he might contract tuberculosis, which had taken the life of his wife. "The only thing close to flamboyant" about Calvin Coolidge, Sobel writes, "was his bright red hair, which contrasted with his pale, freckled face."

Despite his unimpressive physique, as biographer Donald McCoy details, Calvin pulled more than his weight on his father's farm. He may have done his share of "playing and wasting," but Calvin also fed all the animals, led the cattle to and from their pasture, kept the woodbox filled, planted, raked, mowed, and harvested—much as his father had as a boy. There was no excess of ease, however fondly Calvin recalled his child-hood. His closest companion and playmate was his cheerful, outgoing younger sister, Abbie, who also had bright red hair. She died of appen-dicitis at the age of fifteen. Medical treatment was still rudimentary and remote in the highlands of Vermont. Three of the people Calvin loved best were lost to him early, at six-year intervals: his grandfather, his mother, and his sister. The journalist William Allen White, who wrote the best early biography of Coolidge, noted, "That his emotions were hidden did not lessen their power. . . . The pale, prim young fellow [became] a little more aloof, a little less mischievous, a little more serious for even a serious boy."

Of course, such losses only brought him closer to his devoted father, who knew what it was to be a sole surviving child. John Coolidge worried not only about his son's physical health but also about his emotional well-being. Years later Calvin said to his wife, "I am as interested in human beings as one could possibly be, but it is desperately hard for me to show it." He would always be acutely uncomfortable meeting new people. In that sense, as he admitted, "I've never really grown up."

As more children moved into the neighborhood, Calvin did begin to enjoy playing games, like checkers and backgammon, and joined in husking bees, taffy pulls, group singing, and even acting in informal plays—up to a point. His favorite recreations—reading, walking in the woods, fishing, skating, sledding, and horseback riding—were all still solitary. He had no inclination for team sports. Like the young Ulysses Grant, he seemed always to be observing, taking things in rather than participating in them.

His earliest instruction had been at home. He learned to read before he was five. At six he went to the Plymouth Notch schoolhouse, a small stone structure only a few yards from his front door. By now his father had quietly become a community leader. After the death of Galoosh in 1878, he sold the store, which he now owned, to his brother-in-law. He served as township constable, justice of the peace, tax collector, even pound keeper, and was elected to both the state legislature and the state senate. Calvin first learned about the workings of practical politics by accompanying his father to its most direct manifestation, New England town meetings, and hearing his concise contributions.

Calvin's excitement soared, at least for him, when he learned in 1887 that he would be going, as had his mother, father, and grandmother, the twelve miles down the hill to Black River Academy in Ludlow. Colonel Coolidge, however, who now served on the school's board, intended that Calvin would stay to graduation and then—the first in his line of Coolidges—go to college. The ultimate profession he might follow didn't matter to his father; his education did. On a freezing day they drove to the school in an open sleigh. Reportedly there was another passenger on board—a calf the elder Coolidge had brought along to sell and ship to Boston. Tradition holds that as he bade good-bye to his son, Colonel Coolidge said wryly, "If you study hard and are a good boy, maybe sometime you'll go to Boston too, but this calf will get there first." We don't know if Calvin and his father kissed, but it is certain that both were terribly lonely after Calvin's departure.

It was not until his senior year, his fourth at Black River, that Coolidge, still a gawky, rather solitary teenager, discovered Latin, classical literature, and rhetoric and found that he actually enjoyed recitation and debating. According to White, he also filled out a bit physically. The childhood freckles faded, the red hair toned down. "He was slight but not skinny. His muscles were hard and his jaw was well set, his features clear cut." In short, more like his father. He spoke at graduation on "Oratory in History."

After a semester at prestigious St. Johnsbury Academy, Calvin was admitted to Amherst College. That is all it took in those halcyon days. Just before he departed, his father, seven years a widower, married charming Carrie Brown, who had taught Calvin at his first school. "I hate to go away," Calvin would say, fondest of the people and places most familiar to him, but still "Silent Cal" came to love Amherst. By his senior year, as Fuess writes, he was recognized for "his intrinsic character and ready wit." He didn't drink, smoke, or play cards, and he had never danced before going to college, but in that last year he did finally join a fraternity and was chosen "Grove Orator"—to give a humorous address on Class Day. His pride in being selected, something that would have been inconceivable for Coolidge only a few years before, was undoubtedly shared by his father. Calvin graduated cum laude, just short of Phi Beta Kappa.

Two prominent Amherst alumni practicing law in Northampton, Massachusetts, invited him to "read" the profession in their offices. It was still possible to pass the bar without going to law school. Calvin did so in 1897. He also got involved in local politics, initially by handing out literature for one of the firm's partners, who ran successfully for mayor, and started attending state Republican conventions. At the end of 1898, after opening his own law office, he won his first election, to the city council. From the start he demonstrated surprisingly shrewd political instincts, working smoothly with local Democrats as well as the GOP faithful. Throughout, as Sobel writes, "He had a loving, generous father on whom he could count for anything he needed."

Calvin's first meeting with Grace Goodhue, at least in a manner of speaking, was out of a Mack Sennett silent comedy. She saw him standing in the open window of the Northampton house in which he roomed, shaving himself while dressed in his long underwear and wearing a derby hat, perhaps intended to keep his hair down. Calvin also saw *her,* and with uncommon impulsiveness fell in love with the vision. Despite so inauspicious a start, he managed to meet her. Gradually Grace perceived qualities in Calvin only visible to a discerning eye. They made an unlikely couple, this "odd stick," as Calvin called himself, and his gracious Grace. Vivacious, dark-haired, attractive, and stylish, Grace Goodhue may have been lighthearted but she was hardly light-headed. After graduating Phi Beta Kappa from the University of Vermont, she learned sign language and took a position in 1903 teaching the deaf at the Clarke School in Northampton.

Not long afterward, in Burlington, Vermont, Andrew Goodhue looked up from the magazine he was reading to see a surprise guest in his living room. "Hello, Calvin," he said, "what are you doing in Burlington? Got some business here?" "No," Calvin replied, "came up to marry Grace"— or so the story goes. Apparently Mr. Goodhue suggested that Calvin might want to ask Grace herself. According to Grace, when Calvin got around to it, his proposal consisted of "I am going to marry you." Coolidge put it more tenderly in his autobiography: "We felt we were made for each other. For almost a quarter of a century she has borne with my infirmities, and I have rejoiced in her graces."

They were married at her parents' home in Burlington on October 4, 1905. He was thirty-three and she was twenty-six. His pleased parents were among the fifteen or so guests. At a party the night before, a friend of the Goodhues who had not yet met Calvin, seeing him standing alone and silent in a corner, mistook him for one of Grace's students. Later, according to McCoy, a wag suggested that since Grace had taught the deaf to hear, she might one day teach Calvin to speak. She soon became accustomed to dealing with this sort of comment. Years later, in Washington, after being complimented as a stimulating conversationalist, Grace smilingly replied that, after all, she'd had to learn to speak for two. She was precisely what Calvin Coolidge needed, and he was smart enough to realize it. After a frugal honeymoon in Montreal, they moved into a modest duplex in Northampton, where they continued to live long after they could afford more luxurious accommodations. Their first son, John, was born in 1906. Despite his growing legal practice and political progress, Calvin still needed to reluctantly call on his father for financial assistance from time to time. It was never given with reluctance.

No less an authority than Will Rogers considered that Calvin Coolidge "had more subtle humor than almost any public man I ever met."

There is little doubt that Coolidge eventually turned his wry, cryptic, straight-faced comments into a sort of art form, relishing, in the current parlance, "putting people on." The most celebrated instance was at the sort of dinner party Coolidge detested. A society matron gushed at the president that she had wagered with a friend that she could induce him to say more than two words. "You lose," he replied. Once, he was asked the subject of a Congregational minister's sermon. "Sin," he said. Pressed for more details, Coolidge added, "He's against it." And so on. His father's comments were equally succinct. When a reporter informed the Colonel, "We expect great things from your son," his deadpan response was limited to "I hope you won't be disappointed." Invited to attend a dinner of prominent Amherst alumni to promote Calvin's political prospects, the Colonel responded, "Gentlemen: Can't come. Thank you, John Coolidge."

In his entire political career Coolidge lost only one election, for an unpaid post on the Northampton school board. It was before the birth of his children. When told by a friend that he would have voted for him had he had a child in the public schools, Calvin ruefully replied, "Might give me time." It wasn't many years later that, with the support of some four hundred Democratic voters, Coolidge was elected mayor of Northampton. At his Amherst reunion in 1910, he told a classmate, "I got the job just by keeping my mouth shut so they wouldn't know what a fool I was." To his father he wrote more seriously, "I could not have been Mayor without your help." For nearly the next thirty years, Coolidge, a most unlikely politician, held public office until his surprising, laconic announcement, "I do not choose to run for president in 1928."

It was a lengthier pronouncement that launched him into the national spotlight in 1920. As governor of Massachusetts, Coolidge, after some deliberation, ordered the State Guard to intervene in a Boston strike by policemen, declaring, "There is no right to strike against the public safety by anyone, anywhere, anytime." For the first time Republicans envisioned Coolidge as a potential presidential candidate. He was nominated instead, with unusual enthusiasm, as Warren Harding's running mate.

The affection between father and son had always been mutual, but now so was the regard. Their correspondence became more demonstrative. White concludes that not only did Calvin "in his heart" always seek "the protective shadow of his father's approval," but the son became "his father's idol" as well. Those who caricatured colorless Calvin Coolidge as a chief executive with the sedentary inclination of a domestic feline probably never spent much time with him. He believed in substituting "the midnight oil for the limelight" and that "It is much more important to kill bad bills than to pass good ones." He was not so old-fashioned that he didn't relish talking to the electorate over the radio.

When Coolidge said to William Allen White, "A lot of people in Plymouth can't understand how I got to be president, least of all my father," both knew that it wasn't really true. As McCoy writes, "They loved each other, they trusted each other, they admired each other." Sobel adds, referring to their forty years of correspondence, that John Coolidge was one of few people to whom Calvin "opened his heart completely." When his son was elected vice president in 1920, John's satisfaction was tempered by Carrie's death. Once again he was a widower. Within three years he would swear in Calvin as president and, only nineteen months later, on March 4, 1925, sit as an honored guest at his son's inauguration after Calvin won the office in his own right. Yet even that occasion was diminished by an inexplicable tragedy. If possible, it brought Colonel Coolidge and Calvin even closer together.

In the summer of 1924 Calvin's son Calvin Jr. developed a blister on his toe while playing on the White House tennis court. It became terribly infected, and despite every medical effort, the boy passed away on July 7. He was the first child of a president to die in the White House since Willie Lincoln. Calvin all but blamed it on his unseemly political ambition. "When he went," he wrote of his son, "all the power and glory of the Presidency went with him." In November 1924, after the election, Grace Coolidge crocheted a bedspread with one square for each month she and her husband must remain in Washington, literally counting the days until their departure. Although it came to the nation as a surprise, it is little wonder that Calvin Coolidge did not choose to run again for president in 1928.

His father, up in Plymouth Notch, was ailing, almost an invalid after undergoing a prostate operation. His condition worsened after a heart attack. In January 1926, Calvin had a direct telephone line put in and called every day, upset that the press of work made him "resort to the poor substitute of a telephone." He had written on January 1, "It is a nice bright day for the new year, but rather cold. I wish you were here where you could have every care and everything made easy for you, but I know you feel more content at home. . . . I suppose I am the most powerful man in the world, but great power does not mean much except great limitations."

John Calvin Coolidge died on March 18, 1926, late in his eightieth year. When informed that the Colonel was failing, Calvin and Grace rushed by a special train up to Vermont, but they were too late. "When I reached home," Calvin wrote, "he was gone. It costs a great deal to be president."

After the simple Episcopal service he had requested, John Coolidge was borne from his farmhouse in the place where he had always lived and laid to rest next to those he loved best—all but Calvin. Colonel Coolidge left an estate of over $70,000, a substantial sum for the times, but then profligacy was never in his nature. Generosity was. It was his hand that Calvin had first grasped after receiving from him the oath of office. After that, John Coolidge's life had never been quite the same, his treasured privacy shattered by future hordes of visitors.

In a letter to his father on August 2, 1925, Calvin recalled, "It is two years since you woke me to bring me the news that I was president. It seems a very short time. I trust it has been a great satisfaction to you. . . . I am sure I came to it largely by your bringing up and your example. If that is what you wanted, you have much to be thankful for that you have lived to so great an age to see it."

## Jesse Clark Hoover

Herbert Hoover was only six when his father died of typhoid fever or heart failure or both, and was orphaned at nine when his mother died of pneumonia. He wrote in his autobiography, considerably longer than Calvin Coolidge's but equally vivid, of "the wonders of Iowa's streams and woods, of the mystery of growing crops. . . . As gentle as are memories of those times, I am not recommending a return to the good old days. . . . Sickness was greater and death came sooner. . . . Medical science was still almost powerless against the contagious diseases which swept the countryside. My own parents were among the victims. . . . My recollection of my father is of necessity dim indeed."

It is tempting to overstate the potential of those who die too young, but there *was* a remarkable inventiveness and energy in Jesse Clark Hoover and exceptional idealism and activism in Hulda Minthorn Hoover. Had Jesse been granted the opportunity for higher education that was afforded his son, it is likely there would have been an earlier "Great Engineer" in the family.

Jesse Clark Hoover

Andreas Huber, Jesse's great-great-great-grandfather, who arrived in Philadelphia in 1738, was from a Swiss family that had moved to the German Palatinate. As biographer George Nash writes, the Hoovers had a "habit of migration." Somewhere between Lancaster County, Pennsylvania, and Maryland, where he farmed, and North Carolina, where he opened a gristmill, Andreas Huber became Andrew Hoover.

Andrew's son John, both a farmer and a millwright, took his family to the more abundant acreage of Ohio, settling in Miami County. He married a member of the Religious Society of Friends and soon joined it himself. These Quakers were also expanding westward. In the mid-nineteenth century they established a settlement in West Branch, Iowa. It grew quickly. Biographer David Burner quotes a journal from 1854: "For miles and miles, day after day, the prairies of Illinois are lined with cattle and wagons, pushing on towards this prosperous state." John Hoover's grandson, Eli, joined the migration, establishing his farm outside West Grove. His large family included his son, Jesse Clark Hoover, who had been born in West Milton, Ohio, on September 2, 1846.

Jesse's childhood in his new home was unexceptional, divided among terms at the local "select school" (which was not selective, but open to all), the seasonal recreations of fishing and sledding, and chores on his father's farm. Writer Gene Smith describes Jesse's daily life: "Hoeing the garden, planting corn, milking the cow, sawing wood for the stove. Christmas was popcorn balls cemented with sorghum molasses. They wore homespun clothes dyed with butternuts, and no shoes in the summer." Self-sufficiency was essential. Nothing was wasted. The women of West Branch canned their own fruits and vegetables and made everything from rugs to soap. The only overabundance was of corn. Local men constructed the spare furniture that went into their homes of unadorned, whitewashed wood. The Hoovers' house had only two or three rooms, its overall dimensions not much larger than John Coolidge's sitting room.

The Indians who still resided nearby taught the local children how to hunt with bows and arrows, in the absence of firearms. West Branch was different in only one respect from hundreds of other rural towns in the growing Midwest—it was a thoroughly Quaker community. There was no saloon in town. Nor would there be a jail until the railroad brought in interlopers. By the time Friends arrived in California, their Western variety of Quakerism employed ministers, called their meetinghouses "churches," and encouraged singing and proselytizing. Friends in the Midwest had established something of a compromise between the restraint of traditional meetings for worship in the East and the churches of the Far West. Even in West Branch there would be a later rift between evangelical and conservative Quakers. Separatist sects seem to spawn such schisms, but all Friends everywhere affirmed the same fundamentals—to be guided by the conscience of one's "inner light." The Friends of West Branch, Iowa, were committed, just as thoroughly as those in Pennsylvania, to such causes as pacifism, temperance, abolition of slavery, and the rights of Native Americans. Dress was sober and restrained; women wore bonnets, and men wore broad-brimmed hats and dark, collarless coats. "Thee" and "thou" were still forms of salutation, and frivolity of all kinds was discouraged.

Jesse's childhood may have been unexceptional, but he early evidenced two distinctive characteristics, one of temperament and one of skill. He was extremely cheerful and outgoing, and he was a natural-born tinkerer and promoter. They combined to make him exceptionally ambitious. The Quaker farmers of Iowa were not opposed to labor-saving devices if they could afford them. Jesse was fascinated by machinery and particularly enjoyed operating his father's thresher. At the age of eighteen he became the town's blacksmith, an essential job, but he had bigger plans, professional and personal.

In part they centered on bright, devout Hulda Minthorn, whom he had encountered at the meetinghouse. He had also heard her, for the spirit often moved Hulda to speak, with uncommon eloquence for one so young. At her father's funeral, she even broke into song. Most of the community shared the opinion of Hulda's sister that "she was such a gifted girl." Hulda had attended the University of Iowa when higher education for women was still rare. She taught school for several years, wrote verse and music, and became deeply involved in her religion and the enlightened reforms she believed it to inspire, particularly women's suffrage. Hulda was far ahead of her time, and perhaps her place, but gave every evidence of future leadership. Nor did she neglect domestic virtues, learning to sew and cook and care for others. Herbert remembered her as a "sweet-faced woman" who tried nobly to keep her family together.

Jesse Hoover, twenty-four, married Hulda Randall Minthorn, twenty-two, in the West Branch meetinghouse in 1870. Jesse and Hulda had three children—Theodore Jesse, called "Tad," in 1871; Mary, called "May," in 1876; and, in between, Herbert Clark Hoover, called "Bert" or "Bertie," on August 10 or 11, 1874. The confusion results from his having been born just before or just after midnight. In either case, around dawn, as Burner recounts, Jesse Hoover tapped on the window of his sister-in-law's house, across the street. "Well, Agnes," he exclaimed, "we have another General Grant at our house!" He was a "sweet baby," Agnes recalled, "round and plump and looked about very cordial at everybody."

Robust or not, little Bertie nearly didn't survive. At the age of two he had such severe croup that he nearly choked to death. The village doctors were unable to keep him conscious, but by a stroke of fortune Hulda's uncle, Dr. John Minthorn, came by just in time and brought the child back to life through artificial respiration. For days his parents never left his side, taking turns monitoring his temperature. Reportedly his grandmother Minthorn predicted, "God has great work for that boy to do. That is why he was brought back to life." His childhood was much like his father's—a mix of meetings, school, and chores, but with a good measure of mischievous fun.

As he grew older, Jesse had the longest beard of any first father. He looked rather like an Old Testament prophet—at least, one with a rather jovial demeanor. He was tall and thin, almost gaunt, but very strong. Herbert could dimly remember riding with his feet hanging down from the family buggy, getting stuck in the muddy roads, and hearing his father call him a "little stick-in-the-mud." Barefoot Bertie also stepped on an ember at his father's shop, leaving a lifelong scar.

By 1878 Jesse was doing well enough to sell the blacksmith shop and start devoting all his business efforts to a farm implements store. He moved his family of five to a more spacious, trim, white five-room home. Jesse was also named town assessor and councilman, although many in the community considered him a bit too worldly. He often teased Hulda about her excessively public professions of faith. However, by all accounts, theirs was a most happy marriage. Despite all Hulda's activities, her home, as her sister noted, was "always so clean and neat"— high praise in West Branch, Iowa. Herbert's memories of the abundant surrounding fruit trees and fragrant flowers were undimmed by time. His cousin Harriette insisted that the Hoover household was a "merry place"—the parents involved, the children lively and hardly repressed.

Jesse sold everything an up-to-date farmer could use, including his own inventions and those of his father. His sons would be the third generation of inventive Hoovers (although, no, they did not develop the vacuum cleaner). As boys, Bertie and Tad improvised a mowing machine tied to a calf, their own attempt at a labor-saving device. Both would grow up to be engineers. Jesse purchased a machine for manufacturing single-strand barbed wire, coating it with hot tar to inhibit rust. In 1880 he and a friend applied for a patent for a cattle stile and hog guard, which adroitly separated the two types of animals. Later that year his father patented an automatic pump that Jesse manufactured and sold. Burner recalls Jesse's catchy newspaper ads, the promotional side of his enterprise: "Ho, for Kansas! But if you do not go there go to J. C. Hoover and buy your Farming Implements including Three leading Sulky Plows, New Departure Tongueless Cultivator, Orchard City Wagon, Buck Eye Reaper, Rubber Bucket Pumps . . . and Lightning Rods." Nor were overburdened farm wives neglected: "Do not go to Iowa City to buy Sewing Machines when you can get any kind you want [at] J.C. HOOVER and save FIVE DOLLARS."

Jesse died on December 13, 1880, of typhoid fever, just as the business was really gaining momentum. He was only thirty-four. The local newspapers praised his "pleasant, sunshiny disposition," his kindness, and his contributions to the community. His stalwart wife paid off his debts, invested carefully from his $1,000 life insurance policy, sold the business, and worked as a seamstress to keep the family going. Then she, too, was gone. Hulda died a few months short of her thirty-fifth birthday, on February 24, 1884, of pneumonia. However, she had managed to accumulate some $2,000 for the education of her children, who were separated and sent to a succession of relatives.

They were kindly enough, but it was the Stanford University community that became Hoover's true family. A member of its first class, Hoover found there his vocation, his future wife, and himself. His innate humanity, submerged under his shy surface, would have been more evident had his remarkable parents lived only a few more years to nurture it. Suffering so swift a transition during his presidency from the most admired American to the most reviled, Herbert Clark Hoover was more fortunate than his parents. He lived long enough for a fuller understanding of his great contributions to be appreciated.

# 12

## "Most Generous and Kindly of Men"

### James Roosevelt

ALTHOUGH OVERSHADOWED IN BIOGRAPHIES by his formidable wife Sara, James Roosevelt, until slowed by age and illness, was his son Franklin's closest companion and confidant, enabling the pampered youth to gain the confidence to thrive on his own.

Unfortunately, the two most frequently quoted references to James Roosevelt portray him as rather a shallow snob. He is reputed to have told his wife to decline a dinner invitation from his far wealthier Hudson Valley neighbors, the Cornelius Vanderbilts, because the Roosevelts would then be obliged to reciprocate. Apparently James viewed the Vanderbilts as pretentious parvenus. He may have had to sit on business boards with Cornelius, but he wasn't about to share dinner with him. The second story is a relative's derisive description of the English-emulating Roosevelt as trying to pattern his appearance on Lord Lansdowne's, "sideburns and all," but succeeding only in looking like Lansdowne's coachman.

Both assertions may well be true, but neither reflects a rounded picture of the real James Roosevelt. One tends to see this genuinely interesting man, if at all, in only one dimension. If Roosevelt, derived from such solid Dutch antecedents, was offended by the flaunted new wealth of Gilded Age acquisitiveness, he was hardly alone. James did indeed admire the lifestyle of the English country gentry, but one imagines that his prominent muttonchops, his preference for riding clothes, and his thorough enjoyment of his estate were more than examples of slavish imitation. James was a self-confident man who lived his life as he pleased.

His son Franklin, whose childhood was as brightened by his own father as his cousin Theodore's was by his, said of James Roosevelt, "He

James Roosevelt and
the infant Franklin

was the most generous and kindly of men. . . . My father was no snob."
Geoffrey Ward, the noted biographer of Franklin Delano Roosevelt's
youth, refers to the temperamental similarities of James and Franklin:
"The conservative and the gambler warred within James Roosevelt all of
his life, just as they would later within his son." In short, James was not
solely the settled, self-satisfied, and all but sedentary country squire portrayed in too-brief accounts of his life.

Descended from the same Claes van Rosenvelt (the original family
name meant "from the rose field") as the Theodore Roosevelts, by the
nineteenth century the Hudson Valley branch was as much English as
Dutch. James Roosevelt was born on July 16, 1828, at "Mount Hope,"
his family's home near Poughkeepsie on the heights overlooking the
Hudson River. His father, one of many Isaac Roosevelts, was surely the
most eccentric—a reclusive, hypochondriac physician who refused to
practice and was obsessed with death. Fortunately, James's doting mother

was a good deal more normal, and James had additional relatives nearby. As Ward writes, "He was free to roam with his black dog Billy; he hunted and fished, built a water wheel on the ice pond; learned to ride and care for the fine horses his grandfather bred and trained." He seemed a rather serious child, but there was already a streak of rebelliousness, resulting in a succession of schools.

Somehow James persuaded his father to let him attend New York University, but the blandishments of the metropolis proved too tempting. In May of his freshman year he was reprimanded for causing "disorder," and the following year was transferred to small but well-regarded Union College in upstate Schenectady. James continued to lead an active social life, joining a fraternity that, to his father's dismay, met in a tavern. James may have majored more in carousing than serious scholarship, but he did graduate in 1847.

Dr. Isaac rewarded his son with a grand tour of Europe. For eighteen glorious months James traveled from England to the Middle East, even spending time in Italy as a volunteer with Giuseppe Garibaldi's "red shirts." Upon his return, he entered Harvard Law School, did surprisingly well in his studies, and graduated in 1851 on his twenty-third birthday. As evidence of the esteem in which he was held, he would later be made an honorary member of Porcellian, the most prestigious of Harvard's clubs.

James had little difficulty attaining a coveted position with a major New York law firm but found its routine work dry and tedious. He craved action. Fortunately, the firm had corporate clients, and with the aid of family connections James launched his career as what Ward calls a "genteel gambler." He was elected to the board of the Consolidated Coal Company of Maryland, the first of several increasingly ambitious business ventures. His goal was to amass a fortune to rival those being accumulated by families like the Vanderbilts, however he might disdain them socially.

James was equally active in the romantic realm. He met, courted, and married his lovely twenty-two-year-old cousin, Rebecca Brien Howland. He had inherited Mount Hope, viewing it less as a showplace than as a working farm that should be self-supporting. He bred cattle, raised a variety of crops, and attended to local events and charities so energetically that he earned the warm regard of his neighbors. His enjoyment of this bucolic life was enhanced when his wife gave birth to a lively, healthy son. He and Rebecca settled on the peculiarly redundant name of James Roosevelt Roosevelt. The boy would always be known as "Rosy." James delighted in teaching his receptive son horsemanship, hunting, fishing, and a love of the outdoors that were decades later also to be imparted to a second son.

Such idyllic times as a country gentleman in verdant Dutchess County, punctuated by trips abroad, alternated with James's other life in the great metropolis. He invested in railroads, banks, and trust companies. Unfortunately the Civil War intervened. Although a robust thirty-two in 1861, James did not choose to serve, probably hiring a substitute for $300 when the draft took effect, as did many other young men of wealth. During a postwar trip to Europe, a fire of mysterious origins burned his home to the ground. James bought and greatly expanded a comfortable cottage near the pleasant town of Hyde Park, renaming it "Springwood." Amassing over a thousand acres of rolling countryside, he made this new estate, as he had Mount Hope, into a working, profitable farm. He became, in effect, the squire of Hyde Park, serving as town supervisor, overseeing all the local institutions, and becoming the senior warden of St. James Episcopal Church. One day a window there would memorialize him. But, to his wife's immense relief, although James was often proposed for elective office, he had no desire to widen his modest domain.

In the city James's ambitions were less inhibited. A town house on fashionable Washington Square was his second home. He belonged to almost every prominent New York club, and he set out with renewed vigor to make himself a multimillionaire. It never happened. Perhaps he was not quite ruthless enough to bring it off. His venture in coal fell victim to the Panic of 1873. Fortune may go to the brave, but it also favors the lucky. His attempt to gain control of the railroads of the Southeast also failed. His most ambitious venture, to build a canal through Nicaragua, finally collapsed as the twentieth century dawned. Ironically, it would be his cousin Theodore who developed a more viable route, through Panama. James took such disappointments with apparent equanimity; he was still quite wealthy, but in the future his business activity would be largely limited to investments and advice.

No other loss remotely compared to his personal tragedy in 1876. His supportive wife, Rebecca, died of a massive heart attack. It seemed to James that his productive life was over. Writer Jeff Young describes James Roosevelt in his early fifties as "still a strikingly handsome man. His rust-colored muttonchops were now speckled with gray, and his

waist was thickening, but his deep-set eyes, firm jaw, and poised, dignified, and urbane manner compensated for what age had taken away." His
return to a more active social life was hastened by the festive marriage of
his son to a member of the prominent Astor family. Rosy, who also held
Hyde Park close to his heart, purchased a house next to his father's. By
1877 James had found a soul mate in serious, bright Anna Roosevelt, the
"Bamie" treasured by her parents, the senior Theodore Roosevelts. She
seemed as lonely as James, particularly after the death of her beloved
father in 1878, but she had no remote interest in marriage. Still, James
continued to enjoy visiting Bamie and her mother at their New York
home. It was there, in 1880, at a small dinner party, that he met their
close friend, the stately Sara Delano. His gaze met hers, and lingered.

One of the four "beautiful Delano sisters" celebrated by New York
society, twenty-six-year-old Sara was easily the most formidable. Standing
nearly six feet tall, she presented almost a regal elegance. Called "Sallie"
by her friends, Sara was celebrated for her impeccable manners and taste.
She had lustrous, upswept brown hair and a chin as strong as James's.
Moreover, her zest for life was apparent. She had traveled with her dashing father, Warren Delano II, all over the world.

Perhaps James Roosevelt at fifty-two reminded Sara of a more sedate
version of her father. She knew he had a son her age, but at twenty-six
was she content to wind up as simply sad "old Miss Delano"? She
accepted his invitation to a house party at Springwood. In the minuet of
Victorian courtship, when of all his guests James asked Sara to arrange
the flowers on his luncheon table, both appreciated the significance of
such an invitation. James must have had at least an intimation that she
reciprocated his sentiments when he went to call on her father. It took
some time for Warren to discern his guest's intentions. They were already
acquainted and served on some business boards together, although the
Delano fortune dwarfed the Roosevelts'. Warren liked the fellow well
enough, even allowing that James made him "realize that a Democrat can
be a gentleman," but what about his age? It took some discreet urging
from Sara, a favorite of her father, to bring Warren around.

The couple were married in the resplendent setting of "Algonac," the
Delano estate, in 1880. Sara and James enjoyed a leisurely ten-month
honeymoon, more like another grand tour. Whatever his age, James was
still ardent. Sara became pregnant in Paris. On January 30, 1882, in an
upstairs bedroom at Springwood, their child was born. It was a most difficult delivery, taking well over a day. James stayed by his wife's bedside

all night. There was nothing restrained about his reaction the following morning. "At a quarter to nine," he wrote in his diary, "my Sallie had a splendid large baby boy. He weighs 10 lbs. without clothes." They named him Franklin Delano Roosevelt.

Much has been written about the impact of this special child on Sara, a transformation that would dominate future interest in anyone or anything else—"her reason for being," as biographer Ted Morgan puts it. However, the two remaining decades of Sara and James's life together were clearly amiable. Affection was not so overtly displayed by the Hyde Park Roosevelts as by those in Manhattan, but the love of both his parents was no less evident to Franklin, who had no siblings at home vying for their attention.

It was James who kept Franklin from becoming overwhelmed by what I called, in a prior book, Sara's "smothering mothering." Even at fifty-four, James Roosevelt devoted every available hour to Franklin. Sara recalled the joyous equity of their relationship: "His father never laughed at him," she said. "With him, yes—often." When discipline seemed called for, James would sternly remonstrate to Franklin, "Consider yourself spanked."

James taught his son to hunt, fish, and skate; to swim and sail; to go ice boating; to learn to control a sled and ride a thoroughbred. James loved horses, his special pride a matched pair, Top Mast and Top Royal. Father and son would travel together in James's private railroad car, a reminder of past ventures and a special pleasure to a young boy. They would ride together over the estate, Franklin learning to appreciate the natural world. Franklin's son Elliott relates, "James . . . taught his son to recognize the various birds whose habitat was the Hudson Valley and to make a collection of them. . . . With their favorite dog they would go together, Frank and his 'Popsie,' " a companion he could never replace but a relationship he would try to replicate. Franklin Roosevelt's biographer Frank Freidel describes a later time when FDR would take his own children around the estate, just as his father had taken him.

At their summer cottage at Campobello Island in Canada, just off the Maine coast, a splendid place for sailing, Franklin learned to cruise on his father's prize auxiliary cutter, the *Half Moon,* and later to sail his own knockabout in the chilly waters. He embarked on a lifelong love of the sea, collecting ship models along with his stamps and birds. Ward writes, "Mr. James was never distant, and for the first half of their lives together . . . he and Franklin were vigorous and almost inseparable companions."

At least the spontaneity of their relationship ended when Franklin was eight. In 1890 his father had a heart attack. The bond with his son remained as close as ever, but James was never to be so energetic again. The three Roosevelts traveled to Europe together a total of nine times, but during the final decade of James's life it was particularly to seek out the curative potential of spas. Franklin even went to a German school for a time. There were few children on the neighboring estates at home to whom he could relate.

Such isolation would end when, at the age of fourteen, Franklin went off to Groton, the highly regarded new boarding school in Massachusetts. His letters from Groton, and later from Harvard, are not quite so spontaneous as were Theodore Roosevelt's letters home. They read almost as if Franklin carefully couched his reports to "Dearest Mummy and Papa" to tell them what they wanted to hear—that all was well and would surely continue to go well. Biographer Doris Kearns Goodwin considers that from the time of his father's first heart attack, Franklin feared "that if he ever appeared other than bright and happy it might damage his father's already weakened heart."

Even as James lapsed into invalidism, his letters to Franklin remained frequent, solicitous, and tender. In his last semester at Groton, Franklin heard from his father, "Do you realize that you are approaching manhood and next year, when you begin your university life, you will be away from the safeguards of school and will have to withstand many temptations? . . . But I always feel your character is so well formed and established I have no fear as to your future career."

More and more, in 1899 and 1900, Franklin's letters from Harvard were solely to his "Dear Mummy," inquiring after the state of his father's health. She had taken her "beloved invalid" to the softer climes of South Carolina, where he insisted on continuing to ride, however slowly, his wife by his side. He even dashed about, despite her protestations, on a motorized tricycle and later an unreliable "locomobile" auto, alarming horses and nearby spectators alike.

In November 1900, however, back at Hyde Park, he suffered a more severe heart attack. His son Rosy hastened over from next door, and Franklin hurried home from college. Eventually James was taken to New York City to be closer to his doctors. A nurse moved in with them. The vigil began. Franklin came back from Cambridge on December 5, sat for hours with his father, and ran errands for his mother. "James was so glad" to see him, she wrote. Sara and both of James's sons were with him when he died, on December 9, 1900. His last words to his wife were "Only tell Franklin to be a good man." James was seventy-two.

On January 30, 1898, he had sent a telegram to his son: "My Dear Franklin, Only a few lines before we leave for church to wish you many happy and prosperous birthdays in your future life, and may you always bear in mind that in the past on both sides of your ancestors they have a good record and have borne a good name. God bless you my dear boy. We shall think of you often today and drink your good health at dinner this evening. Your affectionate father, James Roosevelt."

# 13

# FROM THE HEART OF AMERICA

## John Anderson Truman • David Jacob Eisenhower

FROM SIMILAR TOWNS in Missouri and Kansas, each denied the success he sought, pugnacious John Truman inspired his son Harry's love of politics, while stolid David Eisenhower toughened all his sons to fear failure even more than their father.

## John Anderson Truman

To potential biographers, Harry Truman would invariably insist, "Don't overlook my father." It was easy to do so. As Truman's daughter, Margaret, points out, there was "an extraordinarily strong intellectual-emotional bond" between Harry Truman and his mother. Widowed for thirty-three years, Martha Ellen Truman became her son's closest confidante—and, at least until his marriage, his best friend as well.

In his memoirs, Truman described both his parents as "sentimentalists" who equally encouraged his appreciation of literature, history, and music—but that wasn't the great contribution of his father. John Anderson Truman gave Harry his profession. A love of politics is what they most shared. Pugnacious, diminutive John Truman also inspired the persona that Harry took for his own. As he proudly proclaimed, his father "would fight like a buzzsaw for what he believed in," even the candidates he favored. Harry, who never had a fistfight in his life, contested equally vehemently, only with words. How John Truman would have loved his son's "Give 'em hell" campaign of 1948.

John Anderson Truman's whole life was a struggle for stature. He couldn't do much to heighten his physical size, five-four and perhaps 140 pounds, although no one dared call him "Peanut" to his face. But size alone need not inhibit success. The Trumans were "yeoman gentry" in the new world as in the old. The lure of abundant land brought them

Wedding portrait
of Martha and John
Anderson Truman

west from Virginia to Kentucky to Missouri. John's parents, Anderson
Shippe (or Shipp) and Mary Holmes Truman, were a hardworking, soft-
spoken, pious, respectable, and respected couple. The third of their five
children, John Anderson, was born on December 5, 1851. His small size
concerned his parents, but he grew into a vigorous young man, a verita-
ble bantam rooster of surprising physical strength and great inventiveness.
Although he loved his gentle parents, his role model for life was the less
easily contented Solomon Young, his future father-in-law.

Perhaps being orphaned early fired the ambition of both Solomon
and his equally formidable wife, Harriet Louisa Gregg Young. While
Louisa oversaw farms that grew to thousands of acres, risk-taking stock
dealer Solomon led cattle drives and wagon trains all the way to the West
Coast. He was as much at ease on the Santa Fe Trail as at home in Missouri, where the clouds of conflict were already gathering in the 1850s.

The Civil War came early to Missouri. John was only five when the first "bushwhackers" came over from "bleeding Kansas" to terrorize any who dissented from their views. Both Anderson Truman and Solomon Young owned slaves, but their Southern sympathies were more by heritage than conviction. Taking oaths of loyalty to the Union didn't help them. Particularly the Young homestead was devastated by the boys in blue and their partisans. Until her dying day Harriet Louisa Young viewed the Republican Party as the embodiment of evil. Her unreconstructed sentiments were imparted to her children, and to their children. Eighty years later her daughter would refuse to sleep in the Lincoln bedroom of the White House. The Trumans would always be Democrats.

Both families, however, recovered quickly from the war. The Youngs moved to a large farm around Grandview. Their daughter Martha Ellen, next to the last of their nine children, had been born in 1852 and was growing into a lively, accomplished, self-confident young woman. Everyone called her "Mattie." David McCullough, who won a Pulitzer Prize for his massive biography, *Truman,* describes her as about five foot six and slender, "with dark hair, a round bright face, and a way of looking directly at people with her clever gray-blue eyes." One of those she looked directly at (or down on, since she was two inches taller) at one of the frequent socials for young people in the area was John Anderson Truman. Describing herself as a "lightfoot Baptist," Mattie loved to dance and play the piano. Soon she was accompanying John, who had a fine singing voice. In this company he was unfailingly polite and took great care with his appearance. He combed his thin dark hair over to one side. His shoes were brightly polished, his clothes immaculate. Although generally sunburned from all those hours out in the fields, John's facial features were delicate, almost feminine. He had a long, thin nose and mouth and heavy-lidded eyes. He was always clean-shaven.

Still, it surprised many of their friends when popular, cultivated Mattie, who had been to a women's college, became engaged to this rather somber school dropout. They were married near the end of 1881 in the Youngs' spacious parlor at Grandview. In the town of Lamar, some ninety miles away, John Anderson Truman would start accumulating his fortune by trading in horses and mules. Their first child was stillborn, but on May 8, 1884, Mattie gave birth to a healthy son. They named him Harry after her favorite brother, Harrison. "They'll call him Harry anyway," John said. For a middle name they settled on just the letter "S," wanting to honor both grandparents but unable to choose between Shippe and Solomon.

Restless John Anderson Truman moved many times in his pursuit of prosperity, but it always eluded him. Three years later they were back at Grandview, with two additional children, John Vivian and Mary Jane. It was not that John hated farming. He was an excellent, innovative farmer. He simply wanted more out of life.

In 1890 the Trumans moved to the county seat of Independence. Both Solomon Young and Anderson Truman had died. Uncle Harrison had come over reluctantly from Kansas City to help run the farm. With a modest inheritance from his father, John was itching to invest again. Most important, six-year-old Harry's new eyeglasses opened vistas for learning beyond the capacity of the rural schools around Grandview. Independence offered many amenities, including excellent schools. Its colorful history as a jumping-off point for the West had been overlaid with an aura of respectability. The Trumans' spacious Crysler Street home, with its menagerie of animals, became headquarters for all the neighborhood children. Because of his thick but fragile glasses, Harry couldn't play rough games, but his role as an impartial arbiter won him at least grudging acceptance. At Sunday School he shyly spied the little girl who would be the one love of his life, Elizabeth Virginia "Bess" Wallace.

John Truman was at his most productive during this period, supervising everything—and even showing an inventive bent. His laborsaving devices, had they been properly promoted, might have provided an additional source of family income. John had met a successful investor from Kansas City named William Kemper and was busily engaged in emulating his example. Through Kemper he also became acquainted with the emerging Pendergast political machine that was being developed by three ambitious brothers. Business and politics went hand in hand. Jackson County, Missouri, at the center of the United States, was a microcosm of the evolving nation, its diverse western end anchored by burgeoning Kansas City, its homogeneous eastern end rural and settled. To the Pendergasts, Truman looked like an ideal representative for that region—seemingly related by birth or marriage to half the electorate out there in the boondocks. The whole of Jackson County was important in many elections.

Harry was doing well in school. He particularly loved history, and reputedly would eventually read every book in the Independence public library. However, to his no-nonsense father, his bespectacled boy seemed almost a sissy. John's tough younger son, Vivian, who wanted nothing more than to be a good farmer, was a more natural companion. Except for politics. Like his father, Harry was fascinated by the compelling entertainment of all-day picnics, rallies, and torchlight parades, of seemingly perpetual campaigning. Politics was their shared enthusiasm, their bond.

John was particularly thrilled with Grover Cleveland's return to the White House in 1892. Harry recalled his father riding "a beautiful gray horse in the torchlight parade" and decorating a weathervane on the roof of their home with a flag and bunting. At the Democratic National Convention in Kansas City in 1900, while his father sat proudly in Kemper's private box, Harry served as a page. Both were overwhelmed by the dramatic oratory of William Jennings Bryan. Politics could be inspiring as well as fun.

However, Harry was also thinking about what to do after high school. By the end of 1902 college of any kind was out. In a final gamble, John Anderson Truman lost everything in grain futures trading. After trying a number of alternatives, he was reduced to working as a night watchman for wages. Incisive biographer Alonzo Hamby concludes, "Still a tough, feisty man, he seems never to have recovered."

Meanwhile, Harry, too, had to find work. He wound up as a bank clerk in Kansas City, well regarded by his superiors, with the likelihood of advancement. On his own for the first time, he lived in a lively boardinghouse and—playing the piano for his friends—was overcoming his shyness and enjoying the social and musical life of the city. In a way, this was his college. It must have been an immense disappointment in 1905 when the call came to return to Grandview.

John had agreed to go back to running the farm, but he needed help. After Vivian married a neighboring farmer's daughter and went off to manage his own acreage, the Grandview farm became truly "J. A. Truman and Son." Only twenty-two when he returned, to the incredulity of his Kansas City friends, Harry would remain for eleven years. Working side by side with his demanding father, Harry became stronger physically, five inches taller and twenty muscular pounds heavier than John Truman, and the two became closer.

However, like other presidents with roots in the soil, dutiful Harry Truman longed to leave it. In later years he would tell young people that some experience in agriculture, business, and the military was the ideal combination for a career in public service. But it was in the army during World War I that he really found himself, and prior to that he tried to emulate his father as an investor, only with more success. As noted Truman scholar and biographer Robert H. Ferrell writes, father and son still debated politics. John supported Champ Clark for the Democratic presidential nomination in 1912, while Harry favored Woodrow Wilson.

Somehow Harry managed to spend so much time off the farm in every conceivable organization that it is almost as if he were already running for office. Richard Lawrence Miller, in his controversial biography of the young Truman, observes that all of Harry's extra activities made him "a community leader with connections throughout the business and political circles of western Missouri" years before he seriously contemplated a political career. One of these key contacts was Mike Pendergast, the brother consigned to the eastern region. Even Harry Truman's factional loyalties were inherited from his father.

John Truman had not worked with the Pendergasts to make money or to run for office. He had hoped to become wealthy through his investments, with political activity as a fulfilling avocation. He dutifully championed Pendergast candidates and served as a delegate to the state party convention and as elections judge in Grandview. In 1912, however, he agreed to become local road overseer, a part-time job others found profitable. The condition of rural roads in Missouri was critical to local farmers. Many overseers used these coveted political appointments simply to line their own pockets. Not John Truman. He became renowned for demanding as much from his road crews as from himself. As Harry later wrote, he learned from his father that "the expenditure of public money is a public trust. . . . Grandview had the best roads in the county."

Characteristically, it was John's stubbornness that led to his death. Impatient with his workmen's hesitation to remove a large boulder, John did it himself. The strain caused an intestinal blockage. After months, he finally agreed to an operation, but he never really recovered. On the morning of November 2, 1914, Harry by his side, John Anderson Truman died, shortly before his sixty-third birthday. The Independence *Examiner* eulogized him under the headline, "An Upright Citizen Whose Death Will Be a Blow to His Community," but a few days earlier, to visiting friends, John had pronounced his life a failure.

Harry Truman disagreed. John Truman "worked from daylight to dark all the time," Harry recalled, "and his code was honesty and integrity. His word was always good . . . and he raised my brother and myself to put honor above profit. He was quite a man, my dad was . . . a doer, not a talker." Harry Truman would do more talking, but he viewed himself, as did others, as a plain talker, and as straight a shooter as his father.

He, too, in his own way, was tough. Only in private did those closest to him rediscover the more authentic Harry Truman—thoughtful and particularly considerate of those who worked for him. The toughness was a façade, perhaps still in emulation of a father who was never afraid to fight. "My father was a very honorable man," Truman concluded. That constant, after all, transcended toughness or tenderness.

## David Jacob Eisenhower

Hadn't he been right all along? Here were all six of his sons, reunited back in Abilene, Kansas, every one a success. Arthur, the oldest, who had lived in that lively Kansas City boardinghouse with a young Harry Truman, was now vice president of a major bank. Edgar, despite his parents' antipathy to lawyers, had persevered to become a prominent attorney. Roy's pharmacy was flourishing. Earl was an engineer. Milton, the youngest, who would go on to become president of three major universities, held an important position in the Department of Agriculture.

Dwight, a major in the United States Army, made less money than any of his brothers, and his prospects in the glacial peacetime military seemed the least promising. Yet he had recently graduated at the top of his class at the elite Leavenworth Command and General Staff School. At thirty-six he was noticeably more tanned and fit than the others, who ranged from twenty-seven to forty, and his natural ebullience hadn't diminished. He admired but didn't really envy his brothers. Only Dwight had traveled all over the world

Retaining their unbreakable bonds, as biographer Piers Brendon writes, all six "swaggered through the streets of Abilene lined up abreast with arms linked," as of old. They even played golf at the country club, a new avocation for Dwight, unimaginable in his threadbare youth. Theirs had been such a hard-pressed family, from quite literally the wrong side of the tracks. It was June 1926, the only reunion all six sons would enjoy as adults.

Their proud father, David Jacob Eisenhower, still the picture of Teutonic stolidity at sixty-three, had to smile for once. Here were the living results of his harsh patrimony. He had beaten even the possibility of failure out of his sons, disciplining them so that they could learn to direct themselves. Once, in his fury, when he had whipped Edgar with a horse's harness because he had skipped school, twelve-year-old Dwight had tried to intervene. David finally relented, still furious but perhaps also in silent admiration for such a display of fearlessness. Dwight had originally been named for him—David Dwight. Only when he went to West Point would his name be officially registered as Dwight David. Even at twelve,

David Jacob
Eisenhower

"Little Ike" was showing signs of a sort of instinctive leadership. "President of the Roughnecks," he would be called as a teenager.

Why hadn't David's father, that good, generous, pious Dutchman, Jacob Eisenhower, understood his children as David did? He was never cut out to be a farmer like his forebears or brothers, but an engineer. The Eisenhauers, or "iron hewers" of the Rhineland, had become Eisenhowers in the New World, and it was the land they worked, from Pennsylvania to Kansas. Known as the River Brethren, as journalist Marquis Childs writes, they believed in "hard work, temperance, self-denial, simple living, an ordered, almost Biblical simplicity." Their disdain for the worldly trappings of materialism, however, did not deter their own prosperity. Their farms were as fertile as their large families. Jacob Eisenhower, both their temporal and their religious leader, expected his young son, David, to follow in that tradition. Born on September 23, 1863, David was one of the fourteen children of Jacob and Rebecca Eisenhower.

However, this boy hated the dawn-to-dusk, monotonous drudgery of farming. The only thing he enjoyed about it was working with its primitive machinery. In the most extensive biography of Dwight Eisenhower, Stephen Ambrose wrote of David, "He was, according to neighbors, a 'natural-born' mechanic," and wanted to be more, a professional engineer. His father, conditioned to patient contemplation, took the long view. He indulged the youth by sending him to a college, but it was hardly the school of engineering David had envisioned. At Lane University, a small River Brethren institution in Lecompton, Kansas, David was indeed enabled to take courses in mechanics, but greater emphasis was placed on reading the Bible in Greek. By his sophomore year, his attentions were diverted to another student, vivacious, enterprising Ida Stover, who had come all the way from Virginia in search of higher education.

They made an attractive, if contrasting, couple. Ambrose describes David, still clean-shaven, as darkly handsome, "tall, muscular, broadshouldered . . . [with] a thin, hard-set mouth, thick black hair, dark eyebrows, deep set, penetrating eyes, and a large rounded chin. His legs were long, his hands large and powerful." Ida was slender, fair, with lustrous brown hair, cheerful, and outgoing—not so much beautiful as glowing, with a ready smile her sons, one in particular, would inherit. She loved music. Throughout her life a piano would remain her most prized possession. They were married in the Lane University chapel on September 23, 1885, David's twenty-second birthday. In their wedding picture, unlike the John Trumans', both were standing; David taller than his wife.

Generous as always, and perpetually hopeful, Jacob Eisenhower gave the couple $2,000 and a 160-acre farm of their own, his customary wedding gift to each of his sons. David promptly mortgaged the farm to his brother-in-law and opened a general store in the town of Hope, south of Abilene. Anything was better than agriculture. The couple lived above the store. Arthur, the first of their six sons (a seventh died in infancy), arrived in 1886. David demonstrated little talent for retailing, and enjoyed less luck. He took in a more experienced partner named Milton Good, who turned out to be a crook. As Brendon observes, Hope did David "no good, and neither did Good." Moreover, a rural depression in 1888 severely hurt all retail businesses. The venture was a disaster. A lawyer hired to clean up the mess took everything but Ida's piano.

David was obliged to move four hundred miles away, to Denison, Texas, where he found work at ten dollars a week as a railway mechanic. After giving birth to their second son, Edgar, Ida joined him. They lived in a tiny frame house, little more than a shack, near the railroad tracks.

Here, on October 14, 1890, she gave birth to their third son. He was named David Dwight, but his parents would always call him Dwight. By now it must have been clear even to Jacob Eisenhower that at least one of his sons wasn't cut out to be a farmer, but the Brethren still looked after their own. They needed a plant engineer to take charge of the machinery at their creamery back in Abilene, an ideal job for a man with David's skills. Although the pay was modest and the hours long, he was happy to bring his family home from Texas after two trying years. Dwight Eisenhower would always view himself as a Kansan. The Abilene of the Eisenhowers was not unlike the Independence of the Trumans, a comfortably placid place with a similarly colorful past featuring such legendary lawmen as Wild Bill Hickok.

When a brother moved to California, he offered his house at a modest rental to David, so long as he agreed to take in and care for their widowed and ailing father. To the Eisenhowers even such a small home seemed of palatial proportions, although with the birth of their last child, Milton, in 1899, they were obliged to house nine people. Surrounded by three acres, it became a self-sufficient farm, with every square foot utilized to sustain the family larder. They had a cow, chickens, ducks, pigs, a vegetable garden, an apple orchard, cherry and pear trees, even a smokehouse to cure meats. Best of all, there was a barn for the boys to play in. Of course, there wasn't much time for play. Just as with John Truman in Independence, David Eisenhower, even if often absent, ruled over this domain—making it as productive as possible.

There is no denying that, even as their habitation improved, all the boys were frightened to death of their father. Life was simple. Right and wrong were clear and nonnegotiable. As Dwight recalled, his father, who communicated with his strap or a maple switch, had "quick judicial instincts"; his mother was more patient and sensitive. Milton added, "Dad had the authority." However different their methods, both David and Ida instilled ultimate self-reliance and confidence. As family biographer Steve Neal puts it, "By setting standards and values of high principles the parents had given their sons a quiet strength."

Ambrose describes Dwight at nine or ten as normal-sized, wearing clean but hand-me-down clothes, generally barefoot, "with a shock of light-brown hair, blue eyes, a friendly disposition, and his mother's grin." However, he could flare up "in red-faced anger," much like his father. As he grew older, he tried to restrain both his temper and the profanity he never used around his parents. Dwight was noted for his restless energy and love of the outdoors. An average student overall, from an early age he enjoyed reading, particularly history. He loved sports. His athletic prowess and his good looks made him effortlessly popular, although, like the young Harry Truman, he was very shy around girls. In later years David must have regretted the time not spent with his sons, particularly this one. Other first fathers whose ambitions were thwarted found satisfaction in the company of their children. David's satisfaction came later, when his sons were grown.

The most traumatic incident in Dwight's youth lends credence to the trusting relationship between the Eisenhower boys. When he was fourteen, a freshman in high school, he scraped his knee, a not-infrequent occurrence. This time, however, it became infected, and the infection spread to the extent that doctors actually contemplated amputating his leg. Vowing that he would rather die than be crippled, Dwight made Edgar, "Big Ike," promise that should he fall asleep, Edgar would stand guard by his bedside to prevent an operation. His father pondered as his mother prayed, but they also acquiesced. It was a close thing, but the leg was saved. When Edgar went off to the University of Michigan, Dwight finally became "Ike," not merely "Little Ike." He graduated from high school in 1909. Yearbook predictions envisioned Dwight as one day teaching history at Yale and Edgar as destined to become president of the United States.

As adulthood approached for each son, their father finally loosened the bonds of discipline and their mother the restraints of tradition. Bible readings and prayer sessions became less frequent. As writer Doris Faber puts it, "Cards made their appearance and in time cigarettes were allowed; music, secular as well as devotional, tinkled from Ida's still prized piano in the parlor. All this was in a real sense a preparation for what lay ahead." When Ike went off to West Point, his aim was more to play football and receive a solid, free education than to pursue a military career. But it was still an affirmation of the constancy of his parents, Brethren pacifists. In her room that night, his mother cried.

Dwight managed to come home at least once a year, even as his army career took him to foreign postings. Brigadier General Dwight David Eisenhower was unable to return, however, for his father's funeral. On March 10, 1942, after recurrent illnesses, David Jacob Eisenhower died. Immersed in the War Plans Division in Washington, all Ike could do was reflect in his diary, "I have felt terribly. I should so like to be with my Mother. . . . But we're at war! And war is not soft . . . I loved my Dad." The following day, he eulogized David: "My father was buried today. I've shut off all business and visitors for thirty minutes—to have that much time, by myself, to think of him. He had a full life. . . . He was not quite 79 years old. . . . He was a just man, well liked, well educated, a thinker. He was undemonstrative, quiet, modest, and of exemplary habits. . . . His finest monument is his reputation. . . . His word has been his bond. . . . His sterling honesty . . . his pride in his independence earned for him a reputation that has profited all of us boys. . . . I'm proud he was my father!"

"I come from the very heart of America," Ike said to the British, who honored him in 1945. No less did Harry Truman. Both future presidents, born in bordering states, reared in America's heartland, were encouraged by mothers who are so easily admired that the influence of their fathers can readily be overlooked. One can almost hear Eisenhower, too, protesting, "Don't forget my father." And one can imagine Truman reflecting, as Eisenhower did in his tribute to his father, "My only regret is that it was always so difficult to let him know the great depth of my affection for him."

# 14

## "WE DON'T WANT
## ANY LOSERS"

### Joseph Patrick Kennedy Sr.

THE MOST RELENTLESSLY AMBITIOUS of all first fathers, initially with his own personal political goals, Joseph Kennedy Sr. committed his considerable resources to the conviction, ultimately shared by his sons, that their electoral success was synonymous with the nation's.

John Fitzgerald Kennedy was his father's third choice to be president of the United States. Joseph Patrick Kennedy Sr.'s first choice was himself. His second choice was his eldest son, Joseph Patrick Kennedy Jr. It looked as if John Kennedy, whom everyone called "Jack," was headed for a career in journalism or academia. Instead, circumstances impelled him to become, in effect, a substitute for a substitute—the standard-bearer of his father's political ambitions.

Only twenty years before Jack Kennedy's narrow election as president, his father realized that any such intentions for himself were no longer viable. He had come down on the wrong side of history. Yet his regret was probably tinged with relief. By 1940 it was apparent that the political prospects of his son Joe Jr. were far more realistic than his own. Fairly or not, having been viewed as almost favorable to fascism, Joe Sr. was now fully free to plot his oldest son's political future. Joe Jr. not only duplicated his father's drive, he had a stronger presence, a more appealing personality, and no hint of controversy—and he was being more thoroughly prepared for leadership. Most of all, he had so much more time to rise to the top. Young Joe's sudden death late in the European war in 1944 put a violent end to that vision. It was felt so deeply and personally by Joe Sr. that for a time he lost his will to live. Future tragedies that took the next two of his sons were at least shared with the nation.

Joseph Patrick Kennedy
Sr. with Joe Jr. and Jack
(right)

There may be more biographies of Abraham Lincoln than of any other American president, but no family rivals the Kennedys for the sheer weight of the works written about them—with no end remotely in sight. In many of them, the ambition of Joseph P. Kennedy Sr. has been portrayed as an amalgam of the philosophies of Niccolò Machiavelli, Friedrich Nietzsche, and Ayn Rand. A more balanced view might include Thomas Jefferson and John Adams. Like Jefferson, Kennedy believed that the new American aristocracy should be based on achievement, not lineage. However, like Adams, he also affirmed that each generation should enhance opportunities for the next. Unlike either, he amassed a fortune to forward his aims. Money was never more than the means to his ends, but with their trust funds his children would never have to worry about it.

What biographers often overlook is Kennedy's fundamental patriotism. His methods may have been excessive, even amoral, but his ambition for his sons was not solely for personal satisfaction—or to validate that all Americans, including Catholics of Irish extraction, share a birthright of aspiration to the nation's highest office. Kennedy believed that *because* of the way his sons had been raised, they were better qualified for leadership than others. In effect, to paraphrase General Motors' Charlie Wilson, what was good for the Kennedys must also be good for the nation. In business Kennedy was a combination of lone wolf and buccaneer, in politics an advocate of overkill, but his philosophy in both was profoundly conservative. He believed in sound money and national self-interest. When the time came, he insisted that Jack Kennedy go into politics, but ultimately this second son became a willing convert. He, too, had come to share the view that no one else was better prepared to get the country "moving again."

It was ambition more than destitution that brought the Kennedys to these shores in the first place. County Wexford, from which they came, was not so afflicted by the terrible Irish potato famine as most of the Emerald Isle. The Fitzgeralds, with whom the Kennedys would be inextricably intertwined, came over a few years earlier from the same locale. What is extraordinary, as opposed to the slow but steady saga of millions of other immigrant families, is that from the year they arrived, it took the Kennedys of Massachusetts no longer to achieve the presidency than it did the Washingtons of Virginia.

By the time the immigrant population in Boston exceeded the native-born, and its political structure became dominated by Irish Catholics, in only their second generation in America, the patriarchs of the Kennedy and Fitzgerald families were already wealthy and powerful. In every other way, "P. J." Kennedy and "Honey Fitz" Fitgerald were so different from each other as to destroy anyone's ethnic stereotypes. It is not surprising that they also profoundly disliked each other.

His education limited to a few terms in parish schools, tall, handsome, deliberative Patrick Joseph Kennedy Jr. had risen from working the Boston docks to owning saloons, importing liquor, investing in a hotel and a coal company, and becoming a banker. By the age of thirty he enjoyed a mansion, servants, a sixty-foot cabin cruiser, and vacations at the most fashionable watering holes. In 1887 he married Mary Augusta Hickey, the bright, assertive, socially ambitious daughter of one of Boston's most prominent Irish families. The next year, on September 6, 1888, she gave birth to the first of their four children, a boy. Naturally, P. J. wanted to name him Patrick Joseph Kennedy III, but his wife insisted that reversing the names would make him sound "less Irish." Joseph Patrick Kennedy it would be.

Because his father had managed to achieve more materially than had Kennedy's father, dapper, gregarious, lively John Francis Fitzgerald had the advantage of an education at the elite Boston Latin School and studied medicine at Harvard. His father's death, however, obliged him to seek more immediate employment, at the Boston Customs House. Contacts there helped him launch an immensely successful insurance business and later his own newspaper. In 1889 Fitzgerald married his extremely shy and devout second cousin, Mary Elizabeth Hannah. The first of their six children, a girl, was born on July 22, 1890. They named her Rose Elizabeth Fitzgerald.

All P. J. and Honey Fitz had in common was wealth, energy—and politics. P. J. was elected to the Massachusetts House of Representatives and State Senate, but his real interest was in exerting power behind the scenes, particularly as a member of the Board of Strategy that selected and endorsed Democratic candidates for office. Honey Fitz, although also a powerful ward leader, was an instinctive, irrepressible politician. He was elected to the United States House of Representatives but in 1905 decided that he wanted even more to be mayor of Boston, by then considered the "Irish presidency." The polo-playing proletarian was already playing the role of vaudeville "stage Irishman" on the hustings—in biographer James Hilty's words, the "back-slapping, quintessential Irish politician who knew every voter's name," wept at every wake, and concluded most appearances by leading supporters he called his "dearos" in a stirring rendition of "Sweet Adeline."

In short, he was precisely the sort of person that responsible, dignified leaders like P. J. Kennedy didn't want representing Irish Americans to the still socially dominant "Brahmins" of the Protestant establishment. Moreover, there were already ugly rumors about Fitzgerald's corrupt campaign practices. Nonetheless, he ran and he won. By his side at every rally was not his reticent wife but his vivacious fifteen-year-old daughter, Rose, his "shining star." Slender, dark-haired, and poised, she had been acclaimed "Boston's prettiest high-school senior" and added a touch of class to the crass. After the election she became in effect the official hostess of Mayor Fitzgerald. She hoped to go on to Wellesley College, but Boston's archbishop prevailed on her father to set the right example. She went, instead, to Manhattanville College, her entire education in Catholic or public schools.

There had been no such inhibitions on young Joe Kennedy. At Boston Latin he excelled at sports and was popular enough to be elected class president. It still wasn't enough to get him invited to the parties hosted by his classmates' snobbish parents. As Rose later put it, there were parallel social circles in Boston, "one for them, and one for us." At Harvard Joe enjoyed success, but not nearly enough to suit him. He made more acquaintances than intimates, played baseball, and gained admission to a number of clubs, but not the most coveted, Porcellian. He resented such exclusion, but had made a significant discovery. He had the knack of making money on his own. Kennedy invested in real estate and ran a profitable bus tour company. More than politics alone, money meant power and might ultimately lead to social acceptance on every level.

With Fitzgerald in office, whether P. J. liked it or not, they managed to patch things up. Unlike the Montagues and Capulets, political feuds rarely draw blood. When, even if uneasily, their families vacationed together, the attraction between Rose and Joe was immediate. Although he may have looked a bit like silent film comedian Harold Lloyd, as Rose got to know bright, lean, sandy-haired, freckle-faced Joseph Patrick Kennedy, she viewed him as "open and expressive, yet with youthful dignity. . . . He neither drank nor smoked. . . . He was serious but with a quick wit and a spontaneous infectious grin. . . . Even then he had an aura of command." Joe was similarly smitten. Their summer romance had a happy ending, or at least a happy beginning.

It took some time, but on October 7, 1914, twenty-six-year-old Joseph Patrick Kennedy married twenty-four-year-old Rose Elizabeth Fitzgerald in the private chapel of William Cardinal O'Connell, merging Boston's two most prominent political families. Joe, who was already president of a small bank, set out to make his first million within ten years. The couple settled into a comfortable nine-room house in suburban Brookline. It would soon be full of little Kennedys. Rose's "precious package," Joseph Patrick Kennedy Jr., arrived on July 15, 1915; John Fitzgerald Kennedy, called "Jack," on May 29, 1917; Rose's first "dainty daughter," Rosemary, christened "Rose Marie," in 1918; and Kathleen, called "Kick," in 1920. They were followed by Eunice in 1921, Patricia in 1924, Robert Francis, called "Bobby," in 1925, Jean in 1928, and finally Edward Moore Kennedy, called "Teddy," in 1932.

During World War I, Joe Sr. helped manage an immense Bethlehem Steel shipbuilding facility, during which time he had a run-in with the youthful assistant secretary of the navy, Franklin D. Roosevelt. After the war, Kennedy joined the well-established Boston investment house of Hayden, Stone & Company, but not for long. The shingle of the office he opened in 1923 said simply "Joseph P. Kennedy, Banker." At his Harvard reunion, he listed his profession as "capitalist." There followed two decades of often-mysterious machinations, from Wall Street and real estate to liquor importing and Hollywood. Well diversified, Kennedy adroitly got out of the stock market before the crash of 1929 and made far more than his first million well ahead of time.

The irony is that, so anxious for social acceptance, Kennedy did little to court it after college. Everything he achieved was on his own. He wanted it all, and felt he had earned it all, but his family was still excluded, in Brookline as in Boston, by the "best" Brahmin families. "I was born in this country," Joe exclaimed. "My children were born in this country. What the hell does someone have to do to become an American?" Rose pondered plaintively about when the "nice people" would accept their family. When it finally came—the Kennedys elevated to little less than American royalty—it no longer mattered. The price had been too high.

But Rose had a more immediate problem. She had been deeply distressed when she found that her father had been blatantly unfaithful to her mother. She was stunned to discover that the husband who had pursued her so avidly had been repeatedly unfaithful to her—most conspicuously with Hollywood sex goddess Gloria Swanson. If alcohol was the curse of the indigent Irish, was infidelity the affliction of the affluent? After agonized reflection and a lengthy religious retreat, Rose decided to stay with her husband but to pursue her own independent life. They would remain unified by mutual devotion to their children, the first priority of both.

Joe Kennedy had already compartmentalized his life. In his view, religion aside, in a contemporary marriage a strong man could do just about whatever he wanted without compromising a harmonious home. Whatever else one might conclude, there is no denying Joe Kennedy's commitment to his children. Jack reflected, "My father wasn't around as much as some fathers when I was young, but whether he was there or not he made his children feel that they were the most important thing in the world to him. He was so terribly interested in everything we were doing. He held up standards for us, and he was very tough when we failed to meet those standards." His disapproval was conveyed by a stare over his glasses. No more was necessary. That he was so often away only made him seem more formidable to his nine children. If their mother, as Jack put it, was the "glue" that held their family together, their father had assembled the framework of the structure. He was, as Rose affirmed, "the architect of all our lives," even as she sometimes sought the solitude of her separate room. To Joe Kennedy, "The measure of a man's success in life isn't the money he has made—it's the kind of family he has raised." Two decades later he reiterated, "My wife and I have given nine hostages to fortune. Our children . . . are more important than anything else in the world."

There was an order of precedence, however, particularly as the older two sons grew into their teens. "My father wanted his oldest son in politics," Jack recalled. "He demanded it. . . . It was like being drafted." Moreover, since the oldest son, Joe Jr., "was the star of our family [who] did everything better than the rest of us," he was the obvious candidate for high office. With their mother increasingly away in the 1930s, often on buying trips to Paris, as their father had been in the 1920s, the children looked increasingly to Joe Jr. as a sort of surrogate parent. He taught the others how to swim and sail, how to play every sport. Much as he loved his parents, Jack vowed never to have a large "institutional" family of his own. The Kennedys may have invented the premise of "quality time."

Presiding over the dinner table with the older children, Joe Sr. grilled everyone on national and world events, his daily seminars reinforced by an endless stream of letters when he was away. Money and business were never discussed. Arthur Schlesinger Jr., the distinguished scholar who worked in the Kennedy administration, writes, "No child could doubt the order of priority. . . . The father confronted the children with large questions, encouraged them to have opinions of their own . . . and instilled convictions of purpose and possibility." To Bobby Kennedy, even at the younger kids' table, public life seemed "really an extension of family life." Of course, it was all supplemented by the advantages of wealth—travel, education, exposure to the world of ideas—but instruction began at home, wherever that might be.

Deciding that Boston was "no place to raise children," or at least *his* children, because of the impenetrable snobbery of its self-appointed elite—"You can go to Harvard and it still doesn't mean a damned thing"—Joe Sr. moved his entire brood to Riverdale, north of Manhattan, and then to an immense estate in Bronxville, in Westchester County. Summer residences were established in Hyannis Port, on Cape Cod, and Palm

Beach, Florida. Wherever they settled for a season was their own exclusive enclave, outsiders admitted only as they accommodated to the Kennedys.

The locale made little difference to their lifestyle, but the regimen was most rigorous, physical as well as mental, at Hyannis Port, the closest to a true Kennedy home—from touch football on the beach to debates in the dining room. Toughness was a virtue, competition a constant, their father's mantra drummed in daily: "We don't want any losers around here. In this family we want winners." At Choate, the elite establishment boarding school, Joe Jr. predictably excelled in everything. Jack, slender, more reflective yet fun-loving, but too often ill, just seemed to plod along. "You have the goods," his father encouraged him. "Why not try to show it?" Yet Joe Sr. already sensed his second son's different sort of potential—more urbane and subtle than Joe Jr.'s robust natural leadership. "The first Irish Brahmin," Massachusetts governor Paul Dever would call Jack Kennedy. Al Smith had been simply "too Irish" and urban to win the presidency in 1928. Perhaps, Joe Kennedy pondered, it might take qualities personified by both Joe Jr. and Jack. One might learn from the other.

It was clear that the Democrats had a great chance to win in 1932. Kennedy put his money on Franklin Roosevelt and raised funds from a good many others as well. After he won, Roosevelt named Kennedy to head the new Securities and Exchange Commission and later the Maritime Commission. In 1937, after his reelection, Roosevelt made an extraordinary decision. Although, as Kennedy's granddaughter Amanda Smith writes, Joe Kennedy "lacked both diplomatic experience and a diplomatic nature," the president named this son of an Irish saloonkeeper to be ambassador to the Court of St. James.

To Rose Kennedy, their too-brief time together in Europe would be the "happiest years" of her married life. As Joe Sr. said to her while dressing for dinner at Windsor Castle, "Well, Rose, this is a helluva long way from South Boston, isn't it?" The whole handsome photogenic family, an early example of "celebrity," was warmly embraced not only by the British media—"eleven ambassadors for the price of one"—but throughout the entire country, king and queen to commoners. Invitations flooded in from the cream of English society. Ironically, full social acceptance finally arrived for the Kennedys in class-conscious Great Britain.

Encouraged by his father, Jack took full advantage of the opportunity to soak up all he could about world events. He even studied for a time with Harold Laski at the London School of Economics, and served as his father's secretary at the embassy. Forced to leave Princeton because of illness, he transferred to Harvard. His senior honors thesis was adapted into a well-received book, *Why England Slept,* reportedly rewritten by Joe Sr.'s journalist friend Arthur Krock. For the first time, Joe Jr., now at Harvard Law School, may have experienced something approaching sibling envy.

Ambassador Kennedy made a good start, his refreshing candor appealing to the English. Unfortunately, the aristocrats he admired most were the "Cliveden set," who felt at least some affinity for fascism, and Kennedy imprudently intruded into domestic British politics. He not only became a personal friend of Prime Minister Neville Chamberlain but an overt supporter of his policy of appeasement of Nazi Germany. At the outbreak of war in 1939, Rose and the children returned to the United States. Joe's letters to his "Rosa" were particularly tender during this time, as if he had never strayed. "I love you devotedly . . . more every day," he wrote her in 1940.

Kennedy's overriding concern in London was what he viewed as protecting America's interests, but President Roosevelt was deeply distressed at his defeatist tone. After he was recalled for "consultations," Kennedy gave a radio address supporting FDR's bid for an unprecedented third term. Kennedy had considered making a run for the presidency himself, or doing so at least by 1944, when Joe Jr. would be ready to run for governor of Massachusetts. After increasingly reckless comments in the press criticizing the president's internationalist policies sundered any productive relationship with the administration, Joe Kennedy Sr. was permitted to resign and return home.

Increasingly branded as a misguided isolationist, an appeaser of the evil Axis, and worse, Kennedy realized that he would never have a political career of his own. Although he was now free to promote Joe Jr. in his stead, it would have to be behind the scenes. After Pearl Harbor he wired Roosevelt, "In this crisis all Americans are with you. Name the battle post. I'm yours to command." All he received back was a belated offer to take a minor administrative post, which he declined. Despite Jack's perennially bad back and his potentially fatal Addison's disease, his father pulled strings to get him a commission as an ensign in the navy. Joe Jr., although he shared his father's views, had volunteered for the naval aviation cadet program six months before the United States entered World War II.

After Jack's heroic and well-publicized exploits as the commander of *PT-109* in the Pacific in 1943 (although his seamanship is still questioned), young Joe wasn't about to be upstaged. In August 1944 he volunteered to fly a plane loaded with explosives to destroy a German rocket site. He was to bail out early, but his plane—essentially a flying bomb—exploded prematurely, killing him instantly. It all but killed his father as well. Joe Sr. blamed Roosevelt, that "warmonger," personally for his son's "murder." Eventually overcoming his grief, Kennedy insisted, "We've got to carry on. We must take care of the living. There is a lot to be done."

It was understood who was now designated to start doing it. As Jack recalled, "I could feel Pappy's eyes on the back of my neck." Joe admitted in a 1957 interview, "I got Jack into politics. . . . I told him he had to." How anxious the potential journalist was to pick up the banner remains a matter of conjecture. But any reluctance Jack may have felt in pursuing a political career was submerged in the excitement of his first race in 1946 for the House of Representatives. Kennedys no longer started at the bottom.

Joe left nothing to chance, investing his money and giving just as freely of his advice, although at this time and place the Kennedy name alone was probably enough to guarantee victory. Joe told his staff, "We're going to sell Jack like soap flakes." Actually he was sold more like a war hero inheriting his brother's mantle. Campaign literature stressed continuity: "The New Generation Offers a Leader. . . . John Fulfills Dream of Brother Joe Who Met Death in the Sky over the English Channel." Rose and her daughters invited thousands of starstruck ladies in the district to take coffee or tea with them. Most significantly, as biographer Nigel Hamilton points out, Jack demonstrated the boyish charm and magnetism of a natural campaigner, beyond his father's expectations. After winning handily, Jack was hardly the most conscientious congressman, although his father pulled strings to have him placed on the most prominent committees. Joe also used his publicity machine to place stories about Jack, "America's most eligible bachelor." The new congressman made friends with other freshman "comers" in the class of 1946, including a Republican from California just down the hall named Richard M. Nixon.

Other than Jack's victory, the 1940s were a devastating decade for the Kennedys, starting with Joe Jr.'s tragic death. In 1948 Kathleen, "Kick," her parents' favorite, died in an airplane crash in England. Rosemary, the oldest daughter, had long suffered from mental illness or retardation or both. She had been making progress in England, but back in the United

States she seemed to regress. Her father agreed to what he understood might be a positive surgical procedure—a prefrontal lobotomy. It didn't work in her case. She was shut away in an institution in Wisconsin, separated from the family. She could never be a "winner."

Joe decided not to have his ghostwritten memoirs published, reasoning, in terms of his sons, "I didn't want them to inherit my enemies. It's tough enough they inherit my friends." The *Saturday Evening Post* predicted that Jack Kennedy would one day be president, Bobby his attorney general, and Teddy a future United States senator. Where did they get that idea? By 1952 Bobby was taking over day-to-day operations of what became essentially the Kennedy political party, leading his well-trained "Irish Mafia." Other Democrats became increasingly offended as Kennedys hogged the credit for future electoral victories. Many who had viewed the old man as impossibly intrusive in 1946 came to miss him in the wake of "ruthless" Bobby Kennedy, almost fanatically devoted to his brother. Still, Joe held the ultimate power, and the purse strings. How many millions he spent between 1952 and 1960—and through whom—will never fully be known, but he kept a businessman's sharp eye on the return for every dollar he invested.

In 1952 Jack ran for the United States Senate against courtly, moderate Republican Henry Cabot Lodge, a pillar of the old Boston establishment. In a statewide race, the Republicans had an equal chance. There were few substantive differences between Kennedy and Lodge, but even in the face of Eisenhower's landslide victory, Kennedy won his Senate race by some 70,000 votes. Reportedly, after Joe gave the *Boston Post* a loan for $500,000, they abruptly switched their support to his son. Even devout Rose Kennedy couldn't resist commenting, "At last the Fitzgeralds have evened their score with the Lodges."

In 1953 Jack Kennedy triumphed again, winning the hand of lovely, stylish Jacqueline Bouvier, in the wedding of the year. Others in the family may have questioned how delicate "Jackie" Kennedy would fit into the rough-and-tumble of touch football at Hyannis Port, but Joe Kennedy knew better. Jackie was just what Jack needed to help forward his political career, adding to his vigor her almost regal elegance.

Despite all her moral ministrations, Rose suffered through the knowledge that there had been a tug-of-war, and Joe had won. Her sons patterned their personal lives after the compartmentalized example of their father. In her long life she would witness at least three generations of Kennedys and Fitzgeralds casually unfaithful to their wives. It is little

wonder that she turned ever more to the solace of her faith, but her support of her husband's and sons' ambitions never wavered. After all, her
boys had been weaned on "political lullabies."

In 1960 she continued to be very effectively out front, Joe even
more behind the scenes. In 1956 Jack, supported by Bobby, had gone
against his father's advice and contested for the Democratic nomination
for vice president. He narrowly lost, but laid the groundwork for a presidential try in 1960, vowing to become a "total politician." During the
next four years he spoke throughout the country for Democratic candidates. Jack's inspirational book, *Profiles in Courage,* written, as biographer
Herbert Parmet points out, by the Kennedy "literary apparatus" and promoted by his father, won the Pulitzer Prize. Many powerful constituencies in the Democratic Party vehemently opposed John F. Kennedy as
their presidential candidate for 1960, at least in part because of residual
suspicion of his father's influence. As journalist Richard Reeves recounts
in his vivid *Profile of Power,* liberal icon Eleanor Roosevelt viewed Jack,
whose charm eluded her, as "just Joe Kennedy's overreaching son, an
arrogant man who would not wait his turn." Harry Truman repeated
Adlai Stevenson's famous line, "It's not the Pope I'm afraid of, it's the
Pop." Lyndon Johnson, a contender for the 1960 presidential nomination,
took off the gloves, labeling Joe a "Chamberlain-umbrella policy-man . . .
[who] thought Hitler was right" and now wanted to run the country
through his "scrawny little son."

There was no refuge remote enough for Joe Kennedy to escape
being a campaign issue. So were Jack's youth, health, and—however soft-
pedaled—his religion. One thing was clear. He would have to win nomination on the first ballot at the Democratic National Convention in Los
Angeles. In early, critical primaries Joe Kennedy invested so much money
that Jack quipped that he'd received a wire from his father, insisting,
"Don't buy one more vote than necessary. I'll be damned if I'll pay for a
landslide." It wasn't entirely satire. In West Virginia, the key primary state,
Kennedy's chief rival, Senator Hubert H. Humphrey, accused the Kennedy steamroller of all manner of "dirty tricks." He wasn't alone.

Kennedy won at the convention and in a razor-thin general election
over Republican Richard Nixon, the outcome in doubt all night. Comedian Mort Sahl quipped, "Joe Kennedy hasn't lost a son. He's gained a
country." The founding father finally emerged on the morning of November 9, 1960, joining the other exhausted Kennedys at the armory in

Hyannis Port. His son Jack said with utter accuracy, "The margin is thin, but the responsibility is clear." Joe Kennedy for once couldn't contain his glee. Even if not as originally planned, it was the fruition of everything— or nearly so. He had only two requests to make of his son, but viewed neither as negotiable. A reluctant Bobby Kennedy, only thirty-four, the confidant Jack could most trust, must be his attorney general. Ted Kennedy, who had worked so hard in the campaign, must, as soon as he reached the legal age of thirty, take Jack's place in the Senate. "You'll learn together," Joe said. "You know my father," Jack explained to friends. When Bobby finally agreed to serve, Jack cautioned him, "Don't smile so much or they'll think we are happy about the appointment." The fact is, he had offered it first to another. Inevitably, as Jack accumulated and exercised his own power, Joe's hold on his sons was slipping. Yet when Jack met a surprisingly vigorous Dwight Eisenhower, he was impressed with how much he reminded him of his father, particularly in the advice he gave.

On December 19, 1961, little more than a year after the election, seventy-three-year-old Joseph P. Kennedy suffered a massive stroke while playing golf at the Palm Beach Country Club. He lay so close to death that he was given the last rites of the church. Rose prayed even more than usual, and bought a black dress for the funeral. Forty-eight hours after he was stricken, Joe still could not recognize Jack, who had rushed to his side. Yet he rallied. Perhaps it was sheer strength of will. Joe Kennedy was incapacitated for life, paralyzed on one side, and unable to speak intelligibly. In this agonizing state he lingered for eight years, his mind apparently still capable of comprehending whatever he was told. Much of the news would be tragic—the violent deaths of two more of his sons and the humiliation of the third. "The New Frontier" would be reached, if at all, by others. "Camelot" had proved to be as ephemeral as the stage play on which Jackie Kennedy's fantasy had been based. To Rose Kennedy it seemed particularly poignant. During the Cuban missile crisis she lamented, "My son, my poor son, so much to bear, and there is no way now for his father to help him."

Joseph Patrick Kennedy Sr. died at the age of eighty-one on November 19, 1969. As family biographer John Davis writes, on the preceding morning, Rose had touched the rosary's cross to her husband's lips and put the beads in his hands while his children recited the Our Father. After the funeral mass in Hyannis, Kennedy was buried in Brookline.

Cardinal Cushing, one of the family's most cherished friends, presided. The senior Joe Kennedy outlived four of his nine children, and a fifth he had put away, finding no other solution to her plight. His wife, Rose, lived for another quarter-century, somehow surviving the same unbearable weight of loss.

When, perhaps in a rare moment of reflection or even uncertainty, Joe Kennedy asked Jack why he wanted to undertake the "appalling burdens" of the presidency, his son replied with a question: "Who can do it better?" The tables had been turned. That had been his father's original justification, first for himself, then for Joe Jr., finally for Jack. Reluctance had been replaced by confidence. In time, Joe Kennedy's vision was shared by his second son.

# 15

## "A Man Who Loved His Fellow Man"

### Sam Ealy Johnson Jr.

EMULATING, DISDAINING, AND FINALLY RETURNING to admiration of his father Sam's example, Lyndon Johnson, a young man in a hurry, was his father in full—a consummate Texas Hill-Country politican, elevated by his energetic efforts to a world stage.

Compare their photographs. The same pale skin, the same slicked-back hair, the same bulbous nose, the same enormous ears, the same penetrating eyes and tight mouth. Both stood well over a slender six feet. Both walked angled forward, the same confident strut, the loping strides. Their clothes, cowboy or cosmopolitan, were cut with care. Imagine them in action, their "treatment" enveloping whoever must be convinced, whether constituent or congressman, one long arm over his shoulders, the other hand grasping his suit lapel or the strap of his overalls, chin lowered to the chest, eyes narrowed, that great nose almost in the face of the prey, yet a slight conspiratorial smile: "We need you to come through." Sam Ealy Johnson Jr. and his son Lyndon Baines Johnson—each viewed at the age of, say, thirty-five or so—in midcareer.

Lyndon Johnson didn't merely resemble his father physically. In his childhood he wanted nothing more than to be like him, to try to replicate him in every way. Yet after Sam Johnson lost everything, proving he had more scruples than sense, Lyndon's admiration vanished. As his brother, Sam Houston Johnson, put it, "It was most important to Lyndon *not* to be like Daddy." Finally, near the end of Sam's life, there was a reconciliation—and more than a measure of redemption. At his core Lyndon had never ceased loving Sam Johnson and admiring what he stood for, the people's causes he championed. In this the son would emulate his

Sam Ealy Johnson Jr.
with Sam and Lyndon
(right)

father, only shrewder, smarter, stronger, and on a larger stage. Lyndon
Johnson was his father in full. One might say bigger than life, bigger even
than Texas.

The Hill Country was in the blood of both. However, Sam's political and business ambitions never really went beyond it. Lyndon's encompassed not only the whole of Texas but the nation, and ultimately the
entire world. At the end, Lyndon too was undone, but not by anything
so trivial as the fall of cotton prices. Lyndon's fall was that of a giant,
brought down as the world watched.

The Texas Hill Country was always Lyndon's home, even though he
spent half his life in Washington. That it was and is a landscape of such
striking contradictions may help to explain both its hold on the Johnsons
and the source of their strength. Its undulating beauty and bounty cover
only a thin layer of tillable soil, over a limestone base. It is a hard place

to farm, afflicted with alternating drought and deluge, a deceptive paradise for dreamers and survivors.

Sam Ealy Johnson Jr., born on October 11, 1877, the first son after four girls, was his father's special joy. Bright "Little Sam" grew up listening to the older Sam, who had known boom and bust, swapping Civil War stories with his neighbors and sharing their plight as small farmers and ranchers unequally ranged against the domination of "the interests." Populist politics was in his blood. Later his father moved to Stonewall, on the Pedernales River, and founded the town of Johnson City.

By passing examinations Sam earned a teaching certificate, taught for several years, and won his first public office in 1902, as justice of the peace for Blanco County. In 1904 he won a seat in the Texas House of Representatives, the first of his six successive terms in the legislature. At least in appearance he seemed the prototypical Lone Star State lawmaker of the old school. LBJ biographer Robert Dallek describes Sam as "six foot two, with coal black hair, a big Stetson hat, hand-tooled boots, into which he stuck his pants." Moreover, he was most convivial, a hearty backslapper. He drank heavily, sometimes too heavily, and was a frequent patron of the Congress Avenue bars in wide-open Austin. Robert Caro, the Pulitzer Prize–winning biographer of Lyndon Johnson, writes that Sam also frequented the lively street's bordellos. Ubiquitous lobbyists "dispensed the 'three Bs' favored by legislators—beefsteak, bourbon, and blondes." But everyone soon discovered what Sam's father already knew. His son was different. He paid his own way for everything.

Many of the causes that Sam Johnson Jr. championed were hardly popular with the powerful. Sam proposed bills to regulate the rates of public utilities. He was for farm relief and the eight-hour day and in favor of establishing pure food standards, levying taxes on corporations and railroads, establishing an equitable justice system in Texas, and limiting the activities of the lobbyists themselves. He might be a bit overbearing at times, but as Texas congressman Wright Patman said of Sam, "He was the best man I ever knew, straight as a shingle."

Politics came first, but Sam was hardly averse to making money. He expanded his ranch, bought and sold livestock, invested in real estate, and traded in high-risk commodities futures. When the bottom dropped out of the market and he was all but wiped out, he started all over again.

One of those who admired him was his predecessor in the legislature, a highly literate lawyer named Joseph Wilson Baines who was down on his luck. He had hoped to be a congressman. Baines had a bright and

beautiful daughter, utterly devoted to him, named Rebekah. She was trying to finish college at Baylor in part by writing stories as a "stringer" for
Austin newspapers. Her father suggested that she go interview Sam
Johnson. She didn't get much of a story. Sam's manners were rough,
almost crude, his language no more literate than that of his backcountry
neighbors, and he was very "cagey" about answering any specific questions. Yet, despite everything, she sensed something "dashing and dynamic"
about him.

As for Sam, while he wasn't about to reveal it straight off, he was
absolutely bowled over by Rebekah Baines. He had never met anyone
like her, a lovely, delicate-looking young lady of quality who actually
enjoyed talking about politics. She was slender but shapely, with pale
skin, her eyes a deep blue. Caro describes her as a "soft-spoken, gentle,
dreamy-eyed young lady who wore crinolines and lace, and lovely bonnets." To Sam, she too seemed to possess an inner quality—a surprising
strength born of character. It was a whirlwind courtship. In November
1906 Joseph Wilson Baines, Rebekah's "adored parent," died. On August
20, 1907, she married Sam Ealy Johnson Jr. She was twenty-six, he
twenty-nine.

Rebekah was quickly disabused of any illusions. Moving to Sam's
three-room shack—it wasn't much more than that, although he painted
it a bright yellow to cheer her up—wasn't so much going to a new
locality as to a new planet. How could any place in the Hill Country be
so desolate? As she reflected in her journal, a comforting habit she continued from childhood, "I was confronted not only by the problems of
adjusting to a completely opposite personality, but also a strange and new
way of life. . . . I realized that life is real and earnest and not the charming fairy tale of which I had so long dreamed." But she coped, her com-
plaints limited to wistful sighs.

On an August morning little more than a year after she had married
Sam, as the creeks were rising, Rebekah went into labor. It was hours
before a doctor was able to make his way to the Johnson cabin. As
Rebekah recounted it, in her rather perfervid style, "It was daybreak,
Thursday, August 27, 1908, on the Sam Johnson farm on the Pedernales
River near Stonewall, Gillespie County. . . . The light came in from the
east, bringing a deep stillness . . . and then there came a sharp, compelling
cry—the most awesome, happiest sound known to human ears—the cry
of a newborn baby, the first child of Sam Ealy and Rebekah Johnson was
'discovering America.' " After hearing the news, white-bearded old Sam

Johnson, oblivious to the weather, mounted his horse and rode wildly from farm to farm, proclaiming, "A U.S. senator was born this morning!" Rebekah's projection, although it sounded like the Nativity, was only for the lower house. Here was the future congressman her husband would never be.

It was months before "the baby" was named. Rebekah and Sam finally settled on the name of a lawyer friend named W. C. Linden, which Rebekah changed to the more "euphonious" Lyndon. Baines would be the child's middle name. There would be four more children—Rebekah, Josepha, Sam Houston, the only other boy, and Lucia.

By the time he was two, little Lyndon was learning the alphabet from his mother. At three, arithmetic was added, and he was already reciting from some of the literary works Joseph Baines had read to Rebekah. Lyndon was an extremely friendly child, very active, seemingly already as natural a politician as his father. Even as a baby he loved to climb from one person's arms to another's. But he craved attention and had to be constantly watched. He loved to crawl away, going quickly and for surprisingly great distances. His mother registered him in the local school a year early.

In 1918, when Lyndon was ten, his father, after a hiatus to look after business, returned to the legislature. The Johnsons had settled into a considerably more spacious home, a six-room Victorian house in Johnson City itself. Sam was able to afford household help for Rebekah. She became a sort of "Lady Bountiful," descending into the benighted village to improve everything and encourage such causes as temperance. Sam himself became more temperate. He drank less, and his affection was more sustained. He even ran Kennedy-like debates around the dinner table, testing his children's knowledge. As Rebekah's expectations for him heightened, Lyndon began to view his father as more emotionally stable than his mother.

In the legislature, Sam found new causes to champion. He fought for pensions for veterans and their widows and opposed the post–World War I anti-German "loyalty bill," pleading for tolerance. Nor did Sam forget his constituents, pushing particularly for graded roads and better schools. Johnson's last bill, the "Johnson Blue Sky Law," protected consumers from unscrupulous stock salesmen. Always there was Lyndon, up in the gallery, following every word intently. His father was now his closest companion. When Sam came home to campaign, Lyndon would join him in the big Model T, going from farm to farm, door to door, cajoling and conversing with everyone. It was altogether wonderful, being with his father at all his rallies and on his rounds. "Sometimes I wished it could go on forever," Lyndon told Doris Kearns, who wrote a particularly personal biography.

It ended when Lyndon was thirteen. In 1919, after Sam's mother died, he bought out all her other children to put together a sort of Greater Johnson City, and moved back to the old farm. The price of cotton fell so low that for the second time in his life Sam was wiped out— only now he had a family to support. He lost everything, even his home. Only the charity of relatives provided food and shelter. The best job he could obtain was as a part-time game warden. Later he was hired as a foreman on the road-building crew that graded the very highway, from Austin to Fredericksburg, that he had promoted in the legislature. Not surprisingly, he began to drink heavily again, perhaps more than ever.

If Sam was humiliated, Lyndon was contemptuous. Of what value now were all his father's high ideals and scrupulous honesty? The first family of Johnson City became its laughingstock. It was particularly bitter for Lyndon, a dapper dresser and president of his high school's senior class. Did he, too, lack common sense? He began running with a wild crowd and, in a final assertion of irresponsible independence, took off with some friends for California, a carefree year of vagabond drifting. It also gave him time to think.

He finally agreed to go to college—Southwest Texas State Teachers College in San Marcos, only thirty miles away. While working his way through, Lyndon also worked his way up, developing the skills he would demonstrate later in public life, placing ambition above ideology. He cultivated older men who had the power to help him. Making himself invaluable to their success hastened his own. The first was the president of his college. After graduation he taught school, then managed the campaign of a candidate for the state senate. In 1934 wealthy Congressman Richard Kleberg made Lyndon his administrative assistant in Washington. Soon Lyndon was running the New Deal's National Youth Administration in the Lone Star State and attracting the attention of President Franklin Roosevelt himself. In 1934 he married refined Claudia Alta Taylor, known as "Lady Bird."

The following year, Sam Johnson, who had followed his son's rise with some satisfaction, had a severe heart attack. Even as Lyndon feared for his father's life, he sought out his advice. Their district congressman had died in February 1937. Although only twenty-eight, Lyndon wanted to run in the special election to succeed him. There were eight other candidates, all older, more experienced, and better known. Lyndon's campaign, his "Blanco Blitz," simply outhustled them all, whom he labeled "eight in the dark." His theme, suggested by his father, "A Vote for Johnson is a Vote for Roosevelt's Program!" was no more true of Johnson than the other candidates, but it was promoted relentlessly.

Lyndon's campaign was launched from Sam's front porch, reversing their past roles. "My father became a young man again," Lyndon told Doris Kearns. Sam Johnson "looked out into all those faces he knew so well and then he looked at me and I saw tears in his eyes as he told the crowd how terribly proud he was of me and how much hope he had for his country. . . . There was something in his voice and in his face that day that completely captured the crowd." Lyndon won. His mother had her congressman; his father had his son back.

That summer, Sam had another massive heart attack. When Lyndon returned for his father's sixtieth birthday, Sam was in the hospital, under an oxygen tent, but he longed to go home. "Lyndon," he said, in words that would resonate, "I'm going back to that little house in the hills where the people know when you're sick and care when you die. You have to help me." Despite the protests of the medical staff, Lyndon took the old man home. Two weeks later, on October 23, 1937, Sam Ealy Johnson Jr. died. He was buried in the family graveyard, by the stream and under the trees he loved.

Lyndon had to settle his father's remaining debts, but the one *to* his father he could never fully repay—the example of a life committed to public service. In Rebekah's words, Sam Johnson was "a man who loved his fellow man."

# 16

## "He Hears the Trains Go By"

### Francis Anthony Nixon • Leslie Lynch King Sr. Gerald Rudolph Ford Sr.

RICHARD NIXON SOMETIMES SOUGHT ESCAPE from his father's excessive volubility, but he also drew strength from Frank Nixon's ceaseless encouragement. Having escaped an abusive marriage, Jerry Ford's mother found in Gerald Ford Sr. a true father for her young son.

## Francis Anthony Nixon

Many of those assembled in the East Room of the White House were getting uncomfortable. They had worked for Richard Nixon, and most of them, whatever the excesses of Watergate, remained devoted to him. Up front, his family fought back tears. It must have been most painful for them to get through Nixon's emotional, rambling farewell to his staff on this, the final day of his presidency, August 9, 1974. It was also, at least in official terms, his farewell to the American people, and it was being viewed on television all around the world.

Eyes moistened when he recalled his two brothers who had died of tuberculosis so many years before and, most of all, his mother. "She was a saint," Nixon said, thinking back to how she had nursed her older son, and other mothers' sons, in their hopeless struggle against tuberculosis. "Yes, no books will be written about her. But she was a saint." (With a bit of chronological license, a book *had* been written about her. Nixon's cousin Jessamyn West made Hannah Nixon the model for her stalwart Quaker heroine in *The Friendly Persuasion*.)

"I remember my old man," Nixon went on. "I think they would have called him sort of a little man. . . . You know what he was, he was

Francis Anthony
Nixon

a streetcar motorman first, and then he was a farmer, and then he had a
lemon ranch. It was the poorest lemon ranch in California, I can assure
you. He sold it before they found oil on it." (This wasn't precisely true,
but close enough.) "And then he was a grocer, but he was a great man.
Because he did his job, and every job counts up to the hilt no matter
what happens." His mother, Hannah Milhous Nixon, was a saint; his
father, Francis Anthony Nixon, was no more than an underappreciated
man who did his job.

Biographers of Richard Nixon invariably dwell on the contrast
between his parents, personifying their ostensibly very different families.
Biographer Stephen Ambrose writes, "On his father's side, his progenitors
were generally loud, boisterous, emotional, and Methodist. On his
mother's side, they were generally quiet, restrained, unemotional, and
Quaker." To biographer Herbert Parmet, this contrast helps to explain
Richard Nixon's "schizophrenic existence." He wanted to be like his
mother but was fated to be more like his father.

But admiring people is not the same as wanting to be like them. The enduring image of Nixon's childhood is the desire to escape its circumstances. In his memorable speech accepting the Republican presidential nomination in 1968, Nixon recalled hearing train whistles at night and dreaming "of faraway places he would like to go." His parents were there to launch him on the journey. He revered his mother, but it was not in her nature to nurture the driven, calculated career of a Richard Nixon. Beyond being tenacious, he was nothing like his father. Frank Nixon was all bluster—imprudent, outspoken, very physical, but bluntly honest. There wasn't a devious bone in his body. His was the greater influence because, as biographer Jonathan Aitken writes, he "fired up" his son. Ambrose calls Frank "the most influential teacher in Richard's life." To Parmet, Frank was "the driving force" in his family. While acknowledging that "I have never known anyone to work longer and harder," Richard stressed his father's encouragement. It impelled the youth to hurl his 140-pound body against bigger opponents on the football field and to be a champion debater, leader, and valedictorian.

Francis Anthony Nixon was born in Ohio on December 3, 1878. His life might have been very different but for two things—his restless nature and the death of his adored mother when he was eight. His brother Ernest stuck it out, survived their cruel stepmother, and eventually earned a Ph.D. to become a respected professor at Pennsylvania State University. Frank could not. He left home in his early teens and made his own way in the world, eventually to Whittier, California. He was at first a streetcar motorman, as he had been in Ohio, and then worked on another's farm. In Whittier he had the good fortune to meet Hannah Milhous. The Milhouses, pious but prosperous Quakers, looked down on indigent, unlettered Frank Nixon, but they tended to look down on everyone.

At least Frank made himself presentable. Ambrose writes that he "wore his dark hair slicked down and precisely parted. He had a fine full face, and a strong but not over-sized nose and jaw, deep penetrating eyes and a firm mouth. . . . His good looks, careful grooming, and animated ways drew people to him, but unfortunately his loud and aggressive personality drove many of them away." It didn't drive away Hannah, who probably didn't mind being hugged and kissed for once. She was not considered particularly pretty, but something about her captivated Frank. Biographer Roger Morris describes her as a "gentle young lady of wasp waist and serious countenance, marked by thick raven hair and eyebrows above dark, limpid eyes." Aitken adds that Frank "saw beauty in her tranquil face, whose high cheekbones and intense, greenish-brown eyes fell away to . . . the Milhous ski-jump nose." Richard would resemble his mother in at least this feature.

On June 25, 1908, in the East Whittier Friends Church, twenty-three-year-old Hannah Milhous married twenty-nine-year-old Francis Nixon. He had also become a Quaker, of its more animated Western variety, and would teach Sunday School with Methodist fervor. Four months later Hannah was pregnant. In June 1909 she gave birth to Harold Samuel Nixon.

It must be said that Hannah's father, however he felt, was generous, first by giving Frank a job, then by helping him buy and seed his own lemon grove in the nearby town of Yorba Linda. The sturdy home Frank built still stands, on the grounds of the Nixon Library and Birthplace. Here Richard Milhous Nixon was born at 9:35 P.M. on January 9, 1913. Hannah marveled at how much noise this healthy, eleven-pound, brown-eyed, black-haired baby managed to make. Harold had been so quiet. Reportedly, Frank danced all around the vicinity, exclaiming, "I've got another boy!" Always fascinated by tales of English royalty, Hannah named her second son for Richard the Lion-Hearted. It was fine with Frank.

For Frank Nixon the years in Yorba Linda were a financial disaster but a social triumph. Although everyone labored, the sandy soil was simply not suitable for producing high-quality lemons. Frank, despite the endless hours in his grove, served on the school board, and Hannah was active in the women's club. They were a popular part of whatever social life the town offered. It didn't matter to Frank that people seemed to prefer his quietly gracious wife; he was proud of her. Forty-four years later he reflected, "I knew I had picked the very best. And I haven't changed my mind." In Yorba Linda Frank experienced a degree of stability, a sense of belonging that he had never known before.

In 1919 oil was found nearby. Soon there was a small-scale boom and at last a potential boon for Frank Nixon. Speculators offered him $45,000 for his property; he turned them down. If there really was oil, he wanted it. Hannah, perhaps on a hunch, suggested that they buy land at Santa Fe Springs, where oil was eventually found. Instead they stayed put, where no oil was discovered. In 1922, when Richard was nine, his father finally sold out, for a fraction of what he had been offered three years before. The Nixons, virtually penniless, moved back to Whittier.

There were now four boys. Francis Donald was born in 1915 and Arthur Burdg in 1918. For once, frugal Frank actually took out a loan.

He opened a gas station and chose a good location. He started bringing in and selling the produce of surrounding farmers, which led to a full-service grocery store, open for extended hours. The family was rarely able to eat together. Hannah, who had studied classical languages and literature, awoke before dawn to uncomplainingly bake dozens of pies to sell in the store. Richard's specialty was sorting vegetables, a chore he particularly disliked. Everyone waited on trade, but when Frank's volatility turned into arguments with customers, he was tactfully reminded that the meats required his expert hand to cut, back in the rear of the store.

Richard learned to gauge his father's moods. Although his years of frustration had seemingly ended, Frank would suddenly strike out with little provocation, argue heatedly with his sons, and settle the issue with his strap. His anger then dissipated as quickly as it had arisen. These outbursts were like summer storms. Richard, however, was rarely their victim. He sensed when to avoid his father, escaping into reading or daydreaming or simply observing from a safe distance. Decades later Nixon reflected, "Perhaps my own aversion to personal confrontations dates back to those early recollections." In the requirements of retailing, only religion and education could not be compromised. Ambrose writes, "There were daily prayers and church services of one kind or another every Sunday." School became almost a refuge. Richard had begun grade school in 1918. Hannah early reflected that her son "was interested in things way beyond the grasp of a boy his age. . . . He always carried such a weight."

In the summer of 1925 Arthur, the youngest son, suddenly fell ill, suffering headaches, indigestion, and exhaustion. The eventual diagnosis was tubercular encephalitis. Neither physicians nor prayer could save him. Richard first saw his father cry when Arthur died. Frank viewed it as a form of divine judgment and never again opened his store or station on Sundays. He began frequenting revival meetings and espousing evangelism to try to find some way to comprehend such tragedy.

All Richard could do to provide any sense of solace was to continue to excel. At his eighth-grade graduation at East Whittier School, he took the spotlight as valedictorian, class president, and "most outstanding student." As in the future, he might be more admired than genuinely liked by his classmates, but his ability was undeniable. "My plans," he said, "are to finish Whittier High School and College and then to take postgraduate work at Columbia University, New York. I would also like to study law and enter politics for an occupation so that I can be of some good to the people." After the Teapot Dome scandal broke, he announced, "When I get big I'll be a lawyer they can't bribe."

Frank could hardly wait for his boy to grow up. With each year he became more involved in Richard's daily life, a school dropout turned debate coach. When Richard, wearing an old brown suit, the only one he owned, won an oratorical contest and some wealthier parents offered to buy him a new blue suit for the state final, Frank was outraged. He wasn't about to accept charity. He couldn't really afford it, but he bought the suit himself. "There was never a day I was not proud of him," Richard wrote.

Then Harold, the oldest son, fell terribly ill. This time the diagnosis was clear from the start—tuberculosis. Frank sold land from behind his store to pay for the best in private care. The family made a hard decision. Hannah would venture with Harold to Prescott, Arizona, to a rented cabin. She took in, cooked, and cared for three other tuberculosis patients as well, to pay for her son's treatments at the local sanitarium. The dry desert climate itself was considered to have curative powers. Frank and his other sons would continue to run the store. For two summers Richard traveled to Prescott, whatever the risks to his own health, holding a variety of jobs there; his favorite was as a carnival barker. Frank made the six hundred–mile round trip as often as he could. The strain was showing on everyone.

Hannah made an immensely welcome surprise trip back to Whittier for Christmas of 1929 and told her incredulous husband that at the age of forty-five, she was again pregnant. Their fifth and final child, a boy like the others, Edward Calvert Nixon, was born in 1930. Finally, Harold insisted that both he and his mother come home for good. However long it might last, he wanted to be near everyone and everything he loved. It lasted until March 7, 1933. Richard returned from Whittier College to see both parents in tears, this time uncontrollably. At twenty he was now their oldest son. Harold, so sunny and spontaneous, was the closest friend Richard Nixon ever had. "From this time on," Hannah reflected, "it seemed that Richard was trying to be *three* sons in one, striving even harder than before to make up to his father and me for our loss."

He excelled at Whittier College, even inducing its staid trustees to permit dancing on campus. "Nixie" was never a "regular guy," but he seemed to loosen up a bit and started dating. Later he would have many nicknames, including "Gloomy Gus." The only one he thoroughly disdained was "Dick," although his father often used it. In a triumphant senior year, he was elected president of the student body, capped by the award of a full-tuition scholarship to Duke Law School. To meet his modest living expenses, he would have to scrimp on everything, but that was nothing new. At graduation he was almost joyous. The president of Whittier predicted, "Nixon will become one of America's important, if not greatest, leaders."

Frank helped him pay his living expenses at Duke, lending him thirty-five dollars a month. The Depression hadn't passed Frank by, severely reducing his liquidity although his business survived. In World War II naval lieutenant Richard Nixon, as usual, did his job, serving for three years. He was married now, having won the hand of Patricia Ryan in 1940. In 1946 he ran for Congress and won, and went on to be elected senator and in 1952 Eisenhower's vice president, his eyes already focused on the ultimate prize.

Frank loved to follow politics and was even an avid reader of *The Congressional Record,* but his loyalties fluctuated. He loved Roosevelt in 1932, for example, and hated him in 1936. Frank's only permanent affiliation was to what one might call "the Richard Milhous Nixon Party." Over his strenuous life Frank Nixon had survived many ailments, including bleeding ulcers, but he appeared healthy enough, not to mention immensely proud (if uncomfortable in his tails) when he and Hannah attended the festivities at Richard's inauguration as vice president in 1953. Living for a time in retirement on a small farm in York, Pennsylvania, both became particularly close to their two granddaughters, Julie and Tricia.

Frank lived until 1956. He was hospitalized during the Republican National Convention, that year being held in San Francisco. On August 22, the day for vice-presidential balloting, Richard Nixon got a call from the Whittier hospital that his father had suffered a ruptured abdominal artery and was sinking fast. Richard and Pat rushed down to see him. As Ambrose writes, "When they arrived . . . Frank Nixon was in an oxygen tent, in great pain, but still able to talk." He gasped out, "You get back there, Dick"—fearful of last-minute "funny business" to deny his son's renomination. Instead, Richard stayed, and they watched it together on television.

Francis Anthony Nixon died at the age of seventy-seven on September 4, 1956. Like Lyndon Johnson's father, he had asked to be brought home from the hospital to die. During Richard's last visit he told his son, "I don't think I'll be here in the morning." Richard replied, "Dad, you've got to keep fighting," and, of course, what he heard back was "Dick, *you* keep fighting." At the restrained Quaker funeral service, the immediate family sat behind a curtain. No photographs were permitted. Frank Nixon might have preferred something more lively.

In his memoirs, Richard Nixon summed up his father's philosophy succinctly. Beyond his love for Hannah and their sons, it was the one constant in his life. "My father's interest in politics made him the most enthusiastic follower of my career from the beginning. My success meant to him that everything he had worked for and believed was true: that in America with hard work and determination a man can achieve anything."

## Leslie Lynch King Sr.

The first time Leslie Lynch King hit his bride was on their honeymoon. In a hotel elevator, a man tipped his hat to Dorothy, and she smiled back in acknowledgment. Once in their room, Leslie became enraged, accused his young wife of flirting or worse, and slapped her repeatedly. She was terrified. All she could do was to tearfully deny it, but she must have realized that she had seen her husband as he really was for the first time.

Their wedding, on Saturday, September 7, 1912, at Christ Episcopal Church in Harvard, Illinois, had been the highlight of the town's social season. Dorothy Ayer Gardner's father, a wealthy businessman, was a former mayor of Harvard. Her mother was descended from the old New England family that had founded the town. At thirty, Leslie King was ten years older than his bride. His parents lived in an Omaha mansion. Leslie had met Dorothy at her college in Illinois, a small, select school for young women that his sister Marietta also attended. The mutual attraction between them was instantaneous. Biographer James Cannon describes Leslie King as "a dashing fellow . . . [a] tall and handsome blond, with his big open face, blue eyes, strong jaw and muscular shoulders," and vivacious "Dot" Gardner as a "fair, buxom brunette with a quick smile, enthusiasm for life and energy." Leslie fascinated her with his plans for the future. Dorothy's father, Levi Gardner, was confident that this strapping fellow, ostensibly a wealthy wool merchant in his own right, could comfortably support his daughter. It was not a protracted courtship.

The wedding gift of Leslie's father, Charles King, was this leisurely, luxurious honeymoon, traveling by Pullman train throughout the West Coast and then back to Omaha, where their new cottage awaited them. For Dorothy each stop became an experience in terror, followed by an emotional reconciliation. He hadn't meant it. It would be the last time. She was frightened to eat in the dining car of the train, should there be admiring glances from the next table. When they finally got to Omaha, it was not to their own home, as her husband had promised, but to live with his parents, including a most domineering mother. After only a

Leslie Lynch King Sr.

week, Leslie not only beat his wife, he threw her out of the house, her trunk and trousseau behind her. Somehow she found her way to the railroad station and back home to her horrified parents.

In a matter of weeks, Leslie appeared on their doorstep, even more contrite than before, and although she must have known better, Dorothy went back to Omaha with him. This time their home was a dingy basement apartment. When Dorothy's mother, Adele, came to visit, Leslie ordered her out. By now Dorothy was pregnant. On July 14, 1913, Leslie Lynch King Jr. was born. It was an impressive name, suitable for a future president, but it wouldn't be the child's name for very long. Leslie became even more abusive. Dorothy wrapped her sixteen-day-old son in a blanket and fled the house. Her parents had been alerted. In December 1913 she obtained a divorce on grounds of "extreme cruelty." The court ordered that King pay twenty-five dollars a month in child support until his son was twenty-one. Unfortunately, he was bankrupt. His father agreed to pay the child support, and did, at least from time to time. Apparently Leslie turned to drink.

After staying for a time with her married sister in Illinois, Dorothy moved back to her parents' home with little Leslie in tow. The Gardners had also moved. Whatever the circumstances, divorce in those times—and in a straitlaced little town in the Midwest—constituted a scandal. Despite being the first family of Harvard, Illinois, the Gardners moved to Grand Rapids, Michigan. Dorothy's son, simply called "Junie" for "Junior," as Cannon writes, "came out of the crib as a healthy, tow-headed boy with a toothy grin and boundless energy."

King, who eventually remarried, moved to Wyoming, inherited some money, and made more, ultimately becoming the proprietor of a large ranch. He saw his renamed son at least twice. The first was when the boy was in high school in Grand Rapids and worked in a diner across the street. Leslie King had tracked him down. Arriving with his new wife and their little girl, King announced to the stunned sixteen-year-old, "I am your father." After an awkward lunch at a different restaurant, King offered to take the boy back to Wyoming to live with them. When the offer was refused, King gave him twenty-five dollars and left in his new Lincoln. After his father died, King had moved from Nebraska to Wyoming at least in part to avoid a judgment Dorothy had obtained to force him to pay toward their son's college education. Working at Yellowstone one summer, Gerry Ford turned the tables and visited King at his spacious spread in Wyoming. This meeting was no more relaxed than the first. Too much had happened, or perhaps too little, in the years of separation.

Leslie Lynch King Sr. died in Tucson, Arizona, on February 13, 1941, at the age of fifty-nine. The cause of his ferocity toward the mother of his son is buried in the mysteries of psychopathology. Although he never really knew his birth father, the man originally named Leslie Lynch King Jr. formed his judgment at their meeting in Grand Rapids: "Nothing could erase the image that I gained of my father that day: a carefree, well-to-do man who didn't really give a damn about the hopes and dreams of his firstborn son."

# Gerald Rudolph Ford Sr.

Grand Rapids in 1915 was a pleasant, prosperous place, described by one historian as "America at its best, a community of great expectations." In one of its more comfortable homes lived the relocated Adele and Levi Gardner, their daughter, and their grandson. At a "social" at Grace Episcopal Church, Dorothy met an amiable young man of twenty-four, only a year older than herself, and was impressed with his earnest manner.

Gerald Rudolph
Ford Sr.

Once stung, she was not about to rush into anything, but she felt he might be worth knowing better. Tall and slender, he was dark and not particularly dashing, physically very little like Leslie King. As she was to discover, to her benefit and that of her son, he could not have been more different in virtually every other way. That he liked Dot Gardner was obvious. His name was Gerald Rudolph Ford.

Ford was a paint and varnish salesman, ambitious to have his own business. Born in Grand Rapids, he had to leave school at the age of fourteen to support his mother and sisters after his father had been killed in a train accident. He was rather shy and serious, yet Cannon also cites his "ready smile" and "booming laugh." Local lawyer Philip Buchen described Ford as "a man of high principles, rather stern looking but not stern acting." Another family friend agreed that Ford was "stern looking [but] very good-hearted, friendly, and very much respected in the community." In essence, Ford was the extraordinary ordinary man.

What Dorothy also discovered was that he was a bachelor who genuinely loved children. There might be nothing flashy about this suitor, but there was nothing contrived about him, either. Dorothy Gardner and Gerald Ford were married where they had met, at Grace Church, on February 1, 1916. They were to have three boys together, Thomas, in 1918; Richard, in 1924; and James, in 1927. They knew their older brother not as Leslie Lynch King Jr. but as Gerald Rudolph Ford Jr. Everyone called him "Jerry." Young Ford himself did not realize that Gerald Sr. was not his birth father until his mother told him when he was thirteen. His new name was not made official until 1935, when he was twenty-two. His stepfather never legally adopted him, probably for reasons relating to any lingering hopes for child support, but it hardly mattered to Jerry. He knew that Gerald Sr. "had as much love for me, if not more, than for his own three sons."

Perhaps it *was* a bit more. Even-tempered Gerald Ford Sr. also sought to be evenhanded, but young Jerry was already at an age where they could be companions, go fishing together, toss a football back and forth. And soon it became clear that Jerry had talent in that area. His stepfather was prospering, so conscientious a salesman that he would personally guarantee the quality of the paints he sold to furniture manufacturers, even if the producers of those paints would not.

In 1919 the family moved from rented quarters into a spacious house, where Dorothy not only presided over a bountiful dinner table but also participated in a multiplicity of activities. It was almost an idealized Norman Rockwellian sort of setting, where family gatherings and traditional holidays were particularly festive occasions. There was something more—an understated commitment to helping the less fortunate, motivated by the shared faith of both parents. Dorothy wasn't simply the prototypical young clubwoman, active in everything. She also volunteered for the Well-Baby Clinic, helped form a community center in the least affluent part of town, and baked bread and sewed clothes for needy families. Similarly, Gerald Sr. wasn't only involved in Masonic, social, and service clubs, the Chamber of Commerce, and the like. He helped form Youth Commonwealth, committed to assisting the poorest children in Grand Rapids. Both were very involved in church work. As a neighbor described the Fords, "They didn't talk religion, they just lived it."

For his sons, Ford had only three rules—always tell the truth, work hard to make something of yourselves, and get to dinner on time. Richard Ford recalled, "It was a very frank, open kind of relationship." Having left school after the eighth grade, Gerald Ford Sr. was particularly concerned with education. Jerry was the other boys' natural leader and role model, although rather reluctantly at first. After all, they were five to fourteen years younger. Headstrong and possessive as a child, he became a thoughtful and protective older brother—his parents' influence at work. His mother was more the disciplinarian in the household than his stepfather, but there were few lapses that required discipline. All the boys became Eagle Scouts and acolytes at church. Although Jerry was popular at school and became renowned for his athletic exploits, he had early difficulties in the classroom, having to overcome a stuttering problem and being left-handed, of some concern to his parents.

By 1922 the senior Ford had more serious problems. A national recession following World War I was felt with great severity in the Midwest. Furniture sales plummeted, and so did his income. The mortgage on their house was foreclosed, and they had to move back to rented quarters. Not everything in Jerry Ford's childhood was idyllic. However, the family members simply turned to each other for emotional support. All the boys had chores, after-school jobs, and thoroughly structured lives. When it came time for Jerry to go to high school, it is instructive that of the three alternatives, his father favored South High, where the poorer and immigrant youngsters tended to go. As Cannon relates, Ford Sr. suggested to his son, although some hard realities might already have sunk in, "It will help you learn about living."

Moreover, South High was noted for the quality of its teaching—and its football team. Only five foot eight and 130 pounds when he entered high school, blond, gangling Jerry Ford became an all-city center on a championship team and a letter-winner in three sports. He did well enough academically but excelled in extracurricular activities. A quiet leader like his father, Ford was voted "the most popular high school senior" in Grand Rapids. The reward was an eye-opening trip to Washington, D.C. Jerry decided he wanted to be a lawyer and perhaps someday a legislator. To many of Jerry's classmates, his family, even in its reduced circumstances, seemed impossibly affluent. One, who happened to be African American, marveled at how such a "rich boy" could be such a "regular guy."

Unfortunately, Gerald Sr. was more noted for tenacity than timing. He finally opened his own firm, the Ford Painting and Varnish Company—in 1929. Three weeks later the stock market crashed. Ford called in his workforce of ten and told them no one would be laid off. Somehow they would get through it together. Everyone would make five dollars a week, including himself, to at least "keep in groceries." The company survived, but it was a close thing. Jerry worked there, and at the diner, as he pondered his future. He obtained a modest scholarship to the University of Michigan. Everyone in the family did their bit to help him out. Michigan's football coach got Jerry a job waiting tables. Through grants and grit he pulled through. By now habits of thrift were ingrained in all the Ford children.

Ford joined a fraternity, managed to enjoy an active if very frugal social life, became an all-American center on two national championship football teams, and graduated with a B average. On the road, Jerry roomed with the only African American on the football team. It didn't seem remotely unusual to him. The Ford home had always been equally hospitable to all of his friends, whatever their ethnicity or circumstances. His parents instilled what are now called "family values," less by preaching than by personifying them. Wherever he played, they tried to be in the stands, but their encouragement went far beyond football.

Perhaps the most practical of the senior Ford's gifts to his oldest son was to whet his interest in politics, a commitment they came to share. As his business gradually recovered, Gerald Ford Sr. became chairman of the Kent County Republican Committee. He was very active in the 1940 presidential campaign of Wendell Willkie. A staunch supporter of "good government," Ford never ran for office himself, but he helped to launch the "home front" that eventually displaced a corrupt, locally dominant political machine. Ford was so involved in this effort that his wife gently remonstrated that if he invested as much time in his business they would all be rich.

Declining a tempting contract to play professional football, Ford pursued his original goals. He gained admission to Yale Law School, helping to pay his way by coaching football, gained his degree, and passed the bar. He joined the navy in World War II and saw action, rising to the rank of lieutenant commander. In 1945 Jerry Ford returned to Grand Rapids to practice law and became involved in local politics. In his first race for the House of Representatives in 1948, Ford—a moderate internationalist—won an uphill Republican primary against an incumbent isolationist and then went on to win the general election. (Shortly before the election, he married Elizabeth Ann "Betty" Bloomer.) Twenty-six years later, when he succeeded Richard Nixon in the presidency, he modestly characterized himself as "a Ford, not a Lincoln." Appropriately, he titled his memoirs *A Time to Heal*. Surely he was the authentic son of Gerald Ford Sr.

He was "the father I loved and learned from and respected. He was my dad," Jerry Ford recalled. His true father, this unobtrusive but "marvelous family man . . . one of the truly outstanding people I ever knew in my life," died on January 26, 1962. He was seventy-two years old. He had slipped on the ice, receiving a concussion, but a heart attack was the immediate cause of death.

It is not too much to say that the entire community was in mourning. Grace Episcopal Church took in all the people it could accommodate, many standing. Gifts in Ford's memory were directed to the Youth Commonwealth he had championed. Gerald Rudolph Ford Sr. left a modest financial legacy sufficient to provide for his wife's welfare. His legacy to his family and his community was hardly modest—particularly to Gerald Rudolph Ford Jr. As Cannon writes, it was "incalculable . . . his own good name, and the example of hard work, integrity, and fair play on which Ford built his public life." An extraordinary ordinary man.

# 17

# "WHY NOT THE BEST?"

## James Earl Carter Sr. • John Edward Reagan

ONLY A BELATED APPRECIATION of his father's beneficence led Jimmy Carter back to Georgia to take over the family business, initiating his political career. Despite his drinking and disappointments, charming Jack Reagan instilled in his son "Dutch" principles to emulate.

## James Earl Carter Sr.

When Lieutenant James Earl Carter Jr. of the United States Navy returned to Plains, Georgia, to visit his terminally ill father, he made two discoveries: "Mr. Earl," as everyone called the senior Carter, was actually a rather small man, shorter even than Jimmy. He had seemed a giant when he dominated the lives of his children—and just about everything else in Plains. Even more remarkable, it was clear from the endless stream of people—black as well as white—who called to pay their respects that James Earl Carter Sr., as staunch a segregationist as any other prominent Georgian in the 1950s, was not merely admired, he was loved. After his father's funeral, Jimmy decided, to the dismay of his wife, that they must return to Plains and take over the family business. Had Carter stayed in the navy, his home for seven years, he might one day have risen to be chief of naval operations. Returning to Plains put him on a different path. Twenty-three years later he was elected president of the United States.

Carters had lived in southwestern Georgia, the most benighted region of a relatively impoverished state, for over 150 years. As biographer Kenneth Morris writes, there was—and to some extent still is—a "gnatline" dividing the northern Georgia piedmont, with its universities and cities, from the more rural and primitive red-clay southern portion of the state. The Carter family tree in the American South has hundreds of branches,

James Earl Carter Sr.

from aristocratic plantation owners in Virginia to dirt-poor farmers in Appalachia. There was some violence in the history of the Carters of Georgia, both before and after the Civil War. Only nine years after James Earl Carter Sr. was born (on September 12, 1894), his father, William Archibald ("Billy") Carter, was shot and killed by a business associate in a mysterious dispute over nothing more consequential than the owner- ship of a desk.

Under the auspices of a more prudent uncle, both Earl, as he pre- ferred to be called, and his older brother, Alton, called "Buddy," attended school regularly. Buddy went on to run the town's profitable general store, the Plains Mercantile Company. Earl had bigger plans. Plains, which at its peak had only about seven hundred inhabitants, was very much like dozens of other dusty southern Georgia towns, but it already boasted a narrow-gauge railroad that served both farmers and passengers. In 1921 Plains achieved another distinction. Three prominent physicians, Sam,

Thad, and Bowman Wise, for some reason established their small hospital in town. It included a nurses' training center. One of its early students was a slender young woman from Richland, twenty miles away, named Bessie Lillian Gordy. "Lilly" Gordy had dreamed of becoming a country doctor, but at that time and place, for a young woman, nursing would have to do.

After Earl Carter finished the ninth and tenth grades at Riverside Academy in Gainesville, Florida—more schooling than any previous Georgia Carter had received—he spent some time in Texas to see what it was like to be a cowboy. Despite his weak eyes, he went on to serve in World War I, emerging as a second lieutenant in the Officer Reserve Corps. By his mid-twenties he was starting businesses that filled gaps in Plains. He opened an icehouse, a small dry-cleaning operation, and a grocery store down Main Street that didn't compete with Buddy's Plains Mercantile. But the key to a man's stature was still land. For the first and only time in his life, Earl borrowed money—to buy farmland.

Energetic Earl Carter wasn't all business. He loved to have a good time. Lilly Gordy also believed in the work-hard, play-hard lifestyle. She enjoyed drinking, smoking, dancing, and partying in general. With her long, lean face, she was by no means beautiful. Her son Jimmy would remember her, when young, as "very slender, almost gaunt . . . but pretty in her own way, with her dark hair parted in the middle and eyes that always seemed to sparkle." Earl covered his natural shyness with an excessively genial demeanor. He stood about five foot eight, an inch or so taller than Lilly, and weighed a stocky 175 pounds. He had light reddish hair and a face sunburned in all seasons from his work outdoors, although he always wore a hat. In a town the size of Plains, it was inevitable that Lilly Gordy would meet Earl Carter.

She didn't like anything about him, from his country looks to his showy open-topped Model T. To her surprise, both her parents and Dr. Sam Wise, the leader of the "three Wise men," had a different view of young Carter. "He's a boy that has more ambition than anyone in this town, and he's going to be worth a lot someday," Dr. Sam told Lilly. For whatever combination of reasons, Lilly and Earl became engaged. It took six months at an Atlanta hospital for her to complete her nurses' training. The two were married on September 26, 1923, by the pastor of the Plains Baptist Church before a modest assemblage in his home. Earl was twenty-seven, Lillian twenty-five. There was neither a reception nor a honeymoon. The potato crop Earl was counting on to finance it had failed to come through. Whatever it was in Earl that had won Lilly over, there was an undeniable affection between them in the early years of their marriage. Their active social life continued. Earl took Lilly to plays in larger Americus. Lilly loved watching baseball as much as Earl, who also enjoyed playing it. They weren't entirely mismatched.

Their first child was born at 7:00 A.M. on October 1, 1924, with Dr. Sam in attendance. Earl had returned from the fields just in time to rush his wife to the Wise Clinic. The boy, named James Earl Carter Jr., would be the first president of the United States to be born in a hospital. His mother pronounced him a "bright, happy baby who needed no extra care." Two years later a daughter, Gloria, was born to the Carters. Two years after that a second daughter, named Ruth. It would be another nine years before the birth of their fourth and final child, William Alton, nicknamed "Billy." Earl teased Lilly that the boy couldn't possibly be his. She didn't find it amusing.

Particularly because he was Earl's only son for the first thirteen years of his life, Jimmy Carter felt most fully both his father's influence and his expectations. "[He] was the center of my life and the focus of my admiration when I was a child," Jimmy recalled. "My daddy was the dominant personality in our family." He also called Earl the "only friend" of his childhood. Earl was often both mother and father to his children. As her husband's landholdings increased, eventually to over five thousand acres, worked by as many as two hundred families of black sharecroppers, Lillian finally became, in essence, the country doctor she had dreamed of being. "Miz Lillian" not only birthed their babies but tended to all their other considerable medical needs. It was laudable, but as a result she neglected her own children. It was Earl who, however demanding his schedule, generally took them to school, to church, and to their social events and helped them with their homework. He was the parent in place, she was the parent on the go.

Earl didn't coddle Jimmy, always telling him he could do better. He called his son "Hot," for "Hot Shot," a term of endearment yet also possibly of derision. He only called him "Jimmy" when he was angry. To Earl's credit, as biographer Peter Bourne points out, he "always reminded his children that there was a world to be conquered outside of Plains." But, like Sam Johnson, "He never saw it for himself. His own ambitions extended to being the most successful person in Plains." When he moved out of Plains, it was only three miles west, to tiny Archery, less a town than a flag stop on the Seaboard Railroad Line.

The Carters converted a clapboard house to their use. It lacked running water and electricity and had only a party-line telephone, shared with others, but Earl built an adjacent clay tennis court. When Jimmy got older, the two would play frequently, the son never beating his father. Jimmy's years in Archery reflected the contrasting ironies of the rural Southern "way of life" in the 1920s and 1930s. For a young boy, it was a *Huckleberry Finn* kind of life, with a touch of *Bleak House* thrown in. Jimmy, red-haired and freckle-faced, even looked like Huck Finn. Barefoot and shirtless, fishing for eels and catfish, shaking down game from the trees, and aimlessly exploring to his heart's content, he seemed carefree. All Jimmy's childhood companions were black, as were the surrogate mothers who helped raise him.

But it wasn't all play. Jimmy plowed and hoed with his playmates and their parents, more each year, his tasks equal to those of his father's tenants—but the expectations greater. Eventually Earl gave him his own acre to be responsible for, to cultivate and make productive. He even sent the apprehensive boy into Plains, which now seemed like a metropolis, to sell boiled peanuts. Jimmy's greatest ambition as a boy was to "be valuable around the farm and please my father," but there was a longer-term goal. Inspired by the colorful postcards he received from his globe-girdling uncle, navy radioman Tom Watson Gordy, Jimmy dreamed of attending the Naval Academy in Annapolis, Maryland, and going on to an exciting career as a naval officer. Would his father let him?

In addition to peanuts, which largely replaced cotton as his staple crop in the 1920s, Carter's diversified farms raised everything from pecans and potatoes to pork and peaches. Every product paid its way—wool from the sheep, syrup from the sugarcane. Earl never worked in the fields himself, as Jimmy did, but he was "omnipresent," putting in the longest hours of anyone. He supervised everything, including a commissary for his workers that sold them every necessity, and eventually the immense peanut warehouse in Plains. Out of his office, he bought and sold real estate, arranged mortgages, brokered commodities, and made loans to other farmers. The Carters lived well, within reason. After getting electricity, they had the first radio in the region, as they would have the first television set, but Earl Carter was not one to put on airs.

Everything was bought with cash. The Great Depression affected almost every family in the vicinity except the Carters. Mr. Earl was also unusually scientific and advanced in his farming methods, diversifying and rotating his crops, using insecticides, and becoming more mechanized.

He was the first local farmer to replace mule drawn plows with tractors. He experimented with a new type of plow and later helped finance an agricultural station at the University of Georgia. From feed and seed to a multiplicity of products, nothing was wasted. Then Earl would go on to think up some new way to make money. His business sense became the stuff of local legend. Yet he also established a reputation for fair dealing and even for generosity, so long as you didn't owe him money.

Earl Carter embodied the contradictions of the society in which he lived, and which he accepted without question. His considerable charity remained largely private until his death. He would help anyone in need, white or black, especially his tenant farmers. Many stayed with him throughout their lives, although his store undoubtedly exploited them. Earl also provided medicines and supplies to his wife, as she made her daily rounds, and probably viewed her work with quiet pride. In the context of the times, he would be considered a political moderate. As a member of the school board, he supported improving the separate black schools. He favored rural mail delivery and electrification. Late in his life he served in the state legislature. The library at Georgia Southwestern College is named for him.

Jimmy had started school in Plains in 1930, at the age of six. This entrance into an all-white world represented a confusing separation from his childhood companions. Undersized, insecure, and wanting to be liked, he decided to take the first step in greeting his new classmates. Smiling broadly, he stuck out his hand and announced, "Hi. I'm Jimmy Carter." Forty-six years later he would add, "And I'm running for president." He did well in school, his imagination enhanced by descriptions of faraway places, the sort he might visit some day in the navy.

Jimmy Carter writes, "By the time I was sixteen I . . . was becoming qualified, if necessary, to succeed my father," although the boy's goal had long been different. Surprisingly, when the time came for decision, Earl did not object—although as an old army man he might have preferred West Point. As his father discussed an appointment to Annapolis with the local congressman, Jimmy started building himself up physically. Once he got to the Naval Academy in 1943, after preparation at the local college and Georgia Tech, his rigorous regimen at home turned out to be an asset. As Bourne writes, Carter had resented his father's strictness, denying him "many of the pleasures he should have had as a teenager," but he appreciated it now. Earl made one request, promising Jimmy a gold watch if he would not smoke until he turned twenty-one. He need not have worried. When he tried it, Jimmy hated smoking. All his siblings were to die of cancer.

With the acceleration of wartime demands, Jimmy graduated in three rather than four years, standing high in his class. Immediately after graduation, at only twenty-one, he married eighteen-year-old Rosalynn Smith, who had lived next door to the Carters in Plains. Carter rose quickly in the navy, finding a second, even more demanding father figure in brilliant, controversial Admiral Hyman Rickover, the pioneer of nuclear submarines. Rickover led by example, like Earl Carter, but he smiled a lot less.

Lieutenant Carter was immersed in his naval responsibilities when his mother telephoned him in 1952. Earl had been diagnosed as suffering from inoperable pancreatic cancer. Jimmy and Rosalynn rushed to his bedside in Plains. For perhaps the first time, as father and son talked together, Jimmy discovered the compassionate side of the man he thought he knew so well. He was even more impressed by witnessing, in Bourne's words, "the hundreds of people of both races who came to express their concern with an unanticipated degree of warmth and sincerity." Morris adds, "Throughout the county [Earl] was esteemed; in Plains he was loved."

James Earl Carter Sr. died at home on July 23, 1953, shortly before his fifty-ninth birthday. As historian Douglas Brinkley writes, "All of Sumter County came to his funeral." He left an estate of over a quarter of a million dollars, a major business enterprise, and a great many people reliant on its retention for their livelihoods.

Miss Lillian, almost in a state of collapse, grieved that Earl "had been a more affectionate father than I had been a mother." She had learned little about his business, and when emotional stability returned, she told her older son that she believed him to be the only person capable of carrying it on. Jimmy had often said, "I want to be a man like my father," but he had not anticipated following him so literally. On his way back from the funeral to Schenectady, New York, where he was stationed, Carter continued to reflect. Rosalynn writes, "He did not think he could ever do anything in his life to have an impact on people . . . like his father's life had made." Jimmy also questioned something else—whether he should invest his whole career on "working on instruments of destruction to kill people." The example of his father resonated in another way. Jimmy, too, liked the idea of finally being his own boss. He decided to go back to Plains and take over the business. His wife, with immense reluctance, finally agreed to return with him.

When Jimmy Carter asked in 1976, "Why not the best?" perhaps he meant values more than personalities. His views of human rights and racial justice came from his colorful mother, eventually known to the nation as "Miss Lillian." But the values of responsibility and charity came from his father, "Mr. Earl." As Senator William Fulbright put it, "Carter had deep roots." Returning to them led to the rediscovery of himself.

## John Edward Reagan

John Edward Reagan, the natural salesman everyone called "Jack," was bigger than his ambitions. He dreamed of having, except for Chicago, the largest shoe store in Illinois. In the pursuit of this goal he took his family all over the state—from Fulton to Tampico to Chicago itself, then to Galena and Monmouth, back to Tampico, and finally to Dixon. Here he had his best chance, as proprietor and part-owner of the town's Fashion Boot Shop. Unfortunately, the Great Depression came early to the Midwest. Shuttering the store drove Jack Reagan to the road and any employment he could find, even hundreds of miles away. To the despair of his wife and the embarrassment of his two sons, the fear of failure, or some other demons, had already driven him to drink.

His pervasive humor, his salesman's patter, had always been tinged with skepticism, but at least until Dixon, his ambition remained. Particularly to the younger of his two sons, he gave two invaluable gifts—one of skill and one of character. As Ronald Reagan said in 1988, "He was the best storyteller I've ever heard and the strongest man of principle I've ever known. He believed in honesty and hard work. He was filled with a love of justice and a hatred of bigotry."

Four years before he made these remarks, President Ronald Wilson Reagan had visited the tiny town of Ballyporeen in County Tipperary, Ireland, and reflected on his roots. "I come back to you as a descendant of people who are buried here in paupers' graves. Perhaps this is God's way of reminding us that we must always treat every individual . . . with dignity and respect. . . . You see, I didn't know much about my family background—not because of a lack of interest, but because my father was orphaned before he was six years old. . . . It is like coming home after a long journey."

John Michael O'Reagan's journey had taken him quite a long way from Tipperary. His grandson, John Edward Reagan, was born in Illinois on July 13, 1883. When he was only six, both of his parents died of tuberculosis, and he was sent to live with a strict elderly aunt in Iowa.

Ronald Reagan with parents, Nelle and Jack

After completing only the sixth grade in school, young Jack Reagan found himself most at home at his uncle's dry-goods store, and set out to make his own way. By the turn of the century he was the star salesman at a much larger store than his uncle's, in Fulton, Illinois.

John Edward Reagan cut quite a figure. He was tall and husky, extremely handsome, and immaculately dressed. As Edmund Morris, who wrote an innovative personal biography of Ronald Reagan, puts it, Jack Reagan possessed a sort of virile elegance: "He was that rare type, the instinctive gentleman." His dark hair, neatly parted in the middle, framed a sensitive-looking face. He was renowned as a bard of the prairies, his gift for telling stories celebrated far beyond Fulton. An experienced salesman at only twenty in 1903, he was anxious to improve his circumstances. Only one factor clouded his future, a drinking problem that would grow more serious with the years.

However, his imbibing didn't inhibit his appeal to young ladies, particularly petite, lively Nelle Clyde, who worked in the same store. Despite Nelle's sharp features, a too-strong chin, and thin lips, she was striking, with beautiful auburn hair, blue eyes, and a slender, graceful figure. Her schooling had been no more extensive than Jack's, but her native intelligence was the equal of his. Unlike his grim childhood and scattered family, she had been raised by loving parents in a large household. Perhaps that is why her sunny, optimistic disposition was not tinged with Jack's cynicism about human nature. A devout convert to the Disciples of Christ, Nelle viewed alcoholism as more a sickness than a sin. She must have felt that her faith and her love could save someone with such obvious ability and ambition as Jack Reagan. She knew that at heart he was a good person.

In deference to Jack's formal affiliation, they were married in Fulton's Catholic church on November 8, 1904. By 1906 they had moved to Tampico, a slightly larger Illinois town. Jack had taken the first step to owning his own establishment, obtaining a better opportunity at the Pitney General Store. In their apartment on Main Street above the town's bank, their two sons were born—John Neil Reagan in 1908 and Ronald Wilson Reagan on February 6, 1911. Neil was nicknamed "Moon" by his father, after the popular comic strip character Moon Mullins. For Ronald, "Dutch" was Jack Reagan's instant appellation. When he saw and heard his loud, ten-pound son, delivered after Nelle had endured a full day's labor, Jack could only exclaim, "He looks like a fat Dutchman." Both nicknames stuck.

The boys would enjoy little stability, moving with their parents to a succession of towns as Jack pursued his retailing goal. It was a challenging childhood, going to a different school every year, moving as often as five times within a single town, always renting their premises and rarely having much in the way of material comfort or possessions. Ron became something of a loner and a dreamer, preoccupied with collections that previous tenants had left in some of the homes they occupied, from toy soldiers to butterflies. He required little inducement to read. Watching his mother trace every line on a page, he absorbed sight with sound, learning "by a kind of osmosis." He read fluently by the age of five. Now his imaginary world expanded to encompass the Rover Boys, Tarzan, Frank Merriwell at Yale, and especially the stories of Mark Twain. He also had a very retentive memory, an immense asset in the professions he would pursue later in his life.

For a time in Tampico, the Pitney store seemed to be doing well, and outgoing Jack Reagan was becoming a community leader. He served as a town councilman, assistant fire chief, and finance chairman of the Catholic church he infrequently attended, and was a member of service clubs. With only the diversion of silent movies for competition, small communities enjoyed active local theatrical and musical troupes. Both of Ronald Reagan's parents delighted in amateur acting and apparently were quite good at it. Just the sound of applause must have been heady for Jack, but he never stopped drinking for long—and sure enough, any prosperity turned out to be transitory.

Nelle explained to her sons their father's "sickness," the addiction he struggled with but simply couldn't always control. "We shouldn't love him any less," Ronald recalled her saying. "We should remember how kind and loving he was when he wasn't affected by drink." It was true enough, but at the age of eleven, Ron was directly confronted by the raw reality of his father's affliction. One night he found Jack sprawled in the snow on the front steps of their home. Should he somehow drag him inside or wait for his mother to manage it, as she normally did? Ron decided to do it himself. To biographer Lou Cannon, that act "represented the first moment of accepting responsibility." But Morris adds that young Reagan's reaction in this pivotal episode in his life was conflicted. He never ceased loving his father, but some of the respect vanished that night, replaced more by pity and even a kind of contempt for such weakness.

After the family moved to Dixon, Ron viewed the place as particularly "sweet and idyllic." It would be fondly remembered as his authentic hometown, the closest to a secure setting he knew in his childhood. Indeed, Dixon was a picturesque place, ten times larger than Tampico, with many more amenities, situated between wooded hills and limestone cliffs. Children could skate on the frozen river in winter, swim and fish in it during the long summer, take canoe trips and explore the cliffs like latter-day Tom Sawyers. Reagan admitted to still being a bit "introverted" when he came to Dixon, but he soon learned to thoroughly appreciate the outdoors, with its abundant wildlife, and began his lifelong love of horses.

His view of everything changed about the time he entered high school. On a Sunday drive with his family, he picked up and put on his mother's eyeglasses and made a startling discovery. Suddenly he could see things with a clarity he had never experienced before. He didn't know he was nearsighted. In high school, coinciding with his physical growth, Reagan emerged, seemingly overnight, into a confident personality. A solid if not outstanding student, he excelled in football and swimming and in every dramatic production. He was elected senior class president and was voted "Mr. Congeniality" by his classmates. He had worked since he was fourteen to help out at home, but his most cherished job was as a lifeguard for seven summers at Lowell Park, overseeing a particularly turbulent stretch of the river. The memory of the seventy-seven people he saved from drowning, encapsulated later by a photograph of himself as a young Adonis, stayed vivid in his mind after much else had vanished.

Jack Reagan's "fondest dream" died when his Fashion Boot Shop closed. It forced him to take to the road. He finally found work two hundred miles away in a dingy store outside Springfield. On one trip, he slept in his car in the middle of a blizzard, nearly catching pneumonia, rather than patronize the only hotel in town, because it excluded Jews. Reagan so detested bigotry that he would not permit his sons to see *The Birth of a Nation* because it glorified the Ku Klux Klan. As with the Fords, the Reagans welcomed warmly all of their sons' classmates and teammates regardless of race—this in the 1920s and 1930s. Politics aside, Ronald Reagan's conviction that people should always and only be viewed as individuals was born in these examples—the ethical application of his mother's faith merging with his father's principles.

Somehow, in the midst of the Depression, his parents managed to get Ron through nearby Eureka College. Even more than in high school, Ron excelled at Eureka, speaking for the entire student body and pushing through a compromise plan when the Depression-plagued college was considering drastic cuts. To biographer William Pemberton, this "was a defining moment for Reagan. He experienced for the first time the thrill of moving an audience." His election as student body president was not based on campaigning or calculation but rather on genuine popularity. Graduating with a degree in economics in 1932, he was already considering acting as a career, with radio as a more viable bridge, but in such bleak times any job prospects were remote. He was encouraged by his father to keep trying. Ron borrowed the ancient family car to look for work in all directions. After months he finally landed a job announcing sports and spinning records at a radio station in Davenport, Iowa. He proudly sent a share of each paycheck back home to help out his parents.

Jack Reagan, back in Dixon, finally got a break of his own. One of few Democrats in the area and committed to the New Deal, he landed a job setting up federal relief programs and later headed the Works Progress Administration in Dixon. It did a good deal for his self-esteem. The whole family supported Franklin Roosevelt, for whom Ronald Reagan cast his first presidential vote. By the mid-thirties he had moved on to Hollywood.

In 1937, after Warner Brothers picked up his option, Ron felt secure enough to bring his parents out to California and give them the only home they would ever own. "Nothing," he said, "has ever given me as much satisfaction." Jack was particularly pleased when Ron landed the role of George Gipp in *Knute Rockne, All-American* and was in his glory at the film's premiere at the University of Notre Dame itself. Unfortunately, he was also in his cups, going on a bender with the film's star, Pat O'Brien, whom he had always admired. At the studio, Jack was given a job handling his son's increasingly considerable fan mail. "I was there," he said with satisfaction, "when my son became a star." He could hardly believe it. Some dreams do come true.

John Edward Reagan died in Hollywood of coronary thrombosis at the age of fifty-seven, on May 18, 1941. After years of such heavy drinking, chain smoking, and frustration, perhaps the only surprise is that his heart didn't give out earlier. It may be, as Morris suggests, that to his second son Jack Reagan really died, at least "morally," two decades before, on those snowy steps in Dixon, Illinois. But, as Cannon points out, "Ronald Reagan was always skilled at softening hard memories with happy stories." So many of them, which he told so well, had been motivated by the father he had never ceased to love. What Jack Reagan accomplished or failed to accomplish is only part of the story of his life. In what he inspired he was so much bigger than his ambitions.

# 18

## "DUTY AND SERVICE"

### Prescott Sheldon Bush

INTIMIDATING AND IMPRESSIVE, Prescott Bush personified the mantra of "duty and service," imparted particularly to his second son, George, who followed business success with a commitment to public service extensive enough to satisfy even his father.

In the Bush household of Greenwich, Connecticut, father knew best. Biographer Herbert Parmet describes Prescott Bush as "austere, regal, dignified, and imperious"—a commanding authority figure. As his grandson George Walker Bush put it, "Grandfather was a stern and formal man. Imposing would be a polite way of describing what we kids sometimes called 'scary.' . . . I think of rules and respect. He expected guests in his home, including his grandchildren, to be on time, well-behaved and properly attired." That meant a coat and tie for boys and neat dresses for girls. Any conversation was initiated from the head of the table. When Prescott was working at home, his wife, Dorothy, ushered guests up the back stairway so as not to disturb him.

Bush was also physically intimidating. His daughter-in-law Barbara described him as "six feet four inches tall with a full head of black hair and a take-charge attitude." Handsome as a movie star of the more somber sort, Prescott Bush, all 250 pounds of him, radiated strength, his most expressive feature the thick eyebrows hooding his blue eyes. His expectations for his five children, four of them boys, represented a daunting challenge. One of them, Jonathan Bush, recalled, "We were all terrified of Dad as boys." As a relative remarked, Prescott's second son, George Herbert Walker Bush, always "placated" his father, but also harbored the hope to eventually achieve independent success. The oldest son, Prescott Jr., admitted that when his father was away, it "seemed like the Fourth of July."

Prescott and George
H. W. Bush

Yet they all loved this man who could be so formidable and even forbidding. In fact, Bush was tender as well as tough and had a lively, unpredictable sense of humor. He was interested in everything his children did and grew to respect each of them as individuals. What they really feared was letting him down.

According to sources like *Burke's Peerage,* there is scarcely any American president, however humble his domestic origins, who is not related in some convoluted manner to European royalty. Of them all, however, the Bush family is unquestionably the most regal, their ties to a multiplicity of monarchs, including Queen Elizabeth II, the most clearly defined. To both George Bushes, this inheritance, supplemented by the material success of their family, has been more a challenge than a boon. Americans tend to prefer politicians who "made it" on their own.

Prescott Sheldon Bush was born in Columbus, Ohio, on May 18, 1895, the only son of a remarkable man named Samuel Prescott Bush and his wife, Flora Sheldon Bush. Son of an Episcopal clergyman and trained in mechanical engineering, Samuel left the Pennsylvania Railroad to make his fortune with the Buckeye Steel Casting Company, producing the framework for railroad cars. A prominent community leader, Bush particularly liked sports. Among other achievements, he founded and is reputed to have been the first coach of the Ohio State University football team.

Despite his wealth, Bush believed in sending his children to public schools, at least for the lower grades. Prescott experienced a healthy melting pot of classmates, including Germans and African Americans, at his elementary school in Columbus. All the Bush children, however, were eventually sent to New England for boarding school—the girls to Westover in Connecticut and Prescott to St. George's School in Newport, Rhode Island. From St. George's, Prescott went on to Yale, establishing a family tradition. An all-around athlete, Prescott excelled in baseball. He was an excellent student and was active in everything from debating to singing. Tapped for the select secret society Skull and Bones, he initiated another Bush tradition. Considering his future, Prescott observed, "Public service would be a wonderful thing to participate in." After graduating in 1917, he joined the "Yale Battalion" of the Connecticut National Guard and saw action in France late in World War I, emerging from the conflict as a captain.

Heeding the advice of a friend, he took a job in St. Louis with the Simmons Hardware Company, launching his business career. Eventually, through a series of moves and mergers, Prescott became an executive of the United States Rubber Company. He also fell in love with vivacious, athletic Dorothy "Dottie" Walker.

They were a contrasting if very handsome couple—Prescott, so dark and tall, hovering over her, so trim and fair. She would be the fire to his ice—outgoing, outspoken, amusing, adventuresome, yet very much a lady. They were married near her family's expansive Walker Point compound in Kennebunkport, Maine, on August 6, 1921, at the Episcopal Church of St. Ann. She was twenty, he twenty-six. For half a century, as Dorothy wrote in a eulogy delivered at Prescott's funeral, he gave her "the most joyous life any woman could experience."

After getting married and moving to Milton, Massachusetts, Prescott pondered another move. Meanwhile, his family was on its way. In 1922 Dottie, although heavily pregnant, had insisted on playing in a local softball game. After, naturally, hitting a home run, she went into labor and was rushed to the hospital, where she gave birth to Prescott Sheldon Bush Jr. Two years later, on June 12, 1924, their second son, named for her grandfather, George Herbert Walker Bush, was born. Almost immediately he was nicknamed "Poppy." (Grandfather Walker had long been known as "Little Pop.") Dorothy and Prescott were to have three more children—Jonathan, William, and a most welcome girl, Nancy.

In 1926 Prescott joined the Wall Street investment house of W. A. Harriman. Eventually the firm merged with Brown Brothers to form Brown Brothers Harriman. Prescott became a partner—and a millionaire. He moved his family to fashionable Greenwich, Connecticut, within easy commuting distance to Manhattan. Their dark-shingled five-bedroom home was more comfortably spacious than ostentatious. Here they raised their children in a personal environment utterly devoid of pretentiousness or snobbery. It was not easy, given the conspicuous affluence and social exclusivity that surrounded them. As Barbara Bush's biographer Pamela Kilian writes, "Both Dorothy and Prescott Bush hewed to the Protestant ethic. They believed in hard work, temperate living, and daily bible readings." However, "even during the Great Depression," Kilian continues, "there were three full-time maids and a chauffeur who took the Bush boys" to school. George Bush recalls his parents' complementary areas of emphasis: "Dad taught us about duty and service. . . . Mother taught us about dealing with life in an old-fashioned way of bringing up a family [with] generous measures of both love and discipline." They were not to be spoiled. "Whatever we wanted," George said, "we had to earn."

Whether at Greenwich Country Day School, at holidays in the South, or at their summer enclave of Kennebunkport, with its physical regimen not unlike that of the Kennedys at Hyannis Port, it was slender, respectful George who apparently had most inherited his parents' athletic prowess. When he went off to elite Phillips Academy at Andover, Massachusetts, his record must have gratified even his demanding father. A fine student, athlete, and president of the senior class, George had intended to go on to Yale. But graduating in the perilous spring of 1942, with the nation at war, made him rethink his plans.

By now they included a lively, attractive young woman from Rye, New York, named Barbara Pierce, whom he had met at a party during Christmas vacation. (Her family was distantly related to President Franklin Pierce.) She was attending Ashley Hall in South Carolina but planned to go to college at Smith. By the time she came up to his Andover senior prom, they considered themselves engaged. The war put everything on hold. Only eighteen, George joined the navy. It was the first independent decision of his life. Bidding farewell to his parents, he saw for the first time tears in his father's eyes. George was sent to preflight school in North Carolina and eventually became the youngest bomber pilot in the naval air service.

For over a decade Prescott Bush had supplemented his business career with increasing community involvement. By the time George left for the navy, Prescott all but ran the governing body of Greenwich. He had helped form the Greenwich Taxpayers Association, streamlined the town meeting organization, and was elected to head it for seventeen out of eighteen years. In addition, he was a director of the local Boys Club and the Greenwich Hospital and was active in the Episcopal church. He also served on the boards of at least seven national corporations.

Prominent Republicans began to ponder—might he not make an attractive candidate for public office? If he would just unbend a little. Why, Prescott was known to have taken his wife home from a party simply because their host told an off-color joke. He was reputed to have cut off his own brother because of his messy divorce (he would later withdraw his support of presidential aspirant Nelson Rockefeller for the same reason). Still, he was a man to watch. During the war Prescott's activities expanded to a national stage. Recognized for his management talents, he was called upon to coordinate over six hundred relief agencies under the National War Fund Campaign. He also raised money, with notable success, for the USO.

While Prescott kept more than occupied with these activities and Dorothy tended her "victory garden," they awaited word from their son. In September 1944, on a bombing mission on the Bonin Islands, after making its run, George's plane was shot down by Japanese antiaircraft fire. Parachuting into the Pacific, he found refuge on a raft and within three hours was picked up by an American submarine. Both other crew members were killed. Bush agonized about whether he had bailed out too soon, or should have crash-landed his plane. He wrote home, "Physically I am O.K., but I am troubled inside. . . . My heart aches for the families of those two boys with me." When he wrote in this vein to the sister of one of them, she replied, "Stop thinking you were in any way responsible. [My brother] had always spoken of you as the best pilot in the squadron." Bush was awarded the Distinguished Flying Cross for completing his bombing mission.

He arrived home on Christmas Eve, greeted by a reception worthy of a hero in a Frank Capra movie. On January 6, 1945, at the First Presbyterian Church in Rye, Barbara Pierce became Mrs. George Herbert Walker Bush. After a brief honeymoon in Sea Island, Georgia, they were sent to a succession of naval bases, finally arriving in Virginia Beach in time to celebrate the startling news that atomic bombs had ended the war. Within two months their 1941 Plymouth had transported them up to New Haven, Connecticut, where Yale offered returning veterans an accelerated program to gain their degrees in only two and a half years.

Miraculously they found a small apartment in a building they shared with other young couples. Barbara was pregnant. On July 6, 1946, the Bushes joined the baby boom. Although the new arrival, George Walker Bush, lacked the full name of his father, in future years he couldn't avoid being called "Junior." The little family had to move twice more before George graduated Phi Beta Kappa in economics in 1948. He had been quite a presence on campus during his truncated time at Yale—baseball captain, a student leader, and, like his father, tapped for Skull and Bones.

Like Prescott, he didn't want to simply duplicate his father's success. Ultimately he settled, and Barbara agreed, on the most remote departure imaginable, to learn the oil business in the wilds of Odessa, Texas. Although the Bushes would soon be joined by many other Ivy Leaguers also searching for "black gold," their move to Texas represented an escape from everything familiar—except the influence of Prescott Bush. He not only gave George a new Studebaker, he found him work with a subsidiary of his friend Neil Mallon's Dresser Industries. By 1950, in partnership with a neighbor, Bush was able to start his own firm in oil exploration, based in Midland and heavily financed by his father and his influential friends.

Prescott finally made his own transition. In 1950, encouraged by many party leaders, he decided to run for the United States Senate, even if he had to make a few speeches to do it. In fact, he campaigned with great vigor, his outgoing wife an immense asset. Bush used a helicopter to get around compact Connecticut in one of the most innovative campaigns that state had seen. He even sang on the campaign trail with other former Yale Wiffenpoofs and strummed a guitar at rallies. There were few substantive differences between Bush and his opponent, the equally moderate Democratic incumbent, William Benton. Bush lost by 1,102 votes out of over 860,000 cast, but he learned a great deal about practical politics.

Only two years later the other Connecticut senator, Brien McMahon, died, and there was a special election to fill the remaining four years of his term. Bush contested the seat with popular Democratic congressman

Abraham Ribicoff and, swept along by the Eisenhower landslide, won with 51.3 percent of the vote. In 1956 Bush won reelection handily. He and Eisenhower became good friends, often golfing together.

In Harry Truman's phrase, Bush was "a workhorse, not a show horse." He espoused fiscal responsibility and supported a strong but efficient national defense, the federal highways program, and both civil rights and voting rights bills. In Connecticut he had been chairman of the United Negro College Fund. Although opposing "socialized medicine," Bush was in favor of moderating the Taft-Hartley Labor Law and easing provisions of the McCarran Act restricting immigration. He opposed the isolationist Bricker Amendment, supported the United Nations, and favored standby price controls should the president need them—all in all, a reasoned, middle-of-the-road approach, reflecting his constituency.

No one ever doubted Prescott's courage. He was one of the first to take on Joseph McCarthy, proposing a "code of fair procedures" for the Senate clearly aimed at the Wisconsin senator. On *Face the Nation* Bush said he hoped the GOP was still the party of Lincoln, but that he had tried to merge the best of the traditions of both major parties. It is very likely that he would have won again in 1962, but, suffering from arthritis and general exhaustion, he decided that at sixty-seven it was time to give others their opportunity to serve. Later, as he recovered his vigor, he regretted that decision. Perhaps he had started in politics too late. In 1953 George had written him about meeting Lyndon Johnson, who described Prescott as "the best thing that had happened to the 83rd Congress."

The last decade of Prescott Bush's life was more fulfilled by the achievements of others. Now increasingly active in Republican politics in Texas, George had lost and won races, was elected to the House in 1967, and was named ambassador to the United Nations in 1971. Based in New York, he was able to see more of his parents, to their immense pleasure. In 1971 George reflected, on attending his father's seventy-sixth birthday in Greenwich, "I think how lucky we are as a family to feel so very, very close." By the following year Prescott was ailing. In September 1972 he underwent surgery for lung cancer at Sloan-Kettering Institute in New York. The cancer had spread too quickly to be contained, but Prescott still could muster a bit of humor. In one of his son's last visits to the hospital, when George told him he'd had dinner with the Russians, Prescott, although heavily sedated, asked, "Who picked up the tab?"

Prescott Sheldon Bush died on October 8, 1972, at the age of seventy-seven. As she was certain her husband would have wished, Dorothy Bush turned his funeral at Christ Episcopal Church in Greenwich into more of a celebration of his life, with bright colors, fond stories, and upbeat music, a parting that was also a party. The grandchildren who had often feared him were his pallbearers. Perhaps the old man was not so somber after all.

To George, Prescott would always be "my mentor, my hero." With the years, he had only learned to appreciate his father more. He wrote, "My dad was the real inspiration of my life. He was strong and strict, full of decency and integrity, but he was also kind, understanding and full of humor." In a later letter to a friend, he added, "Dad was a spectacular man. . . . I guess you . . . knew what he meant to me in terms of inspiration in my own life. . . . He was the incentive behind everything." Most important of all, to his own sons, George Bush wrote in 1974, "My dad felt strongly the firm obligation to put something into the system." Or, as George W. Bush rephrased it a quarter of a century later, "My grandfather Prescott Bush believed a person's most enduring and important contribution was hearing and responding to the call of public service," a determination that inspired a dynasty.

# 19

# "The Name Doesn't Matter"

## William Jefferson Blythe III • Roger Clinton

DENIED BY TRAGEDY the opportunity to know his real father, Bill Clinton was never close to his stepfather until Roger Clinton, dying of cancer, finally realized the import of having such an impressive young man carry on his family name.

## William Jefferson Blythe III

Bill Blythe could charm anyone. How many women he married, how many children he fathered, even the date he was born are not so certain. When nursing student Virginia Cassidy first glimpsed Blythe that night in 1941 as he came into the emergency ward at Shreveport's Tri-State Hospital, it was quite literally love at first sight. Unfortunately, the very tall, sandy-haired, and ruggedly handsome Blythe had another young woman in tow. She needed an immediate appendectomy and was rushed into the operating room. When apprentice nurse Cassidy saw Blythe turn toward her "and his eyes met mine," as she recalled a half-century later, she almost required some resuscitation of her own. She was "stunned. . . . He smiled and the only way I can describe it is that he had a glow about him. I was weak-kneed and also embarrassed." Blythe's girlfriend at the time recovered. Virginia did not. Soon she was seeing Blythe regularly, although she was already engaged, and nursing students were supposed to stay single.

Virginia brought Bill home to Hope, Arkansas, some fifty miles away, to meet her parents. When her cool, exacting mother, Edith Grisham Cassidy, a private-duty nurse with ambitions to better her situation, looked into Blythe's deep blue eyes, her initial reservations dissipated. She saw at least a secure future for Virginia. Blythe was neither rich nor educated, but he seemed to have a great deal of energy, and he certainly exuded charm. As for Virginia's father, Hope's genial longtime iceman, James Eldridge Cassidy, who fondly called his daughter "Ginger," he liked just about everybody.

Blythe was on his way back home to Sherman, Texas, to enlist in the army. He had a good job in Chicago selling heavy automotive equipment, and it would be waiting for him when he came back from the service. For a month or two he romanced Virginia back in Shreveport and took a job selling cars there. They went out every night she could get off, going dancing and seeing movies. Virginia had broken off her engagement to her homegrown fiancé. He was no match for broadshouldered, fun-loving William Jefferson Blythe III. Virginia learned that despite his aristocratic-sounding name, Bill was the oldest son of a poor farming family in Texas. His father had died when Bill was only in his early teens, obliging him to leave school around the eighth grade and work to support his mother and his siblings. His sales job meant being on the road a great deal, but it was a life he liked, and it paid well.

At the time, Virginia Cassidy was still a fresh-faced, spontaneous girl not long out of high school, where she had been quite popular. She had only recently begun to emulate her mother's excessive use of cosmetics. Why Edith was so critical of her daughter, her only child, even abusing her, is difficult to discern. The desire to escape her mother's control and have a career of her own had led Virginia to nurses' training in the nearest city she could find that also offered more of a social life. What she didn't know about Bill Blythe was that he had been married at least three times before, had impregnated other women, and may well have been at least technically married at the time they met. But in her smitten state even that might not have mattered to Virginia.

The two were wed by a justice of the peace in Texarkana, on the Texas-Arkansas border, on September 3, 1943. She was twenty. He was twenty-five, or so he said. A few weeks later he did enlist, or perhaps he returned to the army. He was sent to North Africa and then to Italy, specializing in the repair of vehicles, an area he knew well, and was mustered out at the end of December 1945 as a technical sergeant. Apparently he was an exemplary soldier.

Married or not, Virginia, to her great satisfaction, had obtained her nurse's pin and cap. Meandering or not, Bill came back to her. They moved to Chicago, where he got his old job back, and lived in a hotel in the Loop where they waited to take possession of a home in suburban Forest Park. Housing was scarce, and so many veterans wanted new homes that it would take some months to work out. Virginia was fascinated by the metropolis, if also a bit intimidated, but she loved going out. "I felt like life was a movie and I was the star," she recalled. She was also pregnant, and more than a bit lonely when Bill was on the road. With his agreement, she went back to Hope to prepare for their child, where there was a bit more space and at least some company.

The Blythes' new house was ready for them in May. Over a weekend Bill drove straight through to bring back his pregnant wife. On Highway 60 in Missouri, a tire blew out and he lost control of the car. Apparently he was thrown from it and killed instantly. His body was found in a ditch. Ironically, William Jefferson Blythe III, who like his wife loved the bright lights, was buried in a place he loathed and she sought to escape—that sleepy Arkansas town called Hope.

On August 19, 1946, the boy who was technically William Jefferson Blythe IV was delivered by Caesarean section, a month ahead of schedule. Suspicious tongues wagged throughout Hope that Bill Blythe was not his father. Virginia insisted that the birth was simply premature, and there is no good reason to doubt her. Yet even the first days of the child who would become Bill Clinton were shrouded in an aura of suspicion and scandal. Eventually, when Virginia learned more about her late husband's lurid past, she still remained loyal to his memory, continuing to cherish their brief time together, and insisting that she could judge Bill Blythe only by the way he had treated her. "I'll go to my grave," she wrote, "knowing I *was* the love of his life."

## Roger Clinton

Women have been fighting over Bill Clinton since the day he was born. Moving back to her parents' home must have been difficult for Virginia. The house was big enough to accommodate the new mother and her child, but could it contain two mothers? From the first, Edith Cassidy, only forty-five, viewed herself as better qualified to raise little Bill than her inexperienced daughter. Moreover, to gain her credentials as a nurse-anesthetist and secure her future independence, Virginia had to take courses in New Orleans and leave her boy under Edith's influence. When Virginia returned, she still had to find a job. It's little wonder she was attracted by the blandishments of dapper Roger Clinton. She had met him years before, but after returning from New Orleans in 1947 she got to know him a good deal better.

Bronchial problems had ended Eldridge's career as Hope's iceman. He opened a grocery store in a poor neighborhood. Hope had gone dry in 1944, and the nearest source of alcohol was Texarkana, some thirty-five miles away. Under the counter of Eldridge's store was his stash of bootleg liquor, supplied by Roger Clinton, who also owned, or was reputed to own, the Buick dealership in town. Everyone called him "Dude," and it was easy to see why. As Virginia wrote, "He dressed to kill, with sharp-creased trousers and fine-tailored sports coats and two-toned shoes." He stood about five foot eleven, not quite as tall as Bill Blythe, and had dark curly hair. His eyes twinkled when he talked, as if he was on the verge of saying something funny. He was the life of any party, and he loved partying. Virginia wrote, "Men adored him, women found him charming."

But there was also a sense of danger around Roger Clinton. He drank heavily. He gambled, sometimes recklessly. Gambling was illegal throughout Arkansas, but law enforcement was often influenced to look the other way, particularly in the wide-open resort city of Hot Springs. Roger's older brother, Raymond, who largely ran the lives of his four siblings, was one of the power elite in that "sin city." His major problem was Roger. Raymond was the real owner of Roger's dealership in Hope, where profits were being gambled away by its manager. Roger was also a notorious womanizer—Virginia must have heard the rumors about it—and when things weren't going his way, he could turn violent.

Still, since they had become reacquainted, Roger had been a perfect gentleman, at least around Virginia. She convinced herself that with her love and Roger's money, they could provide a secure home for Bill. She hadn't yet discovered that Roger didn't really have any money, but he did still have a wife. At least it was only one. She divorced him in 1948, on the grounds of physical abuse.

Once again Virginia fell for the blandishments of a fast-talking suitor. This time, however, her mother was not taken in, as she had been by charming Bill Blythe. In fact, Edith Cassidy was so distraught that she threatened to seek legal custody of four-year-old Billy, as she called her grandson. Although the suit never materialized, neither she, her husband, nor the boy attended the ceremony on June 19, 1950, that joined Virginia to Roger Clinton. She was twenty-seven, he was forty.

Even though still in Hope, Virginia, Roger, and Bill moved into a new home in a congenial neighborhood of other young families. For a while, all went well. Roger managed the auto agency and Virginia found work, although it kept her out at all hours. There was a demand for qualified anesthesiologists, even in a small town. A nanny was hired to look after Bill. He was not only bright, he enjoyed playing with other children, so long as he was the center of attention, as he had been with his adoring grandma.

The domestic idyll didn't last long. Roger was at best indifferent or preoccupied when Bill started calling him "Daddy." Worse than his continuing drinking and gambling, which ate up the paychecks Virginia dutifully gave him to help pay the mortgage, Roger became abusive. Precisely what, he wanted to know, was Virginia doing with those doctors after their late-night labors? Of course, his own philandering, no secret to Virginia, had hardly ceased. As his alcoholism became more acute, his accusations turned to violence. He not only hit his wife, he once fired a shot that narrowly missed her head. She had to call the police and send her son to a neighbor's.

What was terrified Bill to make of it? Invariably, after Roger sobered up, he pleaded with his wife for forgiveness and promised to reform. Virginia always took him back, hoping this time it might be true, but her main concern was for Bill. He was special, she told him. She knew it, just as her mother knew it. He must try to block the bad things out of his mind and focus on his bright future.

In 1952, ostensibly to get a new start, the family moved to Hot Springs. The Buick agency in Hope was sold. First they lived on a farm outside of town, but that wasn't at all to Virginia's liking. They moved to a large house she didn't realize was owned not by her husband but by Raymond Clinton. Roger got a job selling auto parts. Hot Springs was nothing like Hope. It was not only much larger, its hilly topography was more enticing than Hope's flatlands. Within the resort city there was an almost startling separation, not unlike that in Las Vegas today—on one side luxurious hotels containing every sort of action, on the other a settled community of neat homes, schools, and churches. Vice and virtue coexisted side by side. Hot Springs not only brought out the worst in Roger Clinton, it embodied the duality of his wife. She was proficient in her profession and very conscientious, but she also wanted to join the perpetual party on the other side of town. She tore around at all hours in her flashy convertible, dressed in a provocative fashion, heavily made up. She, too, gambled, drank, chain-smoked, took in the shows, and at least flirted with other men. The inevitable arguments between Bill's parents rarely ceased.

Yet the turmoil didn't inhibit his progress, in or out of school. Bill did well everywhere, first in Catholic school, then in public school. At the age of ten he announced to the astonished pastor of Park Place Baptist Church that he planned to attend services regularly, with or without his parents. He learned to study and to concentrate, whatever the disorder around him. In 1956 his parents presented him with quite a surprise, a younger brother they named Roger Cassidy Clinton. Anxious to shield little Roger as much as possible from what he had witnessed, Bill became almost a substitute father, a "man-child," as Clinton biographer David Maraniss puts it, the one fully functioning member of an irretrievably dysfunctional family.

In high school Bill really came into his own. He was never formally adopted by Roger Clinton, but from the time young Roger started school, Bill began calling himself Bill Clinton—or, officially, William Jefferson Clinton. It avoided confusion and potential embarrassment for both of them, although Bill always insisted, "The name doesn't matter; it's the man." Except for sports, Bill excelled in just about everything at Hot Springs High. He was an excellent student, the acknowledged leader of his class, and even drum major of its renowned band. (In addition, he played a mean saxophone.) Although rather chunky, he was also quite popular with the girls. During high school his future became the focus of a third maternal figure, principal Johnnie Mae Mackey, a widow who viewed him as her surrogate son.

Bill Clinton had no strong male role models growing up, at least not until he worked for political leaders such as Senator J. William Fulbright. There were men he liked—his gentle grandfather, his pastor, the band director—but to the extent he was influenced by anyone, it was the three women who vied for his affection. Bill's success even brought them together. After Clinton's speech at his high school graduation, Virginia couldn't resist sharing her joy with her mother. "I was so proud of him I nearly died. He was truly in all his glory." Undoubtedly, Principal Mackey felt the same way.

In 1959 Bill had a defining experience not unlike young Ronald Reagan's decision to drag his drunken father into the house. Roger's alcoholism was becoming uncontrollable. After drinking tumblers of whiskey, he strode over, screaming at her as usual, to hit Virginia, as he had so many times before. Bill had seen enough of it. He intervened, grabbing his stepfather and telling him in even tones, "Hear me—never ever touch my mother again." In his teens Bill was already stronger than a stepfather whose health was beginning to deteriorate, but it was not only a rather heroic act, it marked his affirmation that he was now the man of the house.

Virginia, even if no longer physically threatened, finally moved to divorce Roger Clinton. Bill was a witness, testifying to years of rage and recriminations, verbal and physical abuse. The divorce was granted in 1962, but despite everything, within three months Virginia took Roger back. He had taken to sleeping on their front porch, more a pathetic figure than a threatening one. However, this time when he returned home there was a difference. He was more like a visitor. The largest bedroom was Bill's. The property was now clearly his own domain, his launching pad. The first step in his rapid ascent was to attend Georgetown University.

Away from home, Bill reflected on the challenges of his childhood. At home, Roger Clinton reflected on Bill. As he rose and Roger declined, both softened their stances. Roger was diagnosed with cancer in 1965, and although he underwent massive radiation treatments, he knew his time was running out. Maraniss writes that Roger Clinton "had always adored Bill." He simply felt inadequate, unable to express his affection, an alcoholic failure who could see no redeeming social value in his own life. But now there *was* redemption "in his wife's first son, who bore his name."

Bill came down from Georgetown every weekend he could to visit Roger at Duke Medical Center. When he couldn't visit, Bill wrote compassionate, positive letters. "None of us can have any peace unless they can face life with God. . . . You ought to look everywhere for help, Daddy, you ought to write me more. . . . People . . . confide in me. . . . We all have so much to live for; let's start doing it together." In 1967 Roger was moved back home, with constant medical care. Bill returned that fall to stay by his bedside, much between them still unspoken.

Roger Clinton died on November 8, 1967, at the age of fifty-eight. When Bill was named a Rhodes Scholar the following spring, he shed tears of sorrow that he could not share the news with the only father he had ever known.

"The name doesn't matter." Virginia Dell Cassidy Blythe Clinton Dwire Kelley lived to see her son elected president of the United States. She may have been married four times, but Bill Clinton was always the man in her life. William Jefferson Blythe Clinton has his own distinction. He is the third president whose father died before he was born, but he is the only one of them to have had a stepfather. This is a book about inspiration, father to son. With Roger and Bill Clinton, it was more son to father.

# 20

# "If You Need Me, I'm Here"

## George Herbert Walker Bush

MATURITY CAME LATE to George Walker Bush, his own political career rising as his father's receded, their once-uneasy relationship strengthened through the experience of joint efforts, a close-knit family, and the elder Bush's counsel in times of unprecedented peril.

The relationship between George Herbert Walker Bush and his first son, George Walker Bush, has not always been placid. In his twenties, after drinking a bit too much, George W., only twenty-two years younger than his father, even challenged him to go "mano a mano" and settle matters with their fists. Barbara Bush had to separate them. It was not easy living up to a legacy. The heritage of "duty and service" embodied by Prescott Bush and carried forward by his second son, George, was only reluctantly accepted by *his* son George W. If it took him longer not only to put on the mantle but simply to mature, he ultimately arrived at the same place, the awesome responsibility of the American presidency.

The Bushes are only the second father and son in American history to achieve that distinction. The first, John and John Quincy Adams, a father and son utterly devoted to each other, were both men of brilliance but not particularly successful presidents. An equitable evaluation of the tenures of the two George Bushes will, of course, only come with time— just as it took time for them to fully accommodate to each other.

It is ironic that the most authentically Texan of all the Bush children is the only one who was born in the East. His mother called him "Georgie"; most others, "Junior." Odessa, Texas, must have looked to his parents, when they arrived in 1948, more like Mars than the leafy Eastern enclaves they had grown up in. George Sr. was there to learn the oil business from the bottom up—and out. During the next twenty years the Bushes moved to twenty-eight homes in seventeen different cities.

The George Bushes
on Capitol Hill

In California they had a second child, a girl. They named her Pauline
Robinson Bush, "Robin." Soon they were back again in West Texas, but
in the booming town of Midland. Many of their youthful neighbors had
Ivied backgrounds like their own and had also been drawn by the lure
of "black gold." Cocktail shakers and penny loafers merged with overalls
and Friday night football. Young mothers did most of the parenting; their
husbands could be gone for weeks, drilling for oil or, like George Bush,
selling to those who did.

Junior was a typical kid, only more so. He loved all sports, but always
wanted to be captain, and he didn't deal gracefully with losing. At Sam
Houston Elementary School, he was bright but somewhat incorrigible—
both the class clown and the leader of any student pranks. His embarrassed mother was often called in to talk things over with the principal.

Even for no-nonsense Barbara Bush, Junior was quite a challenge. As the Bushes' second son, Jeb, recalled, "Dad was the chief executive officer, but Mother was the chief operating officer." Weekends were special when George Sr. was home. He hosted immense barbecues and taught Sunday school, but best of all, he coached Little League—and sometimes exhibited his own skill with a bat and glove. No one else's father could compare with George Bush, Yale's former baseball captain. His son was envied. The Bush home became the center of activity where the whole neighborhood gathered. "Problem child" or not, there is no doubt that Junior adored his father. George Sr. just wasn't around enough.

After he founded his own firm with a neighbor in 1950, Bush was away even more. He wasn't selling drill bits anymore; he was doing the drilling. It gave him an ulcer, but it also made him a millionaire. He missed his growing family. With the birth of John Ellis, or "Jeb," there were now three children at home. George Sr.'s return was sudden. In 1953 Robin was diagnosed with incurable leukemia. Barbara took her to a New York hospital for treatment with an experimental new drug, but in October she died. Barbara's hair went gray virtually overnight; George Sr. was inconsolable. "Why didn't you tell me?" George W. demanded. At only seven, he had seemed too young to be informed about the severity of his little sister's illness. Junior's reaction, however, was remarkable for one of his age. He tried to cheer his parents up, to lift *them* out of their grief. Although, as he later said, "a little of me died with Robin," he was his parents' rock during this time. Even his humor lightened their load. At San Jacinto Junior High he was still the class clown, but it didn't hurt his popularity.

The business was going so well that George Sr. moved his family to a far more spacious setting in Houston, nearer offshore drilling opportunities. By 1959 their family was completed—two more boys, Neil Mallon and Marvin Pierce, and finally another girl, Dorothy Walker, called "Doro." For the first time, Junior went to a private school, Kinkaid. When he was fifteen, however, he was sent off to his father's old boarding school, Phillips Academy in Andover, Massachusetts. He couldn't understand why. In his experience, only problem children, potential criminals, went away to institutions. To his parents it was simply a matter of providing him with a superior education in preparation for managing the responsibilities that came with being a Bush. To Junior it represented abandonment. First they had kept the truth about Robin from him. Now they were sending him away.

Bush was only an average student at highly structured Andover, but, as always, he had little difficulty making friends. He went on to Yale, the school of his father and grandfather. There, with so much greater freedom, he began drinking in earnest and was even more the life of the party. He was elected president of his fraternity and, like Prescott and George Sr., was tapped for Skull and Bones. The year he graduated, 1968, was a time of turmoil—student unrest over Vietnam—but to Junior it might have been the Roaring Twenties. No longer deferred from the draft, George W. joined the Texas Air National Guard and learned to fly jets. Never reckless in the air, off the base he tended to be a "top gun" on the loose. He later admitted to making mistakes during these "young and irresponsible" years. If drug use was among them, he was hardly alone.

In Houston his father was making the transition to public life. Prescott, ailing, had retired from the United States Senate. In 1964, already chairman of the Harris County Republican Party, George Sr. contested liberal Democratic incumbent Ralph Yarborough for the Senate. He lost, as he was expected to, at a time when the nation was solidly behind President Johnson. But he made a vigorous race, establishing himself as someone to seriously consider for the future. By 1967 Republicans were growing much stronger in Texas. George ran for the House of Representatives, and this time he won.

In 1971 George Sr. was named by President Nixon to represent the United States at the United Nations. In 1972 he moved to Washington to take over the reins of the Republican National Committee. As his siblings continued or completed their educations, Junior went into a kind of uncertain, "nomadic period," toying with jobs, demonstrating little constancy. For years, whenever his conduct lapsed, he had heard the same mantra from his father: "I'm not trying to direct your life, but I'm very disappointed in you. In our family . . . you fulfill your commitments." He was sick of it. That Christmas he and George Sr. had their most direct confrontation. Yet shortly afterward, immature or not, Junior was admitted to Harvard Business School. In 1975 he received his M.B.A., perhaps with an "I'll show him" chip on his shoulder.

Then he went back to Midland, intending to repeat his father's success in the oil fields and in gas. It didn't happen. The 1970s were not the boom times of the 1940s and 1950s. About the time he made a premature bid for Congress, he became reacquainted with an eminently sensible, down-to-earth, attractive young lady he had known back in grade school in Midland, and was "struck by lightning." Her name was Laura Welch. She was now a school librarian. They were married in 1977. Although losing his congressional race, Junior garnered a highly respectable 47 percent of the vote. He was in good company. Both his father and grandfather had also lost their first bids for elective office.

After Laura's ultimatum, "Jim Beam or me," George W. stopped drinking and smoking, and started jogging every day. Then, inspired by Dr. Billy Graham, he found religion. In 1986 George W. declared himself "right with God" and became a committed born-again Christian. He and Laura were already active communicants of her Methodist church. The reformed George W. really emerged after a sort of farewell to his prior life, his raucous fortieth birthday party. And, finally, he found a job he loved. With a syndicate, he purchased the Texas Rangers baseball team. His share gave him only 1.8 percent, but he was the partner out front, the spokesman. Now he could use all of his political and public relations skills, yet carve out an entirely new career of his own. Perhaps one day he might be named commissioner of major league baseball.

Years later George Sr. wrote to a friend, expressing the evident pride he began to feel in the 1980s: "He is good, this boy of ours. He's uptight at times, feisty at other times. . . . He includes people. . . . He's low on ego, high on drive." The elder Bush also wrote to *Time*'s Hugh Sidey, "All the talk about his wild youth is pure nuts. His character will pass muster with flying colors." George Sr. had not always been so dismissive of his son's prior excesses, but family loyalty is a quality all Bushes share.

In 1980 George Sr., after serving as American representative to the People's Republic of China and as director of the CIA, made his first bid for the presidency. Losing the Republican nomination to Ronald Reagan, Bush was chosen by the delegates with visible enthusiasm to be Reagan's running mate. His role as a very involved vice president positioned Bush as Reagan's likely successor.

As his father's campaign kicked off in 1988, Junior attended all the preliminary staff meetings. He bluntly asked strategist Lee Atwater, who had worked for competing candidates in the past, "How do we know we can trust you?" Atwater replied that Junior ought to come to Washington and help in the campaign. "That way if there's a problem, you'll be there to solve it." Junior took him up on it, rendering for his father in 1988 the same sort of service that Bobby Kennedy had provided for his brother Jack in 1960. He thoroughly enjoyed it. "I don't mind a battle," George W. said. "I've got my father's eyes and my mother's mouth."

Young Bush proved to be a more natural politician than either his father or his grandfather, with a peculiarly Texas style of personal campaigning. He defined himself as a "political animal." When a reporter called him less well mannered than his father, Junior replied, "We are different; he grew up in Greenwich, I grew up in West Texas." Later he added, "I was a warrior for George Bush. . . . I would run through a brick wall for my dad. . . . It's one thing to know a guy as your dad and another . . . to be in the trenches with him during a tough political fight." They were never closer, except perhaps in 2001.

After spearheading construction of a spacious new stadium for the Texas Rangers, George W. sold his share of the team at an immense profit. He had decided to run for governor of Texas in 1994. His Democratic opponent would be the "unbeatable" incumbent, Ann Richards. At the Democratic National Convention in 1988, she had ridiculed George Sr. by saying, "He was born with a silver foot in his mouth." It didn't matter what the polls predicted. You don't mess with a Bush. With another son Jeb running for governor of Florida, perhaps George Sr.'s boys were finally being unleashed on the world.

Only a few years before, when his father was president, George W. had introduced himself to White House visitors as "the black sheep" of the family. It had taken him into his forties to reach maturity, spiritually as well as emotionally. Richards called him all sorts of names, from "shrub" to "jerk," but Junior simply plowed ahead. He had a plan, and he stuck with it.

As young Bush's biographer Bill Minutaglio points out, perhaps his father's defeat for reelection in 1992 finally liberated George W. Bush to pursue his own path to extending his family's political legacy. George W. put together what his wife, Laura, called a "lesson plan" of strategy for his campaign: Take nothing for granted, have a clear message, stress it from the start, never lose your cool, recognize even unpleasant realities, stick to a few key issues and hammer them home, don't make promises you may not be able to keep, "vision *does* matter," and "come out swinging."

Against all the odds, George W. Bush was elected governor of Texas in 1994. When opponents, undoubtedly for the final time, accused him of being a transplanted son of the effete Eastern establishment, George replied that it is true that "I was not born in Texas . . . because I wanted to be close to my mother that day." On the day of George W.'s inauguration, his father gave him a gift, accompanied by a note: "Dear George, These cufflinks are my most treasured possession. They were given to me by Mom and Dad on June 9 . . . in 1943 when I got my Navy wings at Corpus Christi. I want you to have them now. . . . You are ready for this huge challenge. You'll do just fine. You'll be a strong, honest, caring governor. . . . You have given us more than we ever could have deserved. . . . We love you. Devotedly, Dad."

On his seventy-fifth birthday, George H. W. Bush wrote a joint letter to all his children: "Remember the old song, 'I'll Be There When You Are.' Well, I'll be there when you are, for there's so much excitement ahead, so many grandkids to watch and grow. If you need me, I'm here." Wearing his grandfather's cuff links, placing his left hand on the same Bible his father had used in 1989, George W. Bush took the presidential oath in January 2001. His wife, Laura, held the Bible that an equally proud Barbara Bush had held for her husband twelve years before. They are a tightly knit family, the Bushes, father and son closer than was once the case. Our presidents—and the American people, of all political persuasions—need such strength and such continuity, perhaps as never before.

# In Conclusion

Here is what a representative sampling of American presidents had to say about their fathers:

**John Adams:** "He was the honestest man I ever knew. In wisdom, piety, benevolence and charity . . . I have never seen his equal."

**Thomas Jefferson:** "Being of a strong mind, sound judgment and eager after information, he read much and improved himself."

**John Quincy Adams:** "All that I dare to ask is that I may live . . . in a manner worthy of him."

**Martin Van Buren:** "My father was never known to have an enemy."

**William Henry Harrison:** "How I wished . . . my father were alive to be with me."

**James Buchanan:** "A kind father, a sincere friend, and an honest man."

**Grover Cleveland:** "Looking back over my life nothing seems to me to have in it more of pathos and interest than the [life story] of my father."

**Theodore Roosevelt:** "I am sure that there is no one [at Harvard] who has a Father who is also his best, and most intimate friend, as you are mine."

**William Howard Taft:** "A man never had a . . . dearer, more considerate father."

**Woodrow Wilson:** "A thinker of singular power . . . a lover and servant of his fellow man, a man of God."

**Calvin Coolidge:** "My father had qualities greater than any I possess. . . . I was exceedingly anxious to grow up like him."

**Franklin D. Roosevelt:** "He was one of the most generous and kindly of men."

**Harry S. Truman:** "My father was a very honorable man. . . . His code was honesty and integrity."

**Dwight D. Eisenhower:** "His finest monument was his reputation. I'm proud that he was my father."

**John F. Kennedy:** "He made his children feel that they were the most important thing in the world to him."

**Richard M. Nixon:** "There was never a day I was not proud of him . . . he was a great man."

**Gerald R. Ford:** "He was the father . . . I loved and learned from and respected."

**Jimmy Carter:** "My daddy was the dominant person in our family and in our life. . . . I want to be a man like my father."

**Ronald Reagan:** "He was the strongest man of principle I ever knew."

**George H. W. Bush:** "Dad taught us about duty and service. . . . My dad was the real inspiration of my life."

Of all the first fathers, perhaps Theodore Roosevelt Sr. comes closest to perfection—but each had his failings. John Adams the younger was inflexible and irascible; Alphonso Taft, excessively intrusive; Joseph Wilson, self-righteous; James Roosevelt, snobbish; John Truman, pugnacious; David Eisenhower, all but abusive; Joseph Kennedy Sr., amoral; Sam Johnson, coarse; James Carter Sr., bigoted; John Reagan, an alcoholic; Prescott Bush, rather intimidating. Yet each in his own way, overcoming the lapses that are our lot in life, provided significant sustenance to a youth who would one day be president of the United States. Most of all, they inspired their sons, as future first fathers are undoubtedly already inspiring *their* sons—and daughters. May they not also inspire us? And when better than now?

# Some Books I've Found Helpful

For some reason, my favorite authors, contemporary and otherwise (other than Bill Bryson), have tended to use their initials—from H. L. Mencken, E. B. White, S. J. Perelman, and C. S. Lewis to P. J. O'Rourke. My favorite historian, the late A. J. P. Taylor, wrote opinionated footnotes far more compelling than the texts of most academics. Having waded through so many endless bibliographic essays, Taylor also made the sensible suggestion that an author's bibliography ought to be limited to books that he or she had at least actually opened.

Since *First Fathers* is in itself a series of forty-four essays, I'm not about to inflict another one on you. And so, after some preliminary suggestions, here are about 250 works of presidential biography and autobiography that I've found useful in this voyage of discovery. I suppose this constitutes a "selected bibliography," although I'm not fond of that term, either.

Having labored in a field so little cultivated, I'm heartened by the conclusions of another historian I admire, John Lukacs. He recently pointed out the irony that at a time when the actual teaching of American history has diminished in our schools to an extent little short of scandalous, interest in popular books about American history, as demonstrated with their dollars by the reading public, is at an all-time high. That has certainly been true of accounts of presidential families, but there are still far too few.

*First Fathers* is only the second book devoted to telling the stories of the fathers of our presidents. I'm indebted to Jeff C. Young, the author of the first, *The Fathers of American Presidents* (Jefferson, NC: McFarland, 1997). In a very thoroughly researched survey, Young lays out the specifics with accuracy and insight.

In all of American history there have been only four books devoted to the mothers of our presidents, two of which are in print—one by an historian, one by a journalist. My book, *Faith of Our Mothers* (Grand Rapids, MI: Eerdmans, 2001), is the only inclusive account of all forty-two first mothers. In it I explored their faith in both the limitless potential of their favored sons and the personal religious faith that many of these women professed. It is the ideal companion to *First Fathers*. *First Mothers* by Bonnie Angelo (New York: HarperCollins, 2000) is limited to only eleven twentieth-century first mothers, but the use of interviews results in a fascinating anecdotal account.

The two earlier books are, alas, out of print but are available through rare book dealers: *The Mothers of American Presidents* by Doris Faber (New York: New American Library, 1968; reprint, New York: St. Martin's Press, 1978), and *Our Presidents and Their Mothers* by William J. Hampton (Boston: Cornhill, 1922).

Accounts of first ladies, for some reason, are the only component of presidential families to be thoroughly—perhaps even excessively—explored. Here are some of the better titles: *Hidden Power: Presidential Marriages that Shaped Our History* by Kati Marton (New York: Pantheon, 2001); *First Ladies: An Intimate Group Portrait of White House Wives* by Margaret Truman (New York: Random House, 1995); *First Ladies: The Saga of the Presidents' Wives and Their Power, 1788–1990* (2 volumes) by Carl S. Anthony (New York: Morrow, 1990, 1991); *Smithsonian Book of the First Ladies* by Doris Faber (New York: Holt, 1996); *American First Ladies: Their Lives and Their Legacies* edited by Louis L. Gould (New York: Garland, 1996).

Another gap has been recently filled by *All the Presidents' Children* by Doug Wead (New York: Simon and Schuster, 2003), detailing the "triumphs and tragedies" of presidential offspring. There are even some short works ostensibly "by" presidential pets. Although coffee table books on the White House tend to be more architectural than personal, some at least touch on presidential parents. The best popular account of life in the White House is *America's First Families: An Inside View of 200 Years of Private Life in the White House* by Carl S. Anthony (New York: Simon and Schuster, 2000). Also of interest is *American Presidential Families* by Hugh Brown and Charles Mosley (New York: Macmillan, 1993). Always worth rereading is *The Presidential Character* by David Barber (New York: Prentice Hall, 1992). An insightful collection of stories was assembled in *Presidential Anecdotes* by Paul F. Boller Jr. (New York: Oxford University Press, 1981).

An excellent account of significant presidential families is *America's Political Dynasties—From Adams to Kennedy* by Stephen Hess (Garden City, NY: Doubleday, 1966). The following biographies of presidents, in chronological order, including some of their memoirs, tell us as much (or as little) about their fathers as we are likely to learn. Some of these books are relatively recent; some aren't. Many are compelling. All are informative.

## Augustine Washington

Alden, John R. *George Washington: A Biography.* Baton Rouge: Louisiana State University Press, 1996.

Bourne, Miriam A. *First Family: George Washington and His Intimate Relations.* New York: W. W. Norton, 1982.

Brookheiser, Richard. *Founding Father: Rediscovering George Washington.* New York: Free Press, 1996.

Cunliffe, Marcus. *George Washington: Man and Monument.* Boston: Little, Brown, 1958.

Fay, Bernard. *George Washington: Republican Aristocrat.* Boston: Houghton Mifflin, 1931.

Ferling, John E. *The First of Men: A Life of George Washington.* Knoxville: University of Tennessee Press, 1988.

Flexner, James T. *George Washington: The Forge of Experience, 1732–1775.* Boston: Little, Brown, 1965.

Freeman, Douglas S. *George Washington: A Biography.* Vol. 1, *Young Washington.* New York: Scribner's, 1976.

Knollenberg, Bernhard. *George Washington: The Virginia Period, 1732–1775.* Durham, NC: Duke University Press, 1964.

Longmore, Paul K. *The Invention of George Washington.* Berkeley: University of California Press, 1988.

Moore, Charles. *The Family Life of George Washington.* Boston: Houghton Mifflin, 1926.

# John Adams Sr.

Butterfield, Lyman H., et al., eds. *The Adams Papers: Diary and Autobiography of John Adams.* Vol. 1, *1755–1770.* Cambridge, MA: Belknap Press of Harvard University, 1962.

East, Robert A. *John Adams.* Boston: Twayne, 1979.

Ellis, Joseph J. *Passionate Sage: The Character and Legacy of John Adams.* New York: W. W. Norton, 1993.

————. *Founding Brothers: The Revolutionary Generation.* New York: Alfred A. Knopf, 2000.

Ferling, John E. *John Adams: A Life.* Knoxville: University of Tennessee Press, 1992.

McCullough, David. *John Adams.* New York: Simon and Schuster, 2001.

Peabody, James B., ed. *John Adams: A Biography in His Own Words.* New York: Newsweek Books, 1976.

Shaw, Peter. *The Character of John Adams.* New York: W. W. Norton, 1977.

Shepherd, Jack. *The Adams Chronicles: Four Generations of Greatness.* Boston: Little, Brown, 1975.

Smith, Page, *John Adams.* Vol. 1. Garden City, NY: Doubleday, 1962.

# Peter Jefferson

Bober, Natalie S. *Thomas Jefferson: Man on a Mountain.* New York: Atheneum, 1988.

Brodie, Fawn M. *Thomas Jefferson: An Intimate History.* New York: W. W. Norton, 1974.

Ellis, Joseph J. *American Sphinx: The Character of Thomas Jefferson.* New York: Alfred A. Knopf, 1997.

Fleming, Thomas. *The Man from Monticello: An Intimate Life of Thomas Jefferson.* New York: William Morrow, 1969.

Gardner, Joseph L., and Julian P. Boyd, eds. *Thomas Jefferson: A Biography in His Own Words.* Vol. 1. Princeton, NJ: Princeton University Press, 1974.

Malone, Dumas. *Jefferson the Virginian.* Vol. 1, *Jefferson and His Time.* Boston: Little, Brown, 1948.

Peterson, Merrill D. *Thomas Jefferson and the New Nation: A Biography.* New York: Oxford University Press, 1970.

Randall, Henry S. *Life of Thomas Jefferson.* Vol. 1. Reading, MA: Perseus Books, 1972.

Smith, Page. *Thomas Jefferson: A Revealing Biography.* New York: McGraw-Hill, 1976.

# James Madison Sr.

Brant, Irving. *The Fourth President: A Life of James Madison.* New York: Bobbs-Merrill, 1970.

Handlin, Oscar and Lilian. *Liberty in Expansion: 1760–1850.* New York: Harper & Row, 1989.

Ketcham, Ralph. *James Madison: A Biography.* New York: Macmillan, 1971.

McCoy, Drew R. *The Last of the Fathers: James Madison and the Republican Legacy.* New York: Cambridge University Press, 1984.

Moore, Virginia. *The Madisons: A Biography.* New York: McGraw-Hill, 1979.

Peterson, Merrill D., ed. *James Madison: A Biography in His Own Words.* New York: Newsweek Books, 1974.

Rutland, Robert A. *James Madison: The Founding Father.* New York: Macmillan, 1987.

Young, Jeff C. *The Fathers of American Presidents.* Jefferson, NC: McFarland, 1997.

## Spence Monroe

Ammon, Harry. *James Monroe: The Quest for National Identity.* Charlottesville: University Press of Virginia, 1990.

Butterfield, Lyman H., ed. *The Adams Papers.* Cambridge, MA: Belknap Press of Harvard University, 1961.

Cresson, William P. *James Monroe.* Chapel Hill: University of North Carolina Press, 1946.

Gilman, Daniel C. *James Monroe.* Rev. ed. Boston: Houghton Mifflin, 1898.

## John Adams

Adams, John Q. *Diary of John Quincy Adams.* Boston: Belknap Press of Harvard University, 1982.

Butterfield, Lyman H., Marc Fridlaender, and Mary Jo Kline, eds. *The Book of Abigail and John: Selected Letters of the Adams Family.* Cambridge, MA: Harvard University Press, 1975.

Ferling, John E. *John Adams: A Life.* Knoxville: University of Tennessee Press, 1992.

Hecht, Marie B. *John Quincy Adams: A Personal History of an Independent Man.* New York: Macmillan, 1972.

Nagel, Paul C. *Descent from Glory: Four Generations of the John Adams Family.* New York: Oxford University Press, 1983.

————. *John Quincy Adams: A Public Life, A Private Life.* New York: Alfred A. Knopf, 1997.

Parsons, Lynn H. *John Quincy Adams.* New York: Greenwood Press, 1993.

Shepherd, Jack. *Cannibals of the Heart: A Personal Biography of Louisa Catherine and John Quincy Adams.* New York: McGraw-Hill, 1980.

## Andrew Jackson Sr.

Davis, Burke. *Old Hickory: A Life of Andrew Jackson.* New York: Dial Press, 1977.

James, Marquis. *The Life of Andrew Jackson.* New York: Bobbs-Merrill, 1938.

Johnson, Gerald W. *Andrew Jackson: An Epic in Homespun.* New York: Minton, Balch, 1927.

Remini, Robert V. *The Life of Andrew Jackson.* New York: Harper & Row, 1988.

## Abraham Van Buren

Cole, Donald B. *Martin Van Buren and the American Political System.* Princeton, NJ: Princeton University Press, 1984.

Fitzpatrick, John, ed. *The Autobiography of Martin Van Buren.* Vol. 1. Reading, MA: Perseus Books, 1973.

Hoyt, Edwin P. *Martin Van Buren.* Chicago: Reilly and Lee, 1964.

Niven, John. *Martin Van Buren: The Romantic Age of American Politics.* New York: Oxford University Press, 1983.

Remini, Robert V. *Martin Van Buren and the Making of the Democratic Party.* New York: Columbia University Press, 1959.

# Benjamin Harrison V

Cleaves, Freeman. *Old Tippecanoe: William Henry Harrison and His Time*. New York: Scribners, 1939.

Hess, Stephn *America's Political Dynasties—From Adams to Kennedy*. Garden City, NY: Doubleday, 1966.

Peterson, Norman L. *The Presidencies of William Henry Harrison and John Tyler*. Lawrence: University Press of Kansas, 1989.

Sievers, Harry J., ed. *Benjamin Harrison, 1833–1901*. Dobbs Ferry, NY: Oceana, 1969.

# John Tyler Sr.

Chitwood, Oliver P. *John Tyler: Champion of the Old South*. New York: Russell and Russell, 1964.

Ellett, Katherine T. *Young John Tyler*. Richmond, VA: Dietz Press, 1976.

Seager, Robert. *And Tyler Too: A Biography of John and Julia Gardiner Tyler*. New York: McGraw-Hill, 1963.

Tyler, Lyon G. *The Letters and Times of the Tylers*. Reading, MA: Perseus Books, 1970.

# Samuel Polk

McCormac, Eugene I. *James K. Polk: A Political Biography*. New York: Russell and Russell, 1965.

Morrel, Martha M. *Young Hickory: The Life and Times of President James K. Polk*. New York: E. P. Dutton, 1949.

Nevins, Allan, ed. *Polk: The Diary of a President, 1845–1849*. New York: Longmans, Green, 1929.

Seigenthaler, John. *James K. Polk: 1845–1849*. New York: Times Books, 2003.

Sellers, Charles. *James K. Polk*. Vol. 1. Princeton, NJ: Princeton University Press, 1966.

# Richard Taylor

Bauer, K. Jack. *Zachary Taylor: Soldier, Planter, Statesman of the Old Southwest*. Baton Rouge: Louisiana State University Press, 1985.

Bent, Silas. *Old Rough and Ready*. New York: Vanguard, 1946.

Dyer, Brainerd. *Zachary Taylor*. Baton Rouge: Louisiana State University Press, 1946.

Hamilton, Holman. *Zachary Taylor: Soldier of the Republic*. Indianapolis: Bobbs-Merrill, 1941.

# Nathaniel Fillmore

Farrell, John J. *Millard Fillmore, 1800–1874*. Dobbs Ferry, NY: Oceana, 1971.

Raybach, Robert J. *Millard Fillmore: Biography of a President*. Buffalo: Stewart, 1972.

Severance, Frank H., ed. *Millard Fillmore Papers*. Vol. 1. New York: Kraus, 1970.

# Benjamin Pierce

Gara, Larry. *The Presidency of Franklin Pierce*. Lawrence: University Press of Kansas, 1991.

Hawthorne, Nathaniel. *Life of Franklin Pierce*. Boston: Somerset, 1972.

Nichols, Roy F. *Franklin Pierce: Young Hickory of the Granite Hills.* Philadelphia: University of Pennsylvania Press, 1958.

## James Buchanan Sr.

Boller, Paul F. Jr. *Presidential Anecdotes.* New York: Oxford University Press, 1981.
Curtis, George T. *The Life of James Buchanan.* Vol. 1. New York: Harper, 1883.
Hoyt, Edwin P. *James Buchanan.* Chicago: Reilly and Lee, 1966.
Klein, Philip S. *President James Buchanan: A Biography.* University Park: Pennsylvania State University Press, 1962.

## Thomas Lincoln

Anderson, Dwight G. *Abraham Lincoln: The Quest for Immortality.* New York: Alfred A. Knopf, 1982.
Beveridge, Albert J. *Abraham Lincoln, 1809–1858.* Vol. 1. Boston: Houghton Mifflin, 1928.
Burlingame, Michael. *The Inner World of Abraham Lincoln.* Urbana: University of Illinois Press, 1994.
Current, Richard N. *The Lincoln Nobody Knows.* New York: McGraw-Hill, 1958.
Donald, David H. *Lincoln.* New York: Simon and Schuster, 1995.
Foner, Eric, and Olivia Mahoney. *A House Divided: America in the Age of Lincoln.* New York: W. W. Norton, 1990.
Guelzo, Allen C. *Abraham Lincoln: Redeemer President.* Grand Rapids, MI: Eerdmans, 1999.
Herndon, William H. *Life of Lincoln.* Reprint, Reading, MA: Perseus Books, 1973.
McPherson, James M. *Abraham Lincoln and the Second American Revolution.* New York: Oxford University Press, 1991.
Peterson, Merrill D. *Lincoln in Modern Memory.* New York: Oxford University Press, 1994.
Sandburg, Carl. *Abraham Lincoln: The Prairie Years.* Vol. 1. New York: Harcourt, Brace, 1974.
Tarbell, Ida M. *The Life of Abraham Lincoln.* Vol. 1. New York: Doubleday and McClure, 1900.
Thomas, Benjamin P. *Abraham Lincoln: A Biography.* New York: Alfred A. Knopf, 1952.

## Jacob Johnson

Stryker, Lloyd P. *Andrew Johnson: A Study in Courage.* New York: Macmillan, 1936.
Thomas, Lately. *The First President Johnson.* New York: William Morrow, 1968.
Trefousse, Hans L. *Andrew Johnson: A Biography.* New York: W. W. Norton, 1991.

## Jesse Root Grant

Anderson, Nancy S., and Dwight C. Anderson. *The Generals: Ulysses S. Grant and Robert E. Lee.* New York: Alfred A. Knopf, 1988.
Barber, James G. *U. S. Grant: The Man and the Image.* Carbondale: Southern Illinois University Press, 1986.

McFeely, William S. *Grant: A Biography.* New York: W. W. Norton, 1981.

Perret, Geoffrey. *Ulysses S. Grant: Soldier and President.* New York: Random House, 1997.

Simon, John Y. *The Papers of Ulysses S. Grant.* Vol. 1, *1837–1861.* Carbondale: Southern Illinois University Press, 1967.

Smith, Jean E. *Grant.* New York: Simon and Schuster, 2001.

## Rutherford Hayes Jr.

Barnard, Harry. *Rutherford B. Hayes and His America.* New York: Bobbs-Merrill, 1954.

Fitzgerald, Carol B. *Rutherford B. Hayes.* Westport, CT: Meckler, 1991.

Williams, Charles R. *The Life of Rutherford Birchard Hayes: Nineteenth President of the United States.* Vol. 1. Boston: Houghton Mifflin, 1914.

## Abram Garfield

Booraem, Hendrik, V. *The Road to Respectability: James A. Garfield and His World, 1844–1852.* Cranbury, NJ: Bucknell University Press, 1988.

Brown, Harry J., and Frederick D. Williams, eds. *The Diary of James A. Garfield.* Vol. 1. Lansing: Michigan State University Press, 1967.

Leech, Margaret, and Harry J. Brown. *The Garfield Orbit.* New York: Harper & Row, 1978.

McElroy, Richard L. *James A. Garfield: His Life and Times.* Canton, OH: Daring, 1986.

Peskin, Allan. *Garfield.* Kent, OH: Kent State University Press, 1978.

Smith, Theodore C. *The Life and Letters of James Abram Garfield.* New Haven, CT: Yale University Press, 1925.

Taylor, James M. *Garfield of Ohio: The Available Man.* New York: W. W. Norton, 1970.

## William Arthur

Doenecke, Justus D. *The Presidencies of James A. Garfield and Chester A. Arthur.* Lawrence: University Press of Kansas, 1981.

Howe, George F. *Chester A. Arthur: A Quarter Century of Machine Politics.* New York: Ungar, 1935.

Reeves, Thomas C. *Gentleman Boss: The Life of Chester Alan Arthur.* New York: Knopf, 1975.

## Richard Falley Cleveland

Brodsky, Alyn. *Grover Cleveland: A Study in Character.* New York: St. Martin's, 2000.

Jeffers, H. Paul. *An Honest President: The Life and Presidencies of Grover Cleveland.* New York: William Morrow, 2000.

Nevins, Allan. *Grover Cleveland: A Study in Courage.* New York: Dodd, Mead, 1932.

Tugwell, Rexford G. *Grover Cleveland.* New York: Macmillan, 1968.

## John Scott Harrison

Hess, Stephen. *America's Political Dynasties—From Adams to Kennedy.* Garden City, NY: Doubleday, 1966.

Myers, Elizabeth P. *Benjamin Harrison.* Chicago: Reilly and Lee, 1969.

Sievers, Harry J. *Benjamin Harrison: Hoosier Statesman*. New York: University Publishers, 1959.

Socolofsky, Homer E., and Allan Spetter. *The Presidency of Benjamin Harrison*. Lawrence: University Press of Kansas, 1987.

## William McKinley Sr.

Higgins, Eva. *William McKinley: An Inspiring Biography*. Canton, OH: Daring, 1989.

Leech, Margaret. *In the Days of McKinley*. New York: Harper & Brothers, 1959.

McElroy, William L. *William McKinley and Our America*. Canton, OH: Stark County Historical Society, 1996.

Morgan, W. Wayne. *William McKinley and His America*. Syracuse, NY: Syracuse University Press, 1963.

## Theodore Roosevelt Sr.

Churchill, Allen. *The Roosevelts: American Aristocrats*. New York: Harper & Row, 1965.

Collier, Peter, and David Horowitz. *The Roosevelts: An American Saga*. New York: Simon and Schuster, 1994.

McCullough, David. *Mornings on Horseback*. New York: Touchstone, 1981.

Miller, Nathan. *Theodore Roosevelt: A Life*. New York: William Morrow, 1992.

Morris, Edmund. *The Rise of Theodore Roosevelt*. New York: Ballantine, 1980.

Morrison, Elting E., and John Blum, eds. *The Letters of Theodore Roosevelt*. Vol. 1. Cambridge, MA: Harvard University Press, 1951.

Pringle, Henry. *Theodore Roosevelt: A Biography*. New York: Harcourt, Brace, 1931.

Renehan, Edward J., Jr. *The Lion's Pride: Theodore Roosevelt and His Family in Peace and War*. New York: Oxford University Press, 1998.

Roosevelt, Theodore. *Autobiography of Theodore Roosevelt*. Reading, MA: Perseus Books, 1985.

## Alphonso Taft

Anderson, Judith I. *William Howard Taft: An Intimate History*. New York: W. W. Norton, 1981.

Pringle, Henry. *The Life and Times of William Howard Taft*. Vol. 1. New York: Farrar and Rinehart, 1939.

Ross, Ishbel. *An American Family: The Tafts, 1678–1964*. Cleveland, OH: World, 1964.

## Joseph Ruggles Wilson

Blum, John Morton. *Woodrow Wilson and the Politics of Morality*. Boston: Little, Brown, 1956.

Heckscher, August. *Woodrow Wilson*. New York: Scribner's, 1991.

Link, Arthur S. *Woodrow Wilson: The Road to the White House*. Princeton, NJ: Princeton University Press, 1947.

———, ed. *The Papers of Woodrow Wilson*. Vol. 1. Princeton, NJ: Princeton University Press, 1966.

Mulder, John M. *Woodrow Wilson: The Years of Preparation.* Princeton, NJ: Princeton University Press, 1978.

Osborn, George. *Woodrow Wilson: The Early Years.* Baton Rouge: Louisiana State University Press, 1968.

Smith, Gene. *When the Cheering Stopped: The Last Years of Woodrow Wilson.* New York: William Morrow, 1964.

## George Tryon Harding II

Downes, Randolph. *The Rise of Warren Gamaliel Harding, 1865–1920.* Columbus: Ohio State University Press, 1970.

Mee, Charles L., Jr. *The Ohio Gang: The World of Warren G. Harding.* New York: M. Evans, 1981.

Russell, Francis. *The Shadow of Blooming Grove: Warren G. Harding in His Times.* New York: McGraw-Hill, 1968.

## John Calvin Coolidge

Coolidge, Calvin. *The Autobiography of Calvin Coolidge.* New York: Cosmopolitan, 1929.

Fuess, Claude. *Calvin Coolidge: The Man from Vermont.* Boston: Little, Brown, 1940.

McCoy, Donald R. *Calvin Coolidge: The Quiet President.* New York: Macmillan, 1967.

Sobel, Robert. *Coolidge: An American Enigma.* Washington, DC: Regnery, 1998.

White, William A. *A Puritan in Babylon: The Story of Calvin Coolidge.* New York: Macmillan, 1938.

## Jesse Clark Hoover

Burner, David. *Herbert Hoover: A Public Life.* New York: Atheneum, 1984.

Hoover, Herbert. *The Memoirs of Herbert Hoover.* Vol. 1, *Years of Adventure, 1874–1920.* New York: Macmillan, 1951.

Nash, George H. *The Life of Herbert Hoover.* Vol. 1, *The Engineer, 1874–1914.* New York: W. W. Norton, 1983.

Smith, Gene. *The Shattered Dream: Herbert Hoover and the Great Depression.* New York: William Morrow, 1970.

Smith, Richard N. *An Uncommon Man: The Triumph of Herbert Hoover.* New York: Simon and Schuster, 1984.

## James Roosevelt

Asbell, Bernard. *The FDR Memoirs.* New York: Doubleday, 1973.

Collier, Peter, and David Horowitz. *The Roosevelts: An American Saga.* New York: Simon and Schuster, 1994.

Freidel, Frank. *Franklin D. Roosevelt: A Rendezvous with Destiny.* Boston: Little, Brown, 1990.

Goodwin, Doris K. *No Ordinary Time: Franklin and Eleanor Roosevelt and the Home Front in World War II.* New York: Simon and Schuster, 1994.

Morgan, Ted. *FDR: A Biography.* New York: Simon and Schuster, 1986.

Schlesinger, Arthur M., Jr. *The Crisis of the Old Order, 1919–1933.* Boston: Houghton Mifflin, 1957.

Ward, Geoffrey C. *Before the Trumpet: Young Franklin Roosevelt, 1882–1905.* New York: Harper & Row, 1981.

———. *A First-Class Temperament: The Emergence of Franklin Roosevelt.* New York: Harper & Row, 1989.

## John Anderson Truman

Daniel, Margaret T. *Harry S. Truman.* New York: William Morrow, 1972.

Ferrell, Robert H. *Harry S. Truman: A Life.* Columbia: University of Missouri Press, 1994.

———, ed. *The Autobiography of Harry S. Truman.* Boulder: Colorado Associated University Press, 1980.

Gullan, Harold I. *The Upset That Wasn't: Harry S. Truman and the Crucial Election of 1948.* Chicago: Ivan R. Dee, 1998.

Hamby, Alonzo L. *Man of the People: A Life of Harry S. Truman.* New York: Oxford University Press, 1995.

McCullough, David. *Truman.* New York: Simon and Schuster, 1992.

Miller, Merle. *Plain Speaking: An Oral Biography of Harry S. Truman.* New York: G. P. Putnam's Sons, 1973.

Miller, Richard L. *Truman: The Rise to Power.* New York: McGraw-Hill, 1986.

Truman, Harry S. *Memoirs.* Vol. 1, *Year of Decisions.* Garden City, NY: Doubleday, 1955.

## David Jacob Eisenhower

Ambrose, Stephen E. *Eisenhower.* Vol. 1, *Soldier, General of the Army, President-Elect, 1890–1952.* New York: Simon and Schuster, 1983.

Brendon, Piers. *Ike: His Life and Times.* New York: Harper & Row, 1986.

Childs, Marquis. *Eisenhower: Captive Hero.* New York: Harcourt, Brace, 1958.

Eisenhower, Dwight D. *Crusade in Europe.* Garden City, NY: Doubleday, 1948.

Ferrell, Robert H., ed. *The Eisenhower Diaries.* New York: W. W. Norton, 1981.

Lee, Alton R. *Dwight D. Eisenhower: Soldier and Statesman.* New York: Nelson-Hall, 1981.

Neal, Steve. *The Eisenhowers.* Garden City, NY: Doubleday, 1978.

## Joseph Patrick Kennedy Sr.

Burns, James M. *John Kennedy: A Political Profile.* New York: Avon, 1960.

Collier, Peter, and David Horowitz. *The Kennedys: An American Drama.* New York: Summit, 1984.

Davis, John H. *The Kennedys: Dynasty and Disaster, 1848–1948.* New York: McGraw-Hill, 1984.

Goodwin, Doris K. *The Fitzgeralds and the Kennedys: An American Saga.* New York: St. Martin's, 1987.

Hamilton, Nigel. *JFK: Reckless Youth.* New York: Random House, 1992.

Hilty, James W. *Robert Kennedy: Brother Protector.* Philadelphia: Temple University Press, 1997.

Kennedy, Rose F. *Times to Remember.* Garden City, NY: Doubleday, 1974.

Parmet, Herbert S. *Jack: The Struggles of John F. Kennedy.* New York: Dial, 1980.

Reeves, Richard. *President Kennedy: Profile of Power.* New York: Simon and Schuster, 1993.

Reeves, Thomas C. *A Question of Character: A Life of John F. Kennedy.* New York: Free Press, 1991.

Schlesinger, Arthur M., Jr. *A Thousand Days: John F. Kennedy in the White House.* Boston: Houghton Mifflin, 1965.

Smith, Amanda, ed. *Hostage to Fortune: The Letters of Joseph P. Kennedy.* New York: Viking, 2001.

Sorensen, Theodore C. *Kennedy.* New York: Harper & Row, 1965.

## Sam Ealy Johnson Jr.

Caro, Robert A. *The Years of Lyndon Johnson: The Path to Power.* New York: Alfred A. Knopf, 1982.

Dallek, Robert. *Lone Star Rising: Lyndon Johnson and His Times, 1908–1960.* New York: Oxford University Press, 1991.

Divine, Robert A, ed. *Exploring the Johnson Years.* Austin: University of Texas Press, 1981.

Harwood, Richard, and Haynes Johnson. *Lyndon.* New York: Praeger, 1973.

Kearns, Doris. *Lyndon Johnson and the American Dream.* New York: Harper & Row, 1976.

Miller, Merle. *Lyndon: An Oral Biography.* New York: G. P. Putnam's Sons, 1980.

Unger, Irwin, and Debi Unger. *LBJ: A Life.* New York: Wiley, 1999.

## Francis Anthony Nixon

Aitken, Jonathan. *Nixon: A Life.* Washington, DC: Regnery, 1993.

Ambrose, Stephen E. *Nixon: The Education of a Politician, 1913–1962.* New York: Simon and Schuster, 1987.

Brodie, Fawn M. *Richard Nixon: The Shaping of His Character.* Cambridge, MA: Harvard University Press, 1983.

Hoyt, Edwin P. *The Nixons: An American Family.* New York: Random House, 1972.

Morris, Roger. *Richard Milhous Nixon: The Rise of an American Politician.* New York: Henry Holt, 1991.

Nixon, Richard. *RN: The Memoirs of Richard Nixon.* New York: Grosset and Dunlap, 1978.

——— . *In the Arena: A Memoir of Victory, Defeat, and Renewal.* New York: Simon and Schuster, 1990.

Parmet, Herbert S. *Richard Nixon and His America.* Boston: Little, Brown, 1990.

## Leslie Lynch King Sr. and Gerald Rudolph Ford Sr.

Cannon, James M. *Time and Chance: Gerald Ford's Appointment with History.* New York: HarperCollins, 1994.

Ford, Betty, with Chris Chase. *The Times of My Life.* New York: Harper & Row, 1978.

Ford, Gerald. *A Time to Heal: The Autobiography of Gerald R. Ford.* New York: Harper & Row, 1978.

Reeves, Richard. *A Ford Not a Lincoln.* New York: Harcourt Brace, 1975.

## James Earl Carter Sr.

Bourne, Peter G. *Jimmy Carter.* New York: Simon and Schuster, 1997.

Brinkley, Douglas. *The Unfinished Presidency.* New York: Viking, 1998.

Carter, Jimmy. *Keeping Faith: Memoirs of a President.* New York: Bantam Books, 1983.
————. *An Hour Before Daylight: Memories of a Rural Boyhood.* New York: Simon and Schuster, 2001.
Mazlish, Bruce, and Edwin Diamond. *Jimmy Carter: A Character Portrait.* New York: Simon and Schuster, 1979.
Morris, Kenneth E. *Jimmy Carter: American Moralist.* Athens: University of Georgia Press, 1996.

## John Edward Reagan

Cannon, Lou. *Reagan.* New York: G. P. Putnam's Sons, 1982.
————. *President Reagan: The Role of a Lifetime.* New York: Simon and Schuster, 1991.
Cardigan, J. H. *Ronald Reagan: A Remarkable Life.* Kansas City: Andrews and McMeel, 1995.
Morris, Edmond. *Dutch: A Memoir of Ronald Reagan.* New York: Random House, 1999.
Pemberton, William E. *Exit with Honor: The Life and Presidency of Ronald Reagan.* Armonk, NY: M. E. Sharpe, 1997.
Reagan, Ronald. *Speaking My Mind.* New York: Simon and Schuster, 1989.
————. *An American Life: The Autobiography.* New York: Simon and Schuster, 1990.

## Prescott Sheldon Bush

Bush, Barbara. *Barbara Bush: A Memoir.* New York: Scribner's, 1994.
Bush, George H. W. *All the Best, George Bush: My Life and Other Writings.* New York: Scribner's, 1999.
Kilian, Pamela. *Barbara Bush: A Biography.* New York: St. Martin's, 1992.
King, Nicholas. *George Bush: A Biography.* New York: Dodd, Mead, 1980.
Parmet, Herbert S. *George Bush: The Life of a Lone Star Yankee.* New York: Simon and Schuster, 1997.

## William Jefferson Blythe III and Roger Clinton

Hamilton, Nigel. *Bill Clinton: An American Journey: Great Expectations.* New York: Random House, 2003.
Kelley, Virginia, with James Morgan. *Leading with My Heart.* New York: Simon and Schuster, 1994.
Maraniss, David. *First in His Class: The Biography of Bill Clinton.* New York: Simon and Schuster, 1995.
————. *The Clinton Enigma.* New York: Simon and Schuster, 1998.

## George Herbert Walker Bush

Bush, George W., with Karen Hughes. *A Charge to Keep.* New York: William Morrow, 1999.
Hatfield, J. H. *Fortunate Son: George W. Bush and the Making of an American President.* New York: St. Martin's, 1992.
Minutaglio, Bill. *First Son: George W. Bush and the Bush Family Dynasty.* New York: Time Books, 1999.

# INDEX

Page numbers in **boldface** indicate articles on individual first fathers.